KANT AND SPENCER

A CRITICAL EXPOSITION

BY

BORDEN PARKER BOWNE

BOSTON AND NEW YORK
HOUGHTON MIFFLIN COMPANY
The Riverside Press Cambridge
1912

PUBLISHERS' NOTE

THIS work does not aim to be an exhaustive treatise on Kant and Spencer, but rather a critical exposition from the standpoint of the author's own system of philosophy.

It is based upon lectures given during many years by Professor Bowne to his students, and is published as left by him at the time of his death. It is a first dictation of the matter to his stenographer, and had not received its final polish from the author's hand. His previous philosophical works were written entirely with his own pen. Had this been the case with *Kant and Spencer*, no such errors would have crept in as have naturally occurred in transcribing the stenographer's notes. It is believed, however, that all these errors have been eliminated by the studious care of friends thoroughly familiar with the author's thought, — the corrections in every case being enclosed within brackets.

April 1, 1912.

CONTENTS

PART I

THE PHILOSOPHY OF KANT

CONTENTS

CHAPTER III

CHAPTER IV

CHAPTER V

CONTENTS

PART II

THE PHILOSOPHY OF SPENCER

ix

CONTENTS

CHAPTER I

CHAPTER II

CONTENTS

CONTENTS

CHAPTER V

PART I

THE PHILOSOPHY OF KANT

THE PHILOSOPHY OF KANT

INTRODUCTION

KANT's great work is his "Critique of Pure Reason." The title itself suggests something of the general thought. It is to discover the scope and limitations of the rational power itself. This undertaking was made necessary by the contradictions into which reason had fallen. In this aim Kant's work is similar to that of Locke in his "Essay on the Human Understanding." Locke says, "If by this inquiry into the nature of the understanding I can discover the powers thereof, how far they reach, to what things they are in any degree proportionate, and where they avail us, I suppose it may be of use to prevail with the busy mind of man to be more cautious in meddling with things exceeding its comprehension; to stop when it is at the utmost extent of its tether; and to sit in a quiet ignorance of those things which upon examination are found to be beyond the reach of our capacities." Kant's aim was similar. Reason he conceived had transcended its own sphere, which was the source not only of speculative error, but also of practical confusion and mischief. To remedy this condition of things he wrote the "Critique of Pure Reason."

Kant's underlying interest in this matter would

3

seem to have been originally ethical. He found that the confused philosophies of his time were such as to throw great doubt upon both moral and religious faith, and Kant regarded the belief in God, freedom, and immortality as things of supreme importance for our human life. But he saw these truths brought into discredit through speculative aberration. He set himself, therefore, to determine more carefully the real scope of reason in such matters, and reached the conclusion that reason itself is a limited faculty, and by means of it we cannot attain to a demonstration of these ideas upon which life is based. But though a limited faculty it is not a deceitful one when critically used. The outcome of this critical inquiry, in his own words, is to destroy knowledge and make room for belief. By means of mere reflection Kant says we can never produce any conviction, and the practical beliefs of men have always been reached in some other way. The great source of difficulty has been the mistaken notion that reason can avail to overturn these things, and hence the objections brought by dogmatism have often availed to shake the people's faith. If now it could be shown that these objections are themselves baseless, then we should be left free to follow our higher spiritual instincts and to fall back on the practical implications of life without being molested or disturbed in any way by the objections of skepticism. This, in a word, was Kant's most general purpose, to criticize reason, to determine its limitations, and to show that beyond the range of the speculative faculty lies the field of practical life where, while we cannot demonstrate, we may yet believe.

4

INTRODUCTION

It is this characteristic of Kant's philosophy which entitles it to be called the Critical Philosophy, in distinction from the philosophy of the preceding period, which Kant described as empirical on the one hand or dogmatic on the other.

The first edition of Kant's work appeared in 1781. In 1783 he wrote a work entitled "Prolegomena to Every Future System of Metaphysics." This was a kind of brief exposition of the "Critique," and puts many of the leading doctrines in a more concise and clear form. In 1787 a second edition of the "Critique" was produced, which contained many changes from the first edition. Concerning the relative merits of these two editions there has been a great deal of debate among Kantian scholars. Some hold that the first edition was the more consistent work, and that the second edition is weak and shows undue concessions to popular philosophical and theological prejudices. In particular the second edition contained a "Refutation of Idealism," and some philosophers looked upon this as a grave inconsistency. The edition also showed, it was said, something of a desire to placate orthodox believers of all sorts, and this was thought by many to show a lack of courage. Schopenhauer in particular was very bitter against Kant on this account. To us who stand far removed from the original controversy there seems to be no justification for this charge of inconsistency, and no more for the charge of cowardice. Kant was only sixty years old when the second edition was produced, and he would not seem to have been a man who would needlessly surrender. It was at a much later period that Kant was silenced by the Minister of Education, but that was in connection with his work "Religion within the Limits of the Pure Reason," and then Kant's silence involved no recantation, but as a loyal subject he ceased to lecture on the forbidden topic.

And as to the philosophical inconsistency there seems to be no good ground for it. Kant was inconsistent in the first edition as well as in the second, and if the inconsistency is a little more prominent in the later edition, it is no more real; for Kant's system cannot be made consistent except by going beyond it. And we may even say that Kant's inconsistency in this matter was one proof of his greatness. Kant struck out a new path and did not succeed in making a perfectly consistent system. He held a number of views which in the form he gave them did not admit of being made consistent, yet all of which really had to be taken into account. Hence, we repeat, while Kant did not succeed in removing all the inconsistencies of his system, his work was all the greater for not making the system consistent by eliminating some factors which had to be retained. Since the second edition no important changes have been made in the text. Only minor emendations and the kind of things that small critics delight in have been produced. The great edition which the Royal Academy of Science in Berlin is bringing out follows the text of the second edition, and gives the variations of the first edition in the appendix. Hartenstein's edition, which for a long time was the standard one, follows also the text of the second edition.

Of translations there are two in English of merit,

that by Max Müller and that by Meiklejohn. Müller's translation follows the text of the first edition, but brackets those parts in it which were left out in the second edition, and then in a series of appendices gives the additions made in the second edition. Meiklejohn follows the text of the second edition. Our quotations are from Müller's translation.

We now proceed to study the work itself as set forth in the "Critique" and the "Prolegomena."

Philosophy had reached a crisis in Kant's time. The empiricism of Locke had ended in Hume's nihilism. Locke had based philosophy on experience, and Hume had shown that experience itself when the mind is purely passive becomes only a vanishing phantasmagoria, which makes all knowledge impossible. In France the empirical doctrine, in the hands of Condillac, had passed into a set of vague and superficial generalizations distinguishing nothing, leading to nothing, and even meaning nothing. Empiricism in ethics had also led to a general low moral tone which was unfavorable to high spiritual living of any kind. And on the other hand, the rational school of Descartes, Spinoza, Leibnitz, had passed into the barren formalism of the Wolfian philosophy, which was scarcely more valuable than the platitudes of the sensational school. In this condition of things either philosophy had to be abandoned or else a new beginning had to be made and some new method initiated. This is the work that Kant did.

Kant says that Hume first woke him from his dogmatic slumber. He had apparently been teaching the traditional Leibnitzo-Wolfian philosophy, but when he came into contact with Hume's dissolving criticism he began to see that the foundations were falling away, and to meet this crisis he made a new examination of reason itself, with the aim of once more establishing philosophy on a solid basis.

In this work Kant appeared as a reconciler of the two previous directions in philosophy. On the one hand, the empirical school had claimed that all knowledge is from experience. And on the other hand, the rational school had maintained that there are sundry rational principles immanent in the mind. Kant claimed to show that both schools were right. On the one hand, there can be no experience, he said, without rational principles, as Hume had clearly shown. Thus the rational school was justified. But on the other hand, these rational principles have application only to experience. When extended beyond the field of experience they become the parent of multitudinous illusions. Thus the empirical school is justified, and thus criticism appears as containing the truth in both empiricism and rationalism, while at the same time showing their limited and partial nature. This view might be called transcendental empiricism. It is transcendental as going beyond the empiricism of sense impressions, but it is empiricism as limiting knowledge to the field of experience. The true view then is neither empiricism nor rationalism of the old type, but criticism which unites and reconciles them.

I

KANT'S DOCTRINE OF EXPERIENCE

KANT does not formally discuss this topic, and yet practically his doctrine of experience is his great contribution to philosophy. For the understanding of his system, therefore, we shall do well to consider what that doctrine is.

According to the earlier empiricists the mind is purely passive in experience. It was a waxen tablet or a *tabula rasa* upon which impressions were made. The mind, then, was simply a recipient and contributed nothing. It received impressions and preserved them, and all that could be later done was simply to read off the impressions in their due order and connection. When this view was taken at all seriously it was seen to lead at once to the overthrow of all reason. Hume took it seriously and held that the original material of all knowledge consists of impressions of which later copies may exist in consciousness. The impressions contain all the reality we have, and all other ideas so far as valid are simply faint copies of the impressions, which are relatively vivid. This certainly led to a short and easy way of dealing with our ideas or beliefs. We had only to ask concerning any idea for the impression of which it was a copy, and if no impression could be shown we must conclude that the idea was a fiction. This at once would limit the mind to impressions of sense and feeling, and anything which could not be thus sensuously or sensibly presented must be set aside as baseless. Elementary ideas, then, of substance, unity, identity, causality, and also the higher ideas of spirit, morality, God, religion, etc., immediately appear as fictions. If we said, But they nevertheless exist as ideas, Hume's reply was that they were due to a "mental propensity to feign"; for by the very terms of the philosophy vivid impressions are the only reality, and faint impressions are either the copies of the vivid impressions or else pure illusions. But on this view no rational experience whatever was possible. Nothing was left but a set of dissolving impressions, no one of which had any identity or abiding character in itself or connection with any other, and all of which vanished with their date, leaving nothing behind. The result was nihilism. Experience itself was impossible.

This shows the significance of the question, How is experience possible? On the purely empirical view, when taken literally and with any precision, experience is not possible. But then as a matter of fact we do have something we call experience, on which life depends and where we meet in mutual understanding. Now, how is this experience possible?

The answer to this is, It is possible only through an activity of the mind itself in accordance with certain principles immanent in the mind, according to which it organizes the impressions of sense into the connected forms of the understanding, and thus only reaches an articulate and connected system of experience. And this is admitted in a kind of left-handed way by Hume himself, for his own doctrine leaves us in this vanishing flux of impressions, but recognizes a "mental propensity to feign" as the source of certain ideas which we call rational, but he calls baseless because of his philosophical position. If we ask, how on the Humian view experience is organized and made articulate, it turns out to be due solely to those ideas which he sought to explain away and which he stigmatized as products of a propensity to feign. We shall see that they are really expressions of the rational nature itself.

A general conviction of superficial thought has been that knowledge is something that can be imported readymade from without, by impressions on the passive mind. The process seemingly admits of being pictured by terms like impression, photograph, and so on, but as soon as we look into the matter with any precision we find how empty all of this is. And, first of all, let us consider the simple impression itself. We shall see that it is not an object of articulate apprehension until it has been made over by the mind into its own rational forms. Let us take, say, a heat sensation. As occurring, this sensation has no unity and no identity of any kind. In order to become anything whatever articulate, the heat sensation must be transformed into a sensation of heat, which is something very different. Of course this impresses common sense as an unreal refinement, but a moment's reflection will show its validity. For let us suppose this impression to last through a minute of time. It is plain that the first second of that minute is not the same as the last second, and it is equally plain that the impression occurring in the first second is not the impression occurring in the last second, and because of the infinite divisibility of time the impression as occurring has no unity and no identity whatever. Each increment of the impression goes away with its date and leaves nothing behind it, and each succeeding increment knows nothing of that which went before nor of that which comes afterward. We have, then, indefinite otherness without identity of any kind. And plainly the only way out of this is that there shall be some rational power that shall react upon this impression, so that instead of being a flux of affections it shall be gathered up into one idea, an impression of heat. When this is done we then have a single and fixed idea, of which the successively occurring impression is the bearer and which in turn expresses the significance of the impression itself. Thus in transforming the heat impression into an impression of heat we have gone beyond the mere affection of the sensibility to the plane of a universalizing intelligence, and that even in this simplest possible sense experience.

The units of sensation themselves, then, by the time they are anything articulate show an activity of the understanding upon them whereby they are made possible elements in a rational experience, and this same fact appears all the more plainly in the so-called recurrence of sensations. It seems very possible to common sense that sensations can recur again and again. But this, too, is possible only to a universalizing intelligence. For any impression whatever as recurring goes away with its date and can no more be recalled than the date itself. When, then, we speak of recurring sensations we really mean the occurrence of something similar. There can never be a recurrence of the same. And this occurrence of the same can be known as such only by a mind which has lifted its impressions to the plane of fixed ideas. And it is through these fixed ideas of the understanding that the mind is able to bring any order whatever into the flux of impressions themselves.

Thus we see an element beyond sense experience entering into it for its organization, and this appears all the more clearly when we come to the higher ideas of the reason. We might conceivably have a succession of impressions, and these might be gathered into systems of sensations in classes of likeness and difference, and still we should not have the actual experience that we possess. In order to this actual experience some ideas must be brought into the sense life.

Thus, suppose we see a moving body. What do the senses really give? Of course at first thought common sense would say, "They give us the moving body"; but plainly this far transcends the fact of sense. All the senses would give us in such a case would be a succession of visual impressions successively changing their apparent place; but this is far enough from the conception of a moving thing. Such an experience could be presented by a series of mirrors or by our familiar moving pictures, where there would be no real motion of a thing at all. When in the moving picture we see the train rush up to the platform and the passengers alight and the train depart, we really see no moving train of passengers but only a set of optical illusions. And yet we really see all that the senses could give in that case or any case. Now, we transcend these data of the senses by importing into the sense experience the idea of objective space with objective reality in it, moving from point to point in space and remaining identical with itself throughout the motion. Not until this is done can we speak of seeing a body move. And in general a little reflection enables us to see that there is a great deal in thought that does not exist in sense at all. The unities, the identities, the causalities, the rational connection which for reason underlie experience cannot be presented to sense in any way. They belong rather to the unpicturable notions of the understanding. Here, then, in sense experience we find a great surplusage over and above anything the senses can give us, and this surplusage is a contribution of the rational nature. According to Hume it is a product of our mental propensity to feign. According to the rational philosopher it is an expression of our reason. It really does not matter much what we call it so long as we see that the work thus described is really done and that the ideas mentioned are really due to the mind itself and that their function is to organize and rationalize experience.

These considerations serve to show the working of immanent rational principles in the mind. And yet it is rather difficult for persons unused to abstract thinking to grasp the fact, because apparently we have such an immediate and undeniable knowledge of things given to us in sense experience. It may be

14

of use, therefore, to take another line of reflection with the aim of bringing this constructive activity on the part of the mind into clearer recognition.

It is commonly supposed by uncritical thought that the existence of things sufficiently explains our perception of them, and when, then, such a question is raised as, How is knowledge possible? we are apt to think that it is no question at all; the things are really there and all we have to do is to open our eyes and see them, or to put forth our hands and touch them, or to walk about among them, and nothing more is needed. But it must be pointed out that this naïve confidence in the reality of things by no means removes the fact that this knowledge is nevertheless the outcome of a highly complex process of interpretation on the part of the mind. This interpretation may go on spontaneously and without any reflective activity on our part; but it goes on nevertheless. If we consider what the physiologists tell us about the conditions of perception we see that the interpretation and the principles of interpretation must necessarily come from within. According to the physiologists' report the condition of perception is some form of nervous change which results in some form of sensitive impression. But no reflection upon the nervous change of which we know nothing immediately, and generally know nothing in any way, will ever give us the world of things as it is. Neither will any reflection upon impressions, as we have just seen, give us a conception of an independent and abiding world of experience. The impressions in themselves are flitting, fleeting, discontinuous. The world of things is

15

continuous and abiding. Now, how can we pass from the vanishing sense fact to the fixed rational fact? This rational fact reports itself only through the sense fact, and the latter is all that we can possibly receive from without. But if this sense fact is to be built into a solid and enduring world it can be only as the mind is impelled by its own nature to work over the sense fact into rational forms, which forms are simply the immanent principles of reason itself. If in this constructive and interpretative process the mind really apprehends the independent fact, it can be only as the independent fact is cast in the moulds and forms of reason, for we can think only in the forms which our rational nature prescribes. But in any case the objective fact can exist for us only through our own mental construction. In further illustration of this, consider what takes place in conversation and mental understanding of persons. Here, of course, there can be no question of thoughts leaving one mind and passing into the mind of another. All the thoughts that can possibly be in a person's mind are the thoughts he himself thinks. And if there be thoughts in others' minds they exist for him only as he thinks them, and he can grasp the thoughts of others only as his own mental nature makes it possible for him to do so.

Thus we see again that experience is possible only through the constructive action of the mind according to principles immanent in it; and thus we see that knowledge in general is possible only in the same way. The early notion of a passive mind passively receiving impressions made upon it must be definitely and finally set aside, and in its place must rather be put the notion of a mind active, constructive, constitutive, a mind which by its own action according to its own rational nature attains to knowledge and systematized experience.

This was not Kant's way of putting his doctrine of experience, but it represents the essential thought of his doctrine and escapes many of the difficulties into which his own exposition falls. And this doctrine is altogether independent of Kant's agnosticism or his peculiar psychology. This is the abiding and imperishable element in Kant's system and constitutes his immortal merit. No critical weapon formed against the view has prospered, and it stands invincible.

But before passing to the discussion we recur again to the ambiguity already referred to in this general doctrine of empiricism. The question between empiricism and rationalism we said may refer to the origin of mental forms or to the validity of knowledge. These two questions are quite distinct. Many empiricists have held that all the higher mental forms and ideas are built up from experience, but they have not questioned the objective validity of knowledge. In a way this is true of Locke. Locke held that all knowledge is from experience, but nevertheless showed no trace of skepticism in his general theory of knowing. Similarly such men as Herbert Spencer have been thoroughgoing empiricists with regard to the higher forms of mentality, but they have been far enough from reducing their beliefs to the limits of this view. And on the other hand, there have been apriorists as to mental forms like Kant, who nevertheless have maintained that speculation cannot demonstrate the validity of these conceptions, but the practical reason demands them, and thus what we lose as knowledge is regained as belief. Meanwhile, reason having shown its limitations is unable to make any protest against the extension of the realm of faith. Thus strangely enough we find these two men who were so opposed in their epistemology practically meeting in their metaphysics. In our future discussion we shall find the two points of view continually mingling and very often without suspicion of the fact. We shall need to keep them separate in order that we may see just what the doctrines we are treating of are and what they are not, how much they establish and how much is left as it was before.

We may also call attention here to a certain fact from oversight of which Kant has involved his system in needless skepticism and much confusion. If we ask concerning the possibility of knowledge or experience we note that there are two sets of conditions, one from the side of the subject and one from the side of the object, and for a complete theory of knowledge both sets of conditions have to be taken into account. Kant, however, took account of only one set, the conditions from the side of the subject. Before his time these conditions had been very largely unsuspected, as they always are by common sense, and it was supposed that knowledge was a simple process, something like the reflection of objects in a mirror, and the fact of its complex conditions from the side of the subject was undreamed of. Hence it was important that the subjective conditions should be emphasized, and this Kant did. And this led him to say that the understanding makes nature, and to represent the mind as acting out of itself alone; and this he did in such a way as almost certainly to imply a species of idealism, if not outright nihilism. We can easily see how Kant was led to extravagances of this kind. It is perfectly clear that the mind can know nothing without except as it constructs it within. As I can grasp another's thought only by thinking his thought for myself, and as that other's thought is immediately my own thought, even though I attribute it to him, so I can grasp the world without, however independent it may be of me and however objective its laws may be, only as I construct that world by my own rational activities for myself. In this sense, then, the mind makes nature in so far as the mind apprehends it. But this is very far from justifying the claim that the mind is absolutely independent in this making. Although I make nature so far as it exists for me, I cannot make it as I please. I cannot fill space with all manner of objects at my pleasure, or invert the laws of the outer world at will. To be sure, I can know things only through my own activity, but I cannot know them even then unless they are in themselves knowable. That is, in the complete theory of knowledge we must consider the nature of the object as well as the nature of the subject, and when we go so far as to make the mind unconditioned in its cognitive activities the result, as said, would be necessarily idealism or nihilism. From failure to note this fact Kant is continually on the borders of an idealism which he repudiated, but into which he was nevertheless driven. When the laws of thought have no application to things, then things themselves are strictly unknowable and the next thing is to deny them altogether. Thus we reach a sort of solipsistic idealism. But there was nothing in Kant's fundamental conception that necessitated this onesidedness. It is entirely possible to retain Kant's doctrine of experience without accepting his phenomenalism and agnosticism. We shall find the contradictions resulting from these two factors continually emerging in Kant's exposition.

The importance of establishing the truth in Kant's system and also the confusion resulting from his phenomenalism leads to another illustration. There is a great deal in Kant's terminology that is exceedingly operose and difficult, which nevertheless when the matter is understood represents a manifest fact of experience. Suppose we assume a manuscript in an unknown tongue which we are to interpret. We may ask, What are the general conditions of its interpretation?

In Kant's exposition of the transcendental analytic he points out sundry fundamental conditions of knowledge. There must be, first, a synthesis of apprehension in intuition; second, a synthesis of reproduction in imagination; third, a synthesis of recognition in concepts; and then finally, as the original and transcendental condition, there must be what he calls transcendental apperception. Now the unpracticed reader might well be excused for saying that he was sure there was nothing whatever of this kind in any of his mental operations, and yet these tremendous phrases cover very simple and undeniable facts. Thus

in studying our manuscript we should find a variety [Carefull
of words and phrases, and if it were not possible for
us to combine these in apprehension we should lose
ourselves in the plurality of words and even of letters,
and no thought whatever would emerge. Now, this
possibility of doing these many things together is the
synthesis of apprehension in intuition. Again, it is
manifest that as we pass from point to point it must
be possible to retain or reproduce the points passed
over in our present consciousness, otherwise each
would be forgotten as soon as it was reached and thus
consciousness itself would vanish. Now, this possibility of retaining and reproducing past facts is all
that is meant by the synthesis of reproduction in
imagination. Further, if the ideas which we have had
in the early stages of our study when reproduced were
not recognized, it would be equivalent to no reproduction, so far as any systematic knowledge goes. The
reproduced idea would be a new one, and this perfectly simple fact is what is meant by the synthesis
of recognition in concepts. And finally, if there were
not an abiding subject throughout the entire process,
in the unity of whose consciousness these various
factors are related to the subject and to one another
in their various temporal and logical relations, there
would be no consciousness whatever. Apart from
the particular objects of consciousness or particular
ideas, it is necessary that they all be grouped and
related in reference to the abiding conscious subject,
without which they fall asunder and cannot become
factors of one consciousness at all. And this obvious
fact is all that is meant by the transcendental unity

of apperception. Thus we see that these high-sounding phrases of Kant's are really perfectly simple and undeniable facts, and moreover they are the indispensable conditions of any knowledge whatever. So then, in the understanding of our manuscript we must assume the facts and activities referred to as absolutely necessary conditions of any knowledge of it by us.

It is further clear that any meaning we get out of our manuscript must be one that we put into it, for clearly the manuscript as such has no meaning in it objectively considered. It has meaning only from mind and for mind, and the meaning it may have for us, the students, must be one that we attribute to it. It is a meaning that we ourselves produce in our own minds and refer to the manuscript, and hence we can say in some sense that we ourselves make the meaning. We have to fix the significance of the terms and unite them in their various logical relations, and all of this is our own activity. From the side of the student, then, we might say that the mind makes the meaning and can never find any meaning other than that it makes. This conclusion necessarily results from the mental activity in all knowing, or from the fact that nothing whatever can exist for the mind except through its own action.

So far we go with Kant; but it is next manifest that unless the manuscript had some meaning apart from our manipulation it would not admit of being understood. The thought we get out of it is in some sense the thought we put into it, but unless there is some thought expressed in it, it would never be possible for us to get any thought out of it. In that case we should simply be seeking to understand random scratches or blotches, which would be a hopeless operation. It would not be much better if we should say that we get only the phenomenal meaning of the manuscript and not the meaning of the manuscript in itself. We get only the meaning which it has for us, but back of this meaning is another transcendental meaning, in which we must believe, but which we can never reach. Every one would see the impossibility of a phenomenalism of this kind. We should never have the slightest reason for affirming any such transcendental meaning, and we never could connect that meaning with the meaning we ourselves discern. If we should further say that the manuscript has no meaning in itself, but that the apparent meaning which we find in it is simply a production of our own ideas without any objective correspondence, we should find ourselves equally blocked, for there would be no possibility of binding an intelligible meaning on to a purely unintelligible and unrelated origin. Plainly we should have to say that our interpretation is not merely conditioned by our own mental nature, but also by the nature of the manuscript itself, and probably we should find no resting-place for the meaning in the manuscript. We posit the mind behind the manuscript, of whose thought the manuscript is the expression. Without insisting on the accuracy of every factor of this illustration, it does serve to show how knowledge can arise only through the mind in its own activity, and how certain conditions must be fulfilled in order that this knowledge shall be possible even as a subjective experience; and it also shows how the knowledge, which as psychological event is our own mental product, is as phenomenon objectively conditioned, so that finally the meaning which we discover is not something that we make, but something that we find. It exists apart from our own thinking, and our thought is simply the instrument for grasping a content beyond itself.

With this general hint of the nature of the work before us we now proceed to expound the system as Kant himself gave it. In general we shall find much labored and operose discussion, some confusion and some error; but along with it all and greatly overbalancing it all, we shall find a system of thought which has taken possession of the modern mind and which constitutes one of the greatest and most important contributions to philosophical thinking.

Kant's approach to the problem was conditioned by the philosophical situation of his time. According to Kant experience is the first product of our understanding. It had been held by the earlier empiricists that experience itself could be given from without by some nervous affection or some simple impression in the sensibility. Sensation at least was regarded as something that could be furnished readymade, but this itself we have seen to be impossible. The constitutive action of the understanding penetrates into sensation so far as it is anything articulate. We have before seen that sensation, without the fixed ideas of the understanding whereby it becomes an abiding and identical content, is strictly nothing for us.

According to Kant, then, even our ordinary sense experience is not a datum from without, but is the first product of our understanding. That all our knowledge begins with experience there can be no doubt, he says. In respect to time, therefore, no knowledge within us is antecedent to experience, but all knowledge begins with it; but though all our knowledge begins with experience, it does not follow that it rises from experience; for it is quite possible that even our empirical experience is a compound of that which we receive through impressions and of that which our own faculty of knowledge (incited only by sensuous impressions) supplies from itself, a supplement which we do not distinguish from that raw material until long practice has arrested our attention and rendered us capable of separating one from the other.

That this is the case is Kant's claim. There exists a knowledge independent of experience and even of all impressions of the senses. Such knowledge he calls a priori and distinguishes from empirical knowledge, which has its sources a posteriori, that is, in experience. He further defines a priori knowledge as follows: "We shall therefore, in what follows, understand by knowledge a priori, knowledge which is absolutely independent of all experience, and not of this or that experience only. Opposed to this is empirical knowledge, or such as is possible a posteriori only, that is, by experience. Knowledge a priori, if mixed up with nothing empirical, is called pure. Thus the proposition, for example, that every change has its cause, is a proposition a priori, but not pure: because change is a concept which can only be derived from experience" (p. 716).[1] The a priori element, then, is one which the mind brings out of its own resources and does not receive from without. This element does indeed emerge out of some experience, but when it does come it is seen to be independent of experience. For example, the truths of mathematics were not perceived before we had some sense experience, but when the mind became capable of reasoning mathematically it saw that those truths stand in their own light and far transcend all experience whatever. The characteristic of all such a priori knowledge is that it is in the strictest sense necessary and universal. No particular experience can give us universal and necessary truth. And when we find judgments of such universality and necessity we come upon a special source of knowledge other than experience.

In further exposition of the subject Kant introduces his distinction between analytical and synthetic judgments. Analytical judgments are those in which the predicate merely expresses what is meant by the subject. They may serve to clarify our thought, but they never extend knowledge. Thus, if I say, a triangle is a three-cornered figure, the predicate only tells the meaning of the subject, but it gives no new information to any one who understands the meaning of the term. If, then, knowledge is to be increased and is not to remain a barren tautology of definition, synthetic judgments must be possible.

But synthetic judgments fall into two classes, synthetic judgments a posteriori and synthetic judg-

---

[1] [Unless otherwise indicated all quotations from Kant are taken from Max Müller's translation of the *Critique of Pure Reason*.]

ments a priori. The former class are simple judgments of experience. They recite what we have experienced, but they never tell what is universal and always true. It is plain that such judgments would simply narrate what has been, and would never give any warrant for saying what will be or must be. In themselves they would not even constitute a probability. Hence it is clear that the problem of knowledge depends on the possibility of synthetic judgments a priori. If the latter are impossible, then we are shut up, as said, to mere narration, and if we eliminate all synthetic elements whatever of an a priori nature we are shut up to the vanishing flux and phantasmagoria of Hume's nihilism. Thus we see how the question of philosophy may be expressed in the form, How are synthetic judgments a priori possible?

It would be easy to cavil against this distinction of Kant's on the ground that there are no purely analytic judgments except such formal ones as $A = A;$ and even this judgment in any concrete application is synthetic, because in the concrete it assumes that A is a definite fixed concept in its several appearances in experience. The judgment of identity in the concrete always presupposes at least two experiences of the identical thing, and the experience itself could never give us more than a similarity of any two experiences more or less exact. To pass from this similarity to the formation of the real identity is something impossible to an analytic judgment. Any judgment whatever that goes beyond the immediate impression of sense contains some synthetic principle in it, but Kant knew this well enough, as clearly

appears in the progress of his work; but the notion
that analytical judgments were fruitful and involved
no rational insight on the part of the mind was current in his time, and moreover Hume by his denial
of causal and substantive connection had thrown
doubt upon the possibility of synthetic judgments in
general. On this account Kant proceeds from the
distinction of the two classes, and aims to show that
a priori syntheses exist and find their possibility in
the nature of the mind itself and its relation to
experience.

Now that such a priori syntheses exist is evident,
according to Kant, from an inspection of the sciences
of mathematics, physics, and metaphysics. Mathematics itself is not a science made up of analytical
judgments, but is rather based upon a priori syntheses
throughout. Thus, to take his example, $7 + 5 = 12$
is not an analytical proposition, for mere analysis
would give us nothing more than $7 + 5 = 7 + 5$. That
$7 + 5 = 12$ is gained only through a synthetic process of counting, whereby we perceive that the problem admits of solution and that the sum is really 12.
No simply analytical reflection under the law of identity will give us this result. We must fall back on the
counting process on which the numerical synthesis
depends. Again, Kant says, geometry as well as arithmetic is likewise synthetic. That a straight line is the
shortest distance between two points is something
which cannot be deduced by any reflection upon the
conception of a line of constant direction. We must
rather construct the process within the spatial imagination itself, and when we do this we see the propo-

sition to be true. Similarly in proving geometrical propositions in general, we do not proceed by any analysis of the lines and figures, but rather by constructing the problem and by producing various auxiliary lines which enable us to see the truth in question.

Mathematics, then, in its two great branches of arithmetic and geometry, is an a priori science, and Kant thought that if Hume had noticed this fact he would not so soon have despaired of philosophy; for here in mathematics we have a priori syntheses, and if the mind is capable of them here it might be capable of them elsewhere. To doubt the truth of mathematics seemed to Kant a piece of frivolity of which no earnest mind could be guilty. Had he, however, been better acquainted with Hume's work he would have seen that Hume had proceeded even to this extreme.

But mathematics is not the only field of a priori syntheses; for natural science also contains synthetic judgments a priori as principles. As examples may be adduced the law of causation, the constancy of the quantity of matter, the equality of action and reaction. Propositions of this kind are plainly not analytical, but they are commonly given as the basis of physical science.

Metaphysics, too, at least claims to contain synthetic knowledge a priori. Its object is not at all merely to analyze our concepts of things, but to go beyond all experience in judgments concerning the nature of the world, its beginning, its cause, etc.; so that at least in intention metaphysics consists entirely of synthetic judgments a priori.

Our original question respecting the possibility of philosophy took the form, How are synthetic judgments a priori possible? We may now specify the question into three others: first, Is pure mathematics possible? second, Is pure physics — that is, natural science in general — possible? and third, Is metaphysics possible? Of the first two sciences Kant says, "As these sciences really exist, it is quite proper to ask how they are possible, for that they must be possible is proved by their reality."

Kant had great faith in both mathematics and physics. With regard to metaphysics the result of his system is to show that it is not possible as a science, but as a general disposition or failing of the human mind, it is nevertheless real. And the reality it has depends upon the a priori syntheses contained in it. It is plain, then, that whether valid or not, a priori syntheses play a great part in actual human thinking: sometimes a valid part, as in mathematics and physics, and sometimes a doubtful part, if not a distinctly misleading one, as in dogmatic metaphysics. In all this we see a vindication of the activity of the mind in knowledge, in reply to all those who have maintained its passivity. It does not follow, however, that these a priori syntheses are necessarily valid, as has just been suggested in the case of metaphysics; but it does follow that the mind is active according to principles inherent in its own rational structure, and that these principles are really determinative of our mental procedure. We now proceed to examine Kant's reply to the several questions just distinguished.

But first of all, a word must be said of Kant's

psychology. He distinguishes between sensibility, the understanding, and the reason. The sensibility merely receives impressions. The understanding works these over in its own forms, and the reason finally prescribes the general outline for our later mental activity. Doubts may be raised concerning this distinction in each case. Thus the separation of sense from understanding is disputed, on the ground that there is no pure sensibility apart from the activity of the understanding. This may be true, but it is really no valid objection to Kant's exposition. His general doctrine so far as true is quite independent of this distinction, and it is not possible to say everything at once. Kant certainly speaks of the sensibility as if of itself it supplied us with intuitions or objects. At the same time Kant very well knew, as later appears, that if we should abstract from any object or intuition whatever the elements contributed by the understanding, there would be nothing articulate left. When, then, in the beginning of the transcendental æsthetics we find Kant speaking as if a world of things in themselves existed outside of us and acted upon us, just as common sense supposes bodies apart from our organisms to affect us, we are not to take the matter too seriously, but only as Kant's way of getting the problem stated. If he had passed at once to his developed view it would have made the exposition much more difficult and really not much more effective. He states the distinction between the sensibility and the understanding as follows: "There are two stems of human knowledge which perhaps spring from a common but to us unknown root, namely,

31

sensibility and understanding." Again he says, "Our knowledge springs from two fundamental sources of our soul; the first receives representations (receptivity of impressions), the second is the power of knowing an object by these representations (spontaneity of concepts). By the first an object is given us, by the second the object is thought, in relation to that representation which is a mere determination of the soul. Intuition, therefore, and concepts constitute the elements of all our knowledge, so that neither concepts without an intuition corresponding to them, nor intuition without concepts can yield any real knowledge. . . . We call sensibility the receptivity of our soul, or its power of receiving representations whenever it is in any wise affected, while the understanding, on the contrary, is with us the power of producing representations, or the spontaneity of knowledge. We are so constituted that our intuition must always be sensuous, and consist of the mode in which we are affected by objects. What enables us to think the objects of our sensuous intuition is the understanding. Neither of these qualities or faculties is preferable to the other. Without sensibility objects would not be given to us, without understanding they would not be thought by us. Thoughts without contents are empty, intuitions without concepts are blind. Therefore it is equally necessary to make our concepts sensuous, that is, to add to them their object in intuition, as to make our intuitions intelligible, that is, to bring them under concepts. These two powers or faculties cannot exchange their functions. The understanding cannot see, the senses cannot think. By their union only can knowledge be produced. But this is no reason for confounding the share which belongs to each in the production of knowledge. On the contrary, they should always be carefully separated and distinguished, and we have therefore divided the science of the rules of sensibility in general, that is, æsthetic, from the science of the rules of the understanding in general, that is, logic." (Page 40.)

The distinction thus made is in the main sound and yet not altogether satisfactory. At all events, it is not satisfactory so long as the two elements are held apart as if they could possibly exist separately in consciousness. It is of course true that to give a conception any connection with reality there must be some kind of perception, and in perception we are passive in this sense, that we cannot have perceptions or intuitions at will or dismiss them at pleasure. Hence all fruitful thinking must connect with reality through perception, which in turn as we are constructed is founded upon some form of affection of our sensibility. Without this our concepts merely float in the air and are purely formal, as when we think of the contents of a new sense which we do not possess. In this case we can talk formally as wisely as we can of a real sense, say that of color, but inasmuch as there is no experience corresponding to it it remains empty. And it is equally clear that impressions without some conception for their expression and understanding are altogether blind. We must, however, be careful not to suppose that the distinction thus made is one which can be clearly realized in experience. We see that the pure sensibility is only a limit to which experience can never attain, for when the last thought element vanishes there no longer is any articulate consciousness whatever. The distinction, therefore, is not to be made absolute, and when Kant extends the sensibility to include the forms of space and time, as if they were a species of passive intuition, the distinction becomes quite untenable; for the spatial and temporal synthesis is also a promiennt form of mental activity and is in no way to be looked upon as a passive reception of forms and figures. It may be said that Kant himself later recognized this fact in the functions which he ascribes to the imagination both in original apprehension and in reproduction. In that case we shall have to regard the distinction as Kant makes it at the start as a kind of provisional one for the sake of getting his doctrine understood, and not as one to be taken with exact literalness.

We now proceed to Kant's doctrine of space and time which gives his answer to the question, How is pure mathematics possible? And first we consider his doctrine of space.

Space

Kant's general doctrine of space is that it is the form of experience and no reality in itself and also no relation of things in themselves apart from intellect. It exists, then, only for and through intelligence; and apart from the experience of which it is the form it is nothing. For this general doctrine, however, he does not give the best of reasons. The exposition throughout is confused and at times inconsequent. This fact is not to be wondered at, since Kant's doctrine in this matter was a new departure in the world of thought, and it seldom happens that such a new departure receives its adequate and final exposition at the beginning.

In the exposition Kant sets forth the following statements: —

1. "Space is not an empirical concept which has been derived from external experience. For in order that certain sensations should be referred to something outside himself, that is, to something in a different part of space from that where I am; again, in order that I may be able to represent them as side by side, that is, not only as different but as in different places, the representation of space must already be there. Therefore the representation of space cannot be borrowed through experience from relations of external phenomena, but, on the contrary, this external experience becomes possible only by means of the representation of space."

2. "Space is a necessary representation a priori, forming the very foundation of all external intuitions. It is impossible to imagine that there should be no space, though one might very well imagine that there should be space without objects to fill it. Space is therefore regarded as a condition of the possibility of phenomena, not as a determination produced by them; it is a representation a priori which necessarily precedes all external phenomena."

3. "Space is not a discursive or so-called general concept of the relations of things in general, but a pure intuition. For first of all we can imagine one space only, and if we speak of many spaces we mean parts

only of one and the same space. Nor can these parts be considered as antecedent to the one and all-embracing space, and, as it were, its component parts out of which an aggregate is formed, but they can be thought of as existing within it only. Space is essentially one; its multiplicity, and therefore the general concept of spaces in general, arises entirely from limitations. Hence it follows that with respect to space, an intuition a priori, which is not empirical, must form the foundation of all conceptions of space."

"Space is represented as an infinite quantity. Now a general concept of space, which is found in a foot as well as in an ell, could tell us nothing in respect to the quantity of the space. If there were not infinity in the progression of intuition, no concept of relations of space could ever contain a principle of infinity." (Page 18.)

In drawing conclusions from these statements Kant holds that space is nothing but the form of all phenomena of the external senses or the subjective condition of our sensibility. And we can affirm space and understand objects only from the human standpoint.

On the first point stated by Kant there need be no question. Space is not a mere abstraction built up in experience. The general fact that nothing whatever can exist for mind except through a constructive activity by the mind makes it necessary to hold that space, supposing it to be objectively real, could not pass bodily into the mind, but could exist for the mind only as the mind gives its experience this spatial form. The other points made by Kant, however, are more questionable. He speaks of space as a necessary representation or perception, as if it were an object and even as if it preceded the perception of other objects. He likewise calls it the form of perception or the form of all phenomena of the external sense. These two conceptions are by no means the same thing. As the form of experience it would not itself be a given object. Furthermore, from the fact that space is originally a form of human experience it does not follow, without further reasons than Kant gives, that space is limited only to phenomena or to the field of human experience. For all that he says it would be possible to view space as universal for all experience of whatever kind, human or otherwise.

The psychology of to-day, even when holding to Kant's general doctrine of space, is compelled to present the matter in a different way. Space is not originally given as one and infinite, neither is it given as a perception which is the condition of other perceptions. The mind on the basis of its sense affections builds up various spatial objects and sets these in spatial relations to one another, without any thought whatever of the unity and infinity of space. Acting as it does under the space law, it produces its limited spatial experience, and it is only later, when reflection begins, that the unity and infinity of space comes into thought. Indeed, in our concrete experience even the unity of space depends upon a certain continuity and quality within experience itself. When we imagine a series of spatial figures at successive times it never occurs to us to think that these figures, though spatial, are yet in the same space. Each is in its own space at the time of imagining, but there is no one space that contains them all. Similarly our sense experience might well have been such that different experiences might each have had the spatial form without, however, suggesting any one space in which they might all be comprised. There are two things in question in this matter, the unity and infinity of the pure geometrical intuition, and the unity and infinity within concrete experience itself. In the former case we find it possible in imagination to posit points and by a continuous process to pass from any one to any other. And as this process of positing points is endless, and as all the points we can posit can be comprised in the one scheme, we come to speak of space as one and all-embracing. But this is nothing that was given as any original perception or intuition. It arises entirely from reflection upon the space law itself. The same is true for the supposed real space. We relate our objects in a common scheme and thus space appears to be one. We relate all our objects in one and the same scheme and thus space appears to be all-embracing. Finally the form of relation admits of indefinite reproduction and thus space appears to be infinite; but the community is simply the community of the law. The all-embracing character of space means simply the applicability of this law to all external objects. The infinitude of space is only the inexhaustibility of the spatial synthesis. None of these properties is an adequate perception of object-ive fact, but only a reflective implication of the space law.

With regard to the space of concrete experience the same fact is evident. We seldom extend the spatial synthesis beyond surrounding objects. These we relate in mutual externality and relative position. Beyond this we seldom go. The unity and infinity of space lie latent in thought and only emerge upon occasion. Often we leave our objects so unrelated that they do not seem to be in space at all. At other times we fail to relate our several groups and seem to have several spaces. We experience something of the same kind in traveling, when we drop out the intermediate links between the successive spatial groups. We believe that they could be united in a common space intuition, but so far as the experience itself goes there is nothing to compel it or even to suggest it. For this there is needed a certain continuity in the experience itself, and it is quite conceivable, as just suggested, that our experience should have been such that we should never have united our objects in a common spatial scheme.

While, then, we may hold to Kant's general conception of the a priori nature of space and even to its subjective character, we certainly cannot hold it in the form in which Kant has presented it nor for the reasons that he has given. Behind the representation of the infinite void, which Kant seems at times to think is given, is a vast amount of reflective activity which does not represent any a priori perception, but rather an a priori judgment. In this use of the term "a priori" Kant is by no means clear and consistent. As applied to judgments a priori it has a definite meaning. It means not that the judgment is prior to all experience, but that it is not based upon experience, its validity depending upon the mind's own insight; but when applied to perception, a priori must mean prior to all experience and in that case it is absurd. There is no such a priori perception. When, then, Kant speaks of the a priori perception of space as conditioning all empirical conception of individual objects in space, he is confused.

The exposition of the doctrine as thus given appears in the first edition. In the second edition the same matter with very slight variation reappears, but some new matter is added. In the later edition Kant distinguishes what he calls the metaphysical exposition of the idea of space and the transcendental exposition of the idea. The metaphysical exposition is that already given. The transcendental exposition is something new. The argument is based on the possibility of geometry and seems to be really the argument on which he most relies. It appears in full in the second edition of the "Critique," but also in the "Prolegomena." He says: —

"Geometry is a science which determines the properties of space synthetically, and yet a priori. What, then, must be the representation of space, to render such a knowledge of it possible? It must be originally intuitive; for it is impossible from a mere concept to deduce propositions which go beyond that concept as we do in geometry. That intuition, however, must be a priori, that is, it must exist within us before any perception of the object, and must therefore be pure, not empirical intuition. For all geometrical propositions are apodictic, that is, connected with the consciousness of their necessity, as, for instance, the proposition that space has only three dimensions; and such propositions cannot be empirical judgments, nor conclusions from them."

"How, then, can an external intuition dwell in the mind anterior to the objects themselves and in which the concept of objects can be determined a priori? Evidently not otherwise than so far as it has its seat in the subject only, as the formal condition under which the subject is affected by the objects and thereby is receiving an immediate representation, that is, intuition of them; therefore as a form of the external sense in general.

"It is therefore by our explanation only that the possibility of geometry as a synthetical science a priori becomes intelligible. Every other explanation, which fails to account for this possibility, can best be distinguished from our own by that criterion, although it may seem to have some similarity with it." (Page 728.)

Here Kant assumes the truth of mathematics and makes its possibility depend upon the doctrine that space is the general form of our external sense, and geometry which gives the laws of that form is therefore valid for all objects that come within the range of our external experience. If we were asked to tell what the colors of objects must be we could not do so. If, however, we knew that the eye in itself prescribes a certain list of colors and that any class falling outside of that list could never be given to us, we could then tell the limits within which all colors in experience must lie, because the ground of color would exist not in the objects themselves alone, but also and more decisively in the eye itself. Again, the objects in a kaleidoscope might have various forms and take on various shapes and we could not tell a priori what forms and shapes they may possess, but if we know the law of the instrument we are able to see that whatever the forms and shapes may be in themselves they will have certain qualities due to the mathematical nature of the kaleidoscope. Now, in the same way Kant would conceive a form of space to be the general law of our external sense and mathematics would be simply specifications of that law. Hence we can say that the laws of geometry will always be apodictically valid for us, because they condition our experience in its spatial aspect and hence we will be sure of their validity for our experience.

This is Kant's transcendental exposition of the idea of space from which he infers its subjectivity. Geometry is something indisputable, its truths being universal and necessary. As such they cannot be gained from experience, but must be expressions of the nature of the mind. This transcendental argument Kant seems to regard as a considerable advance on the metaphysical argument before given. But this argument also is not entirely satisfactory. We may allow that without affirming the a priori character of geometry in the sense of being founded upon our mental nature, there could be no principles in mathematics. This is the truth in Kant's claim. If we take the atomistic and passive conception of the mind held by Hume, it is clear that such a mind would have no logical right to faith in anything. It must be therefore purely descriptive and recitative, telling what it has found in past experience, but utterly unable to prescribe or tell what must be true for all experience everywhere and always. Empiricism of this type, then, is fatal to all knowledge, higher and lower alike, though it seems more fatal to moral and spiritual insight than to ordinary and scientific notions. It reduces the mind to a mere impotency which may not prescribe anything and can at best only be the servant of sense and passion. It is this conception of empiricism that made it such a solvent of all higher faiths and such a servant of sense and sensualism. It is this fact that explains the hostility which has always been felt by earnest and thoughtful persons for the doctrine. The a priori doctrine, then, is a negative condition of geometrical truth, but this view might be held without establishing geometrical truth on a firm foundation; for the question would still arise, What warrant have we for saying that the a priori utterances of the mind are forever valid or even that they are valid at all? There seems to be no reason for saying that a thing is certainly true because it is a priori, for it is still possible that the a priori element may belong to error or that it might undergo change, and the only reply to this would be that the mind must at least have faith in itself and its own rational insight, no matter what we call it. We must of course refrain from views that would undermine this faith, but even then we come at last to a point where we have to fall back on the mind's own trust in itself. The a priori character of knowledge, then, is not decisive. It is a negative condition, but for positive knowledge we have to fall back on our rational insight. In the case of mathematics we fall back on our insight into the nature of space and number and not upon any particular theory of knowledge. The old empirical doctrine would indeed make mathematics impossible, that is, it would undermine our confidence in mathematics; but our confidence in any case does not depend upon our theory of knowledge, but entirely upon the insight we possess into the spatial and numerical intuition. Kant himself would hardly claim that geometry was any more firmly established after his transcendental exposition of the idea of space than it was before. Kant's further conclusion, as a result of his transcendental exposition, that space is subjective and relative to ourselves, is something which is groundless; but this point will come up for later discussion.

It seems then that Kant's a priori conception of space helps us to mathematics only in a partial way. In so far as it rejects the mere passivity of empiricism it is on the right road, but when it rests its positive confidence on apriorism it does not seem to be entirely satisfactory, and all the more so because Kant himself goes on to restrict geometrical truth to the limits of human experience and denies it to things in themselves. But if we allow that the mind has at least some power to know, there seems to be no good reason why the mind might not have insight into space relations as things in themselves, if there were any reason for thinking that space is a thing in itself. The mere fact that space is a thing which we do not make but find, ought not to make our knowledge of it impossible, any more than the same fact with respect to our neighbors prohibits our knowing something about them. The fact that space is a law of thought does not forbid that it should also be a law of things. There is nothing whatever in what Kant has offered thus far to forbid our thinking that space is at once a law of thought and also a form of reality, so that it shall be both subjective and objective. And this looks so much like the plain indication of experience that it would have to be accepted unless some reasons were found for limiting space to purely subjective validity. Such reasons could be found only in the contradictions or impossibilities that emerge when space is taken to be a real thing in itself. All that is done by Kant in this direction is given in the two first antinomies, where the only question raised is that concerning the finitude or infinitude of the world in space and time. The other and deeper difficulties in the case Kant nowhere develops.

We must say, then, that Kant's doctrine of space in relation to geometry is very far from satisfactory, and it is still less satisfactory in its general relation to knowledge. We have before pointed out that knowledge is conditioned partly by the subject and partly by the object, and have said that Kant was very right in emphasizing the conditions that lie in the nature of the subject. The mind that is to know nature must be able to rebuild nature in thought, and it can do that only as it contains the principles of nature within itself as immanent laws of its own procedure. But this fact must not lead us to forget that the object also is equally an important factor in knowing, for if we suppose that the movements of thought and its constructive principles lie in no way parallel to the system of objects and the relations which obtain

45

among them, we are landed forthwith in solipsism
and the object disappears altogether; and not only
the object, but the neighbors, equally disappear, for
we succeed in reaching the existence of our neighbors only through the same constructive activity of
thought; and if we will not allow that this activity
truly grasps things and relations existing apart from
it, then solipsism is the immediate result. As we shall
later see, this point has been entirely overlooked by
Kant. He has a world of things in themselves of
whose existence he appears to have no doubt, but
which he thinks we can never know; and then he proceeds to deal with these things in such a fashion as
to make them utterly empty, without any contents
whatever. And this is true not merely of the world
of things, but also and equally of the world of persons.
But we postpone the discussion of this point to a later
chapter. It suffices here to refer to the matter and to
point out that the doctrine is left in very considerable
confusion. As we have said before, we may hold that
space is simply the form of experience, but we must
hold it for reasons different from what Kant gives
and must also hold it in a somewhat different form
from that which he offers.

Time

Kant's doctrine of time is very similar to that of
space. It is not an empirical concept deduced from
experience, but is a necessary representation on which
all intuitions depend. It is, too, not a general concept,
but a pure form of sensuous intuition, and the original
representation of time must be given as unlimited.

Much the same may be said with respect to this that was said with respect to space. It is not true that time is given originally as infinite and one, and it is not true that it is primarily a representation or perception at all. The time experience arises not through any limitation of the original perception of infinite time, but solely through the relation of the elements of experience to self and to one another under the temporal form. That is, the basal fact is a law of relation in the mind, and the properties of time are to be understood from the side of this relating act. As all events are related by the same law and in a given scheme, time is said to be one. The unity consists entirely in the fact of a single system of relations according to the same law, so that from any point whatever in the system we can find our way to any other by a continuous process. If there were any events which could not be related in one scheme, time would not be one; but as no event can be conceived which cannot thus be related, time is not only one, it is also infinite and all-embracing. But the unity and infinity of time are only consequences of the fact that the law of synthesis is one and extends to all events. Ordinarily we do not extend the temporal synthesis beyond adjacent events. We give these the relation of antecedence and sequence, and ignore their relation to other events or groups of events. The unity and infinity of time commonly lie latent in the background of our thought. Here, then, as in the case of space, we do not believe in the original apprehension of the unity and infinity of time, for this apprehension is consequent and not first. The basal fact is the law of temporal synthesis whereby the concrete temporal experience is made possible, and then by reflection on the nature of the time law we come to affirm its unity and infinitude.

As geometry is the science of space, so for Kant arithmetic is the science of time. There is something a little arbitrary in restricting arithmetic to time, and it was apparently done out of Kant's love of system; for the really important thing in arithmetic is number, and the important thing in number is the discriminability of things and events, whether in space or in time. However, Kant makes number the science of time, and founds the possibility of arithmetic upon the a priori character of time as the form of the internal sense, as space is the form of the external sense.

Here again the previous criticism of the foundation of geometry must be repeated. Without some a priori insight of the mind there could be no science of arithmetic; but after all it depends more upon the insight than upon its a priori character, the a priori element being, as we have said, only of negative use in excluding the passive doctrine of mind which Hume held and the implications of that doctrine.

As to the subjectivity of time or its non-applicability to things in themselves, Kant is even less satisfactory than he is in treating of the subjectivity of space, as indeed the doctrine is more difficult when applied to time. We have in a fashion a certain experience of non-spatial facts in the inner life, but we have no such experience of non-temporality. So far as Kant's argument goes it is entirely possible for

us to believe that time is an a priori element in knowing, and at the same time to hold that it is likewise
a veritable fact in the objective movement of reality.

In general the ideality of time is a more difficult
doctrine than the ideality of space, because we have
in our inner life some illustration of non-spatial
experience, while the time relation enters into consciousness itself. We have, then, no illustration whatever of a timeless experience, while we do have
illustrations of a spaceless one. On this account the
objection was very early made to the ideality of time,
that whether external changes are denied or not, we
are certainly conscious of change in our own mental
states and the change in these states presupposes
change in the external ground. Since, then, we are
conscious of change in our own mental states, the
idea of time is given as a fact which can in no way be
escaped. Kant replies to this by saying that time is
subjectively real or empirically real, but it is not real
for things in themselves. He in no way, however,
succeeds in showing how this distinction can be maintained. Change can never be eliminated from the
world of experience, and this world of experience can
never be in any way looked upon as a manifestation
of a changeless order beyond it. Hence change is
real, and if the reality of change implied the reality
of time, time also is real, not merely for our experience
but for things in themselves. Kant never adequately
considered this difficulty, and indeed it cannot be
solved upon the impersonal plane at all. We must
carry the question of time up into the field of self-
consciousness, and discern its relativity and in what

a possible timelessness would consist. But this question we reserve for later discussion when we come to consider Kant's general doctrine of phenomena and things in themselves.

So much for Kant's general doctrine of the sensibility and its forms, space and time. As already pointed out, many objections could be made to the order in which Kant puts the doctrine, and especially to the utterances here and there where he seems to assume that the sensibility as such can give us the world of spatial and temporal perceptions. Of course this is not the case, as Kant himself clearly recognizes later on. Perception, as he says, is possible only through various functions of the understanding whereby a spatial phenomenon becomes something definite for us. To recur to our illustration of the moving body, we cannot say that we see the body move merely on the basis of what can be sensuously presented, for we have precisely the same sense affection and sense phenomena in the case of moving pictures that we have in the case of a moving body. In the latter case, then, evidently something has been added to sense, namely, an interpretation of the sense impression, a working-over of it into the forms of the understanding. We are therefore to regard the sensibility and the understanding as different aspects of our mental life, and not as things which can go on in complete separation from one another. The distinction between them, however, is important for the understanding of our mental life. Whatever we call the sensibility or whatever our psychological classification of it may be, it is in any case something without which thought remains formal and empty. We get perceptions only through modifications of the sensibility, and apart from these we have nothing but formal conceptions, which as such have no contents, as would be the case when we speak of a kind of sensation lying beyond the ordinary five senses. We can speak of such sensations, but they will be no real experience and therefore are only forms of words.

The distinction between a space and time world and the world of the understanding is very convenient also in the exposition of our problems. The space and time world admits of description in terms of coexistence and succession without making any deep excursion into metaphysics. As in the case of our moving pictures we could name and describe the orders of coexistence and sequence without taking account of the metaphysical elements involved in the realities they may be supposed to represent, so in the space and time world of experience there is a large amount that can be described in terms of coexistence and sequence of phenomena without passing to the unpicturable notions of the understanding. The former realm belongs to descriptive science, the latter realm to philosophical interpretation; and by keeping the two quite distinct we tend to greater clearness both in science and in speculation. We might all agree as to the space and time order, and might differ widely in our conception of the metaphysical system by which that order is to be explained. We now pass to the work of the understanding or the forms of thought.

II

In the introduction to this section Kant gives the general distinction between the work of the sensibility and the work of the understanding which we have before quoted. Through the sensibility we receive impressions and are connected with reality. Kant speaks of the sensibility as the "receptivity of the soul." The understanding, on the other hand, is a reaction against the affections of the sensibility. He calls it "the power of producing representations or the spontaneity of knowledge." Neither of these qualities or faculties is preferable to the other and neither can dispense with the other; for, as we have before quoted, "thoughts without contents are empty; intuitions without concepts are blind." The sense impression without the form of the understanding is no articulate apprehension whatever, and the work of the understanding without the sense impression is itself without material, moving through the air without an object. The understanding, then, reacts upon the sense impression, forms it and lifts it up into articulate conception, and only thus do we attain to any definite knowledge. It should be pointed out also that this work of the understanding is equally necessary to articulate perception. At the beginning Kant is not clear enough on this point and speaks of objects as given us in perception, giving the impression that

52

perception may be complete in itself without the work of the understanding. But whatever Kant's thought in the case was, there is no question nowadays that perception itself, even of a sensation, by the time it is anything articulate for intellect, undergoes the formative activity of the understanding. We have before referred to this fact in connection with the simpler sensations or recurrent sensations of different sorts. So then once more we are not to think that the sense experience, even in its lowest forms, can go on apart from the activity of the understanding.

Kant distinguishes general logic from transcendental logic. The former means simply the traditional logic of the syllogistic type, which takes no account of the contents of knowledge and treats of nothing but the mere form of reasoning. Transcendental logic, on the other hand, does not entirely ignore the contents of knowledge. It always treats of the origin of our knowledge so far as it has an a priori character. This science which has to determine the origin, the extent, and the objective validity of our a priori knowledge he calls transcendental logic. It is then essentially an inquiry into the nature and conditions of our a priori knowledge. This transcendental logic is further divided into transcendental analytic and dialectic.

"In transcendental logic," he says, "we isolate the understanding, as before in transcendental æsthetic the sensibility, and fix our attention on that part of thought only which has its origin entirely in the understanding. The application of this pure knowledge has for its condition that objects are given in intuition, to which it can be applied, for without intuition all our knowledge would be without objects, and it would therefore remain entirely empty. That part of transcendental logic, therefore, which teaches the elements of the pure knowledge of the understanding, and the principles without which no object can be thought, is transcendental Analytic, and at the same time a logic of truth. No knowledge can contradict it without losing at the same time all contents, that is, all relation to any object, and therefore all truth. But as it is very tempting to use this pure knowledge of the understanding and its principles by themselves, and even beyond the limits of all experience, which alone can supply the material or the objects to which those pure concepts of the understanding can be applied, the understanding runs the risk of making, through mere sophisms, a material use of the purely formal principles of the pure understanding, and thus of judging indiscriminatingly of objects which are not given to us, nay, perhaps can never be given. As it is properly meant to be a mere canon for criticizing the empirical use of the understanding, it is a real abuse if it is allowed as an organum of its general and unlimited application, by our venturing, with the pure understanding alone, to judge synthetically of objects in general or to affirm and decide anything about them. In this case the employment of the pure understanding would become dialectical.

"The second part of transcendental logic must therefore form a critique of that dialectical semblance and is called transcendental Dialectic, not as an art of producing dogmatically such semblance (an art but too popular with many metaphysical jugglers), but as a critique of the understanding and reason with regard to their hyperphysical employment, in order thus to lay bare the false semblance of its groundless pretensions, and to reduce its claims to discovery and expansion, which was to be achieved by means of transcendental principles only, to a mere critique, serving as a protection of the pure understanding against all sophistical illusions." (Page 49.)

We are here introduced to Kant's distinction between the understanding and the reason. The understanding has the function of working over sense material into the forms of articulate experience. It does this by virtue of principles immanent in itself which Kant calls the categories, but the field of application of these categories is also and only that of sense impression. In this way the material of sense becomes articulate experience, and in this field the understanding finds its true and proper function. When it ventures beyond this it then loses contact with reality and falls a prey to multitudinous illusions. This is the dialectic of the pure reason, that is of the understanding, when it ventures beyond its realm.

Transcendental Analytic

This section discusses first the concepts, and second the principles of the pure understanding. The concepts are the categories according to which the understanding proceeds, and the principles deal with these concepts as applied to the building-up of the system of knowledge.

The first thing is to discover the pure concepts of

the understanding. And since all knowledge consists in the form of a judgment, Kant thinks by analyzing the forms of judgment to find the ideas according to which it proceeds. In order to lead up to this he defines the understanding as the faculty of judging, and concludes that "the functions of the understanding can be discovered in their completeness if it is possible to represent the functions of unity in judgments." Here Kant has recourse to the table of judgments given in the traditional formal logic as something readymade to his hand. There are four classes of these judgments.

Table of Judgments

I	II
Quantity of Judgments	Quality
Universal	Affirmative
Particular	Negative
Singular	Infinite

III	IV
Relation	Modality
Categorical	Problematical
Hypothetical	Assertory
Disjunctive	Apodictic

From this table of judgments Kant deduces the following table of categories: —

Table of Categories

I	II
Of Quantity	Of Quality
Unity	Reality
Plurality	Negation
Totality	Limitation

56

TRANSCENDENTAL ANALYTIC

III	IV
Of Relation	Of Modality
Inherence and Subsistence (substantia et accidens)	Possibility Impossibility Existence Non-existence
Of Causality and Dependence (cause and effect)	Necessity Contingency
Of Community (reciprocity between the active and the passive)	

It is by no means easy to follow Kant in the details of this discovery, or as he later calls it, "the metaphysical deduction of the categories." He says, "All judgments are functions of unity among our representations, the knowledge of an object being brought about, not by an immediate representation, but by a higher one comprehending this and several others, so that many possible cognitions are collected into one." (Page 57.) It is hard to find the way in which this conception of the judgment as essentially a function of unity among our representations enables us to pass from the table of judgments to the particular categories which Kant enumerates. But not to insist upon this in a general way, we may follow the exposition given by Professor Watson, in his "Philosophy of Kant Explained," as being the most satisfactory and sympathetic account of the matter. "In such a judgment as, 'Man is mortal,' the quantity is said to be universal, because the predicate 'mortal,' is affirmed of every member of the class 'man.' The category corresponding to this subsumption of all individuals under one conception must be totality. No doubt the universal is not an abstract idea, but a combination of perceptual elements, nevertheless the function of thought will be fundamentally the same. A particular judgment, such as, 'Some men are wise,' divides up the abstract conception into its logical parts, and the corresponding category will therefore be a number of separate perceptual elements regarded as several or manifold. The category then is plurality. In the singular judgment, such as, 'Socrates is a man,' we are not dealing with a general or abstract conception, but rather with an individual. In the analytic judgment no distinction is made between the singular and the universal judgment, because the predicate is affirmed of the subject without qualification. But, argues Kant, the function of unity presupposed in the singular judgment must be made explicit when we are dealing with synthetic judgments, because here we have to see the object in the making, so to speak. Hence the function of thought implied in this form of judgment is unity. Taking the categories in the reverse order, Kant enumerates the categories of quantity as unity, plurality, and totality."

In judgments of quality the "function presupposed in the affirmative judgment is the determination of an object of perception as a reality. The negative judgment must yield, when it is interpreted from the synthetic point of view, the category of non-reality or negation. Negation, it must be observed, is not the mere absence of reality, but the negation of a certain given or limited reality. Then, lastly, the infinite judgment which excludes a conception from one sphere and puts it into another, yields the category of limitation, which is just a synthesis of reality and negation."

58

In relation a category "affirms directly or without limitation. Now, when we are dealing with actual objects of experience, simple or unconditional predication must consist in attributing properties to a substance; hence our category is inherence and subsistence." In the hypothetical judgment a predicate is not affirmed without qualification, but only under condition. "Now when we are dealing with actual objects of experience, conditionality, or the dependence of one element upon another, must take the form of real dependence," giving the relation of cause and effect. "In the disjunctive judgment, which takes the form 'A is either B or C,' we have a whole of conception, together with subordinate conceptions, which in their totality constitute the whole. . . . When this principle of the reciprocal exclusiveness of two conceptions which together constitute a totality is applied to real objects of experience, we must have the mutual exclusion and yet relation of real substances, and this is the category of community or reciprocal causation."

"The first form of the modal judgment is the problematic. . . . When this principle is applied to possible objects of experience, we get the categories of possibility and impossibility. The assertoric judgment, again, asserts a connection of ideas without any limitation. The function of thought in the synthetic judgment will, therefore, be the comprehension of a real object of experience as existing or not existing. . . . The category, then, is existence and nonexistence. Lastly, the apodictic judgment asserts the absolutely necessary connection of two conceptions;

that is, its principle is that two given conceptions must necessarily be thought as correlative. And when we apply this principle to objects of experience, we get the categories of necessity and contingency, meaning by necessity the necessity of an object of experience, and by contingency the denial of such necessity."

This is the gist of Professor Watson's explanation of the deduction of the categories from the table of judgments. He adds: "By following the guiding thread of the forms of judgment, as tabulated by general logic, we have thus been enabled to discover the pure conceptions of the understanding, and to discover all of them. These pure conceptions are the functions of unity constitutive of the very nature of understanding; without which, therefore, no knowledge of objects of experience can be obtained; and we may have perfect confidence in the validity of our derivation, because the list of conceptions has not been picked up empirically, but has been derived from a single principle, namely, the faculty of judgment."[1]

Kant himself seemed to think very highly of this deduction. He says: "The classification is systematical, and founded on a common principle, namely, the faculty of judging (which is the same as the faculty of thinking). It is not the result of a search after pure concepts undertaken at haphazard, the completeness of which, as based on induction only, could never be guaranteed. Nor could we otherwise understand why these concepts only, and no others, abide in the pure understanding. It was an enterprise

[1] *Philosophy of Kant Explained*, p. 128.

worthy of an acute thinker like Aristotle to try to discover these fundamental concepts; but as he had no guiding principle he merely picked them up as they occurred to him." (Page 67.)

Kant, then, seems to regard himself as having had a guiding principle which has enabled him to discover the complete table of the pure concepts of the understanding. Nevertheless it is not possible to feel the satisfaction which Kant himself apparently felt. Some of his categories are doubtful, and some other categories quite as important as those he has given are left unmentioned. If his aim had been to show that there are rational categories underlying judgments, without insisting upon calling this a deduction from the nature of the judgment and from the table of judgments in formal logic, his table might be allowed to stand; but as it is, we really have nothing that can be called a deduction, and the relation of the real categories to the table of judgments is certainly highly artificial. In formal logic proper we have nothing to do with the individuals of perception, but only with the subordination of individuals to a class or of lower classes to higher ones. But for the metaphysical purpose which Kant has in view these judgments are neither first nor fundamental. The singular judgment of perception, whereby the mind really gets articulate objects, is something that does not belong to formal logic at all. The mere subsumption of individuals under a class term, with which formal logic concerns itself, will never give us the individual causes of perception with their metaphysical unities and their relations of substance and attribute; and it is these things which Kant especially needs to find. The judgment of perception is one which really takes place according to the categories, but it is one for which the traditional formal logic makes no provision. It hardly seems too much to say, then, that the judgments which Kant adduces as the source of the categories are not the judgments which really give the categories. In the singular judgment or the judgment of perception, the mind does proceed by the categories of substance and attribute, of unity and identity, etc., and thus and thus only does it reach the singular individual things on which our metaphysical system is based. But the mere subject and predicate of formal logic are very far from identical with the relation of substance and attribute, especially as the subject and predicate in formal logic merely include either individuals in a class, or classes in another class, and expressly aim to exclude all metaphysical thought whatever. The unity also, and the quantity which formal logic deals with, are not metaphysical unities. [They have to do simply with the relation of one or more or all of a set of individuals to a class], and this is not a metaphysical unity such as is involved in the relation of substance and attribute, etc. At all events, it is quite as possible to reach the categories by direct observation of the singular judgments, or of the activity of the mind in articulate perception, as it is in this roundabout way through the formal judgment of quantity and quality.

Similarly with the categories of relation. It is a somewhat obscure passage from the hypothetical and disjunctive judgment to causality and interaction.

The necessity of affirming causal action is much more directly and clearly seen by observing the orders of succession and concomitant variation in experience than by any study of the formal judgments in question; and as commonly used, these judgments do not involve any dynamic relations. Thus I may say all triangles are either acute, rectangular, or oblique; but this does not imply that these three classes are in reciprocal dynamic interaction. In other words, the hypothetical and disjunctive judgment oftentimes expresses cases where causality and interaction are in play, but in its general use as such it does not express any dynamic relation among things. Hence the category of causation is not to be found in the hypothetical and disjunctive judgment as such, but only in particular cases, and in those cases we discover the category without regard to the judgment. We may say, therefore, that a study of actual judgments does reveal that the mind proceeds according to certain conceptions which we may call categories, but it reveals them much more directly to immediate reflection upon the facts of experience than it does when we seek to reach them in this roundabout fashion. Kant's deduction here can hardly be viewed as other than a case of the artificial formalism of which he was so fond.

This brings us to the transcendental deduction of the categories, which is meant to be an advance beyond this metaphysical deduction. For in the latter case we have only discovered the fact that the categories exist, but in the transcendental deduction the aim is to show the necessity of these categories as that without which no mental life whatever would be possible. Kant says, "Jurists, when speaking of rights and claims, distinguish in every lawsuit the question of right from the question of fact, and in demanding proof of both they call the former, which is to show the right or, it may be, the claim, the deduction." (Page 70.) Now something of the same kind is necessary in the philosophical field. In the case of space and time Kant gave a transcendental deduction of geometry and number, of which sciences he never had any doubt, but a greater difficulty exists, he thinks, in the case of the pure concepts of the understanding. In the case of mathematics we have clear insight into the existence of our objects and relations, but this is not true with the understanding. Hence some transcendental deduction of the latter is especially necessary, which shall show the absolute need of these categories in order to any consciousness whatever. "It was easy to show before, when treating of the concepts of space and time, how these, though being knowledge a priori, refer necessarily to objects, and how they make a synthetical knowledge of them possible, which is independent of all experience. For, as no object can appear to us, that is, become an object of empirical intuition, except through such pure forms of sensibility, space and time are pure intuitions which contain a priori the conditions of the possibility of objects as phenomena, and the synthesis in these intuitions possesses objective validity.

"The categories of the understanding, on the contrary, are not conditions under which objects can be given in intuition, and it is quite possible therefore that objects should appear to us without any necessary reference to the functions of the understanding, thus showing that the understanding contains by no means any of their conditions a priori. There arises, therefore, here a difficulty, which we did not meet with in the field of sensibility, namely, how subjective conditions of thought can have objective validity, that is, become conditions of the possibility of the knowledge of objects. It cannot be denied that phenomena may be given in intuition without the functions of the understanding. . . . They must conform to the formal conditions of sensibility existing a priori in the mind, because otherwise they could in no way be objects to us. But why besides this they should conform to the conditions which the understanding requires for the synthetical unity of thought, does not seem to follow quite so easily. For we could quite well imagine that phenomena might possibly be such that the understanding should not find them conforming to the conditions of its synthetical unity, and all might be in such confusion that nothing should appear in the succession of phenomena which could supply a rule of synthesis, and correspond, for instance, to the concept of cause and effect, so that this concept would thus be quite empty, null, and meaningless." (Page 74.)

A transcendental deduction of the categories must then be admitted, but before passing to this we must note first that even sensation as anything articulate cannot be given without some function of the understanding, as we have seen. Even space appearances are nothing for us except as the understanding brings them under fixed ideas. And we point out, second, that the formal conditions of the understanding cannot be arbitrarily imposed upon phenomena. As we have before said, the subjective conditions of subjective thought must be harmonious with the nature of the object. The phenomenon must be taken as a thing, otherwise the object is only the subjective illusion projected as real. This objective harmony between the laws of our thought and the nature of the thing cannot be deduced, but only accepted as implied in the possibility of knowledge. At the same time it cannot be rejected, for then we fall into solipsism and nihilism. We must bear in mind what has before been said about the double condition of knowledge, the subjective and the objective. Unless we do this we shall not understand Kant at all.

III

TRANSCENDENTAL DEDUCTION OF THE CATEGORIES

KANT'S discussion of this topic differs considerably in the second edition of the "Critique" from that given in the first edition, and it is obscure and unsatisfactory in both. His general aim is to show that the categories are the a priori ground of experience, so that without them experience would be impossible. In this general showing his so-called deduction of the categories consists. There is an important truth underlying the doctrine, but in the exposition given by Kant there is a great deal that is inconsequent, very much more that is operose, and somewhat also that is distinctly untenable.

In this discussion Kant was led on by the necessity of showing the spontaneity and active nature of thought in opposition to the pure passivity of the traditional empirical school. The same opposition led him to emphasize the synthetic activity involved in thought in contrast to the fancy of earlier philosophers that thought merely analyzes a given matter. If we bear this general fact in mind, we shall better understand some of the forms which the discussion takes on. The traditional view had been that the objects of perception might be given to a passively recipient mind, which should reflect those objects something as a mirror reflects the things which stand before it, without adding anything to them and even without doing anything more than this passive reflection. In opposition to this, Kant strongly emphasizes the synthetic activity in all our mental operations. Accordingly he begins the transcendental deduction by emphasizing the synthetic function in the mental life in general. In the first edition he distinguished three original sources or faculties, "which contain the conditions of the possibility of all experience, and which themselves cannot be derived from any other faculty, namely, sense, imagination, and apperception. On them is founded, —

"1. The synopsis of the manifold a priori through the senses.
2. The synthesis of this manifold through the imagination.
3. The unity of that synthesis by means of original apperception." (Page 78.)

In explanation and application of these conditions he proceeds to point out that every representation contains something manifold and is presented in our consciousness under the form of time. Each momentary impression disappears as soon as it arises, and hence, if we suppose nothing but separate or discrete impressions, there could be no consciousness of these as such. The consciousness of a single impression could not distinguish that impression from the consciousness of succeeding moments. Hence impression implies not merely a succession of impressions, but a consciousness of the succession. These separate impressions must be gathered up in the unity of the single consciousness of the successive impressions as united into a single object. Kant calls this "the synthesis of apprehension in intuition."

The necessity of this synthesis is obvious for both

empirical and pure elements of perception. Without it we should never be able to have the representations either of concepts or time a priori, because these representations — say of a line or triangle — cannot be produced except by a synthesis of the manifold, which their elements offer.

The next form of synthesis Kant calls the synthesis of reproduction in imagination. As the impressions are momentary and are continually passing away, in order that thought shall not cease the mind must be able to reproduce the past data so as to combine them with the present fact. Kant says: "We must admit a pure transcendental synthesis of imagination which forms even the foundation of the possibility of all experience, such experience being impossible without the reproductibility of phenomena. Now, when I draw a line in thought, or if I think the time from one noon to another, or if I only represent to myself a certain number, it is clear that I must first necessarily apprehend one of these manifold represent-ations after another. . . . And if, while I proceed to what follows, I were unable to reproduce what came before, there would never be a complete representa-tion, and none of the before-mentioned thoughts, not even the first and purest representations of space and time, could ever arise within us.

"The synthesis of apprehension is therefore insep-arably connected with the synthesis of reproduction, and as the former constitutes the transcendental ground of the possibility of all knowledge in general (not only of empirical but also of pure a priori know-ledge), it follows that a reproductive synthesis of imagination belongs to the transcendental acts of the soul. We may therefore call this faculty the transcendental faculty of imagination." (Page 84.)

The third synthesis Kant calls the synthesis of recognition in concepts. He says: "Without our being conscious that what we are thinking now is the same as what we thought a moment before, all reproduction in the series of representations would be vain. Each representation would, in its present state, be a new one, and in no wise belonging to the act by which it was to be produced by degrees, and the manifold in it would never form a whole, because deprived of that unity which consciousness alone can impart to it. If in counting I forget that the unities which now present themselves to my mind have been added gradually one to the other, I should not know the production of the quantity by the successive addition of one to one, nor should I know consequently the number produced by the counting, this number being a concept, consisting entirely in the consciousness of that unity of synthesis." (Page 85.)

All of this is only introductory, but already Kant refers here to a presupposition of knowledge, the significance of which he never fully develops or even realizes. He says of the reproductive imagination: "This law of reproduction, however, presupposes that the phenomena themselves are really subject to such a rule, and that there is in the variety of these representations a sequence and concomitancy subject to certain rules; for without this the faculty of empirical imagination would never find anything to do_that it is able to do, and remain therefore buried

70

within our mind as a dead faculty unknown to ourselves. If cinnabar were sometimes red and sometimes black, sometimes light and sometimes heavy, if a man could be changed now into this, and now into another animal shape, if on the longest day the fields were sometimes covered with fruit, sometimes with ice and snow, the faculty of my empirical imagination would never be in a position, when representing red color, to think of heavy cinnabar. Nor, if a certain name could be given sometimes to this, sometimes to that object, or if the same object could sometimes be called by one and sometimes by another name, without any rule to which representations are subject by themselves, would it be possible that any empirical synthesis of reproduction should ever take place." (Page 83.)

Again, he says in the same line: —

"And here we must needs arrive at a clear understanding of what we mean by an object of representations. We said before that phenomena are nothing but sensuous representations, which therefore by themselves must not be taken for objects outside our faculty of representation. What, then, do we mean if we speak of an object corresponding to, and therefore also different from, our knowledge? It is easy to see that such an object can only be conceived as something in general $= x$; because, beside our knowledge, we have absolutely nothing which we could put down as corresponding to that knowledge.

"Now we find that our conception of the relation of all knowledge to its object contains something of necessity, the object being looked upon as that which prevents our knowledge from being determined at haphazard, and causes it to be determined a priori in a certain way, because, as they are all to refer to an object, they must necessarily, with regard to that object, agree with each other, that is to say, possess that unity which constitutes the concept of an object. . . . This unity of rule determines the manifold and limits it to conditions.

"It is clear, also, that as we can only deal with the manifold in our representations, and as the x corresponding to them (the object), since it is to be something different from all our representations, is really nothing to us, it is clear, I say, that the unity necessitated by the object cannot be anything but the formal unity of our consciousness in the synthesis of the manifold in our representations. Then and then only do we say that we know an object, if we have produced synthetical unity in the manifold of intuition." (Page 86.)

There is, then, according to Kant, an original and transcendental condition of experience which outranks and precedes all others. This he calls transcendental apperception. This "must be a condition which precedes all experience and in fact renders it possible, for thus only could such a transcendental supposition acquire validity. No knowledge can take place in us, no conjunction or unity of one kind of knowledge with another, without that unity of consciousness which precedes all data of intuition, and without reference to which no representation of objects is possible." (Page 88.)

TRANSCENDENTAL DEDUCTION

This is the starting-point of the transcendental deduction. It is a little embarrassing to find what seems to be a new faculty suddenly thrust upon us. The reproductive imagination here appears apparently somewhere between sense and the understanding. The understanding was before defined as a unifying power, and now appears another unifying power, the reproductive imagination, without any clear indication of what its relation is to the other two faculties and of what the unity which it produces consists in. Let us suppose that the imagination produces various unities. Are they of the nature of the unity produced by the understanding, or are they something distinct? Is this faculty itself simply the understanding working spontaneously, or is it something distinct? This is a point left very obscure and indeed unnoticed by Kant, although it is one which a student of Kantian psychology would be glad to have cleared up. It must be further noted that the understanding in this transcendental deduction has become very different from what it was in the metaphysical deduction of the categories. There it was apparently based on the table of formal judgments in the traditional logic, but here the unity which it produces seems to be of quite a different kind. It seems to be largely devoted not to the manipulation of principles, which is the great function of formal logic, but rather to the getting of objects to manipulate; and this is indeed the real field of the categories in their concrete and vital application. Formal logic classifies and deals with objects after we have determined them and their relations, but this transcendental logic is getting the world of concrete objects and their relations. Kant himself does not seem sufficiently to have noted the change of ground in passing from the metaphysical to the transcendental deduction. As to the transcendental unity of apperception, that is only a very large phrase for the unity of self. The necessity of this unity as the condition of all judgment is perfectly manifest. If states of consciousness were simply our states without being united in one consciousness that embraced them all, there would be no articulate consciousness whatever. When two of our states A and B are given, each is separate from the other and no provision for their union is made until there is some conscious subject M, which is neither A nor B, but which embraces both in the unity of its own apprehension. Then by distinguishing, comparing, and uniting them in the unity of one conscious act, it reaches the judgment A is B. But so long as we have only the particular states A and B, they remain mutually external and the judgment is impossible. Hence over against the plurality of coexistence of our states the self must be one. Over against the plurality of successive particular states the self must be both one and abiding. The latter necessity is as manifest as the former, for if we suppose the particular states to be in time, they vanish as fast as they are born; and if there be nothing that abides across this flow and unites the past and the present in the unity of its continuous and identical existence, once more the judgment, and with it all articulate experience, becomes impossible.

What Kant says about the object will be considered

later on. We remark here only that it has a pretty strong idealistic flavor and seems to make the object only a function of the understanding itself, that is, of the human understanding, because as yet no other understanding is in sight. He says: "It is we, therefore, who carry into the phenomena which we call nature, order and regularity, nay, we should never find them in nature, if we ourselves, or the nature of our mind, had not originally placed them there. For the unity of nature is meant to be a necessary and a priori certain unity in the connection of all phenomena. And how should we a priori have arrived at such a synthetical unity, if the subjective grounds of such unity were not contained a priori in the original sources of our knowledge, and if those subjective conditions did not at the same time possess objective validity, as being the grounds on which alone an object becomes possible in our experience?" (Page 102.) "However exaggerated therefore and absurd it may sound, that the understanding is itself the source of the laws of nature, and of its formal unity, such a statement is nevertheless correct and in accordance with experience. . . . The pure understanding is therefore in the categories the law of the synthetical unity of all phenomena, and thus makes experience, so far as its form is concerned, for the first time possible. This, and no more than this, we are called upon to prove in the transcendental deduction of the categories, namely, to make the relation of the understanding to our sensibility, and through it to all objects of experience, that is, the objective validity of the pure concepts a priori of the understanding, conceivable, and thus to establish their origin and their truth." (Page 104.)

Such is Kant's transcendental deduction of the categories. In no strict sense of the word can it be called a deduction. At the very best it can be viewed only as a discovery of the categories from another point of view than that taken in the metaphysical deduction, and the discovery itself involves no such operose and tedious considerations as Kant himself has given us. Simple reflection on the nature of thought will show that our principles really become principles for us only as the categories of the understanding appear in them. It is plain that if objects did not constitute some kind of system, so as to stand in some intelligible relation to one another and to admit of expression in terms of our rational ideas, we should have no articulate consciousness whatever. If all objects were incommensurable, there could be no subsumptive judgment. If the category of reality and the relation of substance and attribute were removed from the thought world, there would be little that is intelligible left. Without the connection of cause and effect the causal judgment would be worthless. Without the connection of reciprocity or mutual determination, existence breaks up into unrelated elements and no judgment can find its way from one thing to another. Without the continuity of existence, past and future fall hopelessly asunder and nothing is left but vanishing and groundless shadows. And this was the result implied in Hume's denial of connection. The outer world of coexistences broke up into groups of qualities without any inner union, and the world of cause and effect vanished into an unconnected series of groundless events. Even the externality of the world and the existence of other minds disappear on that view, and nothing is left but a groundless and vanishing phantasmagoria in the consciousness of nobody. In this sense we may say that the categories are the condition of all knowledge and of all objects, but this is by no means to deduce them, it is rather to discover them as the actual conditions of the consciousness we actually possess; but Kant has nowhere succeeded in deducing them from the conception of self-consciousness. He has merely succeeded in showing that self-consciousness realizes itself through the categories, and this is far enough from being anything that deserves the high name of the transcendental or other deduction. Moreover even this does not apply by any means to Kant's entire table of categories, some of which are of very doubtful validity, while other categories of far greater importance are omitted. All that we can allow, then, is that the mind itself actually proceeds according to principles immanent in itself in the attainment of consciousness and knowledge. Whether these principles can all be definitely formulated is a question that we have not to consider.

Furthermore, in order to avoid the apparent absurdity in Kant's doctrine that the mind makes nature, we may recur to what has before been said, namely, that a knowing process must in any case proceed according to rules immanent in the mind. If we allow the world to be as real and as independent of us as the most pronounced disciple of common sense would

77

maintain, we must nevertheless hold that the unity of this world arises for us only through the inner constructive and constitutive action of our own minds. Allowing, then, that the cosmic reality exists in its own right, we may still ask how that existent reality becomes an object of knowledge for us. And when we remember that sense alone can give us nothing but discontinuous sensations, and that unaided sense perception at best could give nothing more than discontinuous presentations, we must ask what weaves this rather flimsy and unsubstantial material into a solid and abiding world. It is the mind, and the mind can do it only because the plan and order of nature is implicit in the mind; for nature as known is our own product, just as another's thought, so far as grasped by me, must be immediately my own thought. It has in it, indeed, the necessity of referring to another's thought of which it grasps the content, but nevertheless the thought is mine. In like manner my thought of nature has in it an objective reference, so that I am grasping a content independent of my thought; nevertheless both the form and content of nature, so far as they exist for me, are my own product. Our understanding, then, makes nature in a real and important sense. It is only through the laws of nature immanent in the understanding that any knowledge of an objectively existing nature can possibly arise. Whether, corresponding to the reason by which nature exists for us, there is cosmic reason by which nature has its existence independent of us, is another question. It is a question which Kant did not sufficiently consider. He was led by his doctrine of the subjectivity of the categories to overlook the fact that the forms of the understanding cannot be arbitrarily impressed upon experience, so that knowledge is finally conditioned, as we have before said, not merely by the laws of our thought, but also by some independent nature of the object. When the latter element is omitted the next thing is agnosticism, and the end is solipsism and nihilism.

The following quotation shows how far Kant could go in the latter direction. He gives what he calls a summary representation of the correctness and of the only possibility of this deduction of the pure concepts of the understanding. He says: "If the objects with which our knowledge has to deal were things by themselves, we could have no concepts a priori of them. For where should we take them? If we took them from the object (without asking even the question, how that object could be known to us), our concepts would be empirical only, not concepts a priori. If we took them from within ourselves, then that which is within us only, could not determine the nature of an object different from our representations; that is, supply a ground why there should be a thing to which something like what we have in our thoughts really belongs, and why all this representation should not rather be altogether empty. But if, on the contrary, we have to deal with phenomena only, then it becomes not only possible, but necessary, that certain concepts a priori should precede our empirical knowledge of objects. For being phenomena, they form an object that is within us only, because a mere modification of our sensibility can never exist outside us. The very idea that all these phenomena, and therefore all objects with which we have to deal, are altogether within me, or determinations of my own identical self, implies by itself the necessity of a permanent unity of them in one and the same apperception. . . . Pure concepts of the understanding are therefore a priori possible, nay, with regard to experience, necessary, for this simple reason, because our knowledge has to deal with nothing but phenomena, the possibility of which depends on ourselves, and the connection and unity of which (in the representation of an object) can be found in ourselves only, as antecedent to all experience, nay, as first rendering all experience possible, so far as its form is concerned. On this ground, as the only possible one, our deduction of the categories has been carried out." (Page 105.)

We shall later discuss Kant's general doctrine of phenomena. We here refer simply to a previous statement, that the a priori character of the categories is by no means a sufficient proof of their validity. We have before said that the a priori doctrine is a kind of negative condition of knowledge in the sense that the pure passivity of the mind which Hume maintained makes the mind really incapable of knowledge of any kind. On this account, then, we must affirm a certain activity on the part of the mind as a necessary condition of all knowledge, and in this sense the a priori doctrine must be maintained. But it by no means follows that things are true because they are a priori. They might well be a priori principles, that is principles derived from the mind itself, which nevertheless lead us astray. And indeed Kant's own view with regard to knowledge comes dangerously near to this conception. Knowledge is a priori, and yet is not true for reality, but only for appearance. Moreover, as we shall also see, this statement that the mind makes the object, while having a certain subjective truth, is only half the matter, for if we take it in strict literalness the result is to shut us up, as we have seen, to solipsistic negation and nihilism.

Analytic of Principles

The analytic, as we have seen, is divided into two parts: the analytic of conceptions, of which the aim is to discover and vindicate the validity of the categories; and the analytic of principles, of which the aim is to determine the use of the categories in judgment or in application. The latter power, which we are now to consider, is also divided into two. We must first determine the conditions under which the categories are used, and next discover the a priori principles involved in the use of the categories under these conditions. The problems then become the schematism of the pure concepts of the understanding and the system of all principles of the pure understanding. It is hard to escape a certain impression of arbitrariness in this section. There seems to be in some respects a reduplication of the work of the previous chapters. When we have discovered what the categories are and determine their validity, it would seem that special conditions of application need not be considered; but in the system of principles Kant proceeds to give new proofs quite independent of those given in the deduction of the categories, as if he had not entirely satisfied himself in the deduction and wished to try again.

The doctrine of schematism is very confused and does not seem to be particularly useful. The problem is stated by Kant in this form: —

"In comprehending any object under a concept, the representation of the former must be homogeneous with the latter. . . . Thus, for instance, the empirical concept of a plate is homogeneous with the pure geometrical concept of a circle, the roundness which is conceived in the first forming an object of intuition in the latter.

"Now it is clear that pure concepts of the understanding, as compared with empirical or sensuous impressions in general, are entirely heterogeneous, and can never be met with in any intuition. How, then, can the latter be comprehended under the former, or how can the categories be applied to phenomena, as no one is likely to say that causality, for instance, could be seen through the senses and was contained in the phenomenon? It is really this very natural and important question which renders a transcendental doctrine of the faculty of judgment necessary, in order to show how it is possible that any of the pure concepts of the understanding can be applied to phenomena. In all other sciences in which the concepts by which the object is thought in general are not so heterogeneous or different from those which represent it *in concreto*, and as it is given, there is no necessity to enter into any discussions as to the applicability of the former to the latter.

ANALYTIC OF PRINCIPLES

"In our case there must be some third thing homogeneous on the one side with the category, and on the other with the phenomenon, to render the application of the former to the latter possible. This intermediate representation must be pure (free from all that is empirical) and yet intelligible on the one side, and sensuous on the other. Such a representation is the transcendental schema." (Page 112.)

There is, then, according to Kant a need of some kind of go-between which shall unite the sensuous presentations of the sensibility with the unpicturable ideas of the understanding. This go-between he finds in the notion of time, or the schemata of the various categories are derived from time.

"The pure image of all quantities before the external sense is space; that of all objects of the senses in general, time. The pure schema of quantity, however, as a concept of the understanding, is number, a representation which comprehends the successive addition of one to one (homogeneous). Number, therefore, is nothing but the unity of the synthesis of the manifold (repetition) of a homogeneous intuition in general, I myself producing the time in the apprehension of the intuition.

"Reality is, in the pure concept of the understanding, that which corresponds to a sensation in general: that, therefore, the concept of which indicates by itself being (in time), while negation is that the concept of which represents not-being (in time). The opposition of the two takes place therefore by a distinction of one and the same time, as either filled or empty. . . .

"The schema of substance is the permanence of the real in time, that is, the representation of it as a substratum for the empirical determination of time in general, which therefore remains while everything else changes. . . .

"The schema of cause and of the causality of a thing in general is the real which, when once supposed to exist, is always followed by something else. It consists, therefore, in the succession of the manifold, in so far as that succession is subject to a rule.

"The schema of community (reciprocal action) or of the reciprocal causality of substances, in respect to their accidents, is the coexistence, according to a general rule, of the determinations of the one with those of the other.

"The schema of possibility is the agreement of the synthesis of different representations with the conditions of time in general, as, for instance, when opposites cannot exist at the same time in the same thing, but only one after the other. It is therefore the determination of the representation of a thing at any time whatsoever.

"The schema of reality is existence at a given time. The schema of necessity is the existence of an object at all times." (Page 116.)

Thus we see that time is introduced as the schema which is to make clear the application of the categories to the intuitions of sense.

This doctrine seems baseless in its reasoning and a failure in itself. First, as to its reasoning. There seems to be nothing whatever which calls for this picturing of the unpicturable categories. There is no subsumption of the principles of sense under, say, the category of cause, like the subsumption of singulars under a universal in formal logic. There is rather the reference of the objects of sense to the principles of causality as their explanation. There being, then, no subsumption, we need not concern ourselves for any schema to mediate the subsumption which does not exist.

There is, however, a difficulty of another kind which Kant himself does not appreciate, as follows. Concepts, we have seen, without intuitions are empty, and the concepts of the understanding cannot be presented in the intuitions of sense. There is nothing whatever in sense that represents to us the concept of substance or cause or identity, etc. The temporal intuition and the spatial intuition alike are useless in this respect. Hence we might raise the question, What do the categories really mean; are they anything more than merely verbal forms without contents? And clearly they must be regarded as such forms unless we find somewhere in our total experience something which will illustrate these categories and assure us that they have some real meaning; and for this we need not a doctrine of schematism, but an examination of experience in order to see the forms these categories take on in the concrete. Then it appears that when abstractly taken the categories not only defy conception, but contradict themselves, and they continue to do so until they are brought out of their abstraction and are looked upon as modes of intellectual manifestation. Thus if we talk of the categories of being, unity, identity, causality, substance, etc., in abstraction from any given experience we find them utterly vacuous, so that we cannot tell whether there be any corresponding fact or not, and it is only as we find these categories realized in living self-experience that they acquire other than a formal meaning or pass from anything more than purely verbal counters. Thus, take the category of being. Suppose we ask what we mean by it. At least it would be found that it means either objectivity in experience or else it means just our own conscious life. Similarly with identity. This may mean the formal identity of logical meaning, or it may signify a continued existence through a period of time. In the latter case, which is supposed to be the metaphysical meaning, we really do not know by speculation whether such a thing is possible or not. Successive experience is not identity, and changeless existence cannot be found. Here again we have to fall back upon experience. Identity is given as the self-equality of intelligence through experience, and any other conception destroys itself. In like manner, when we attempt to think causality abstractly and impersonally, we lose ourselves in the infinite regress, and if we escape it we have no means of telling whether there is anything corresponding to our ideas or not. The categories, then, are simply abstractions from self-conscious life. They are the modes of operation of the intellect and derive their meaning only from that self-conscious life as they find their only realization in it. But this result is far removed from Kant's operose doctrine of the schematism of the categories.

We pass now to consider the system of principles which Kant lays down.

IV

THE SYSTEM OF ALL PRINCIPLES OF THE PURE UNDERSTANDING

In the transcendental æsthetic Kant satisfied himself with presenting the subjectivity of space and time as the foundation for mathematics, but he made no attempt to develop any other principles of mathematical science. The aim of the transcendental analytic was to show how pure physics was possible, and this possibility is found in the doctrine of the categories; but now Kant proceeds in the present section to point out some of the general principles of science. In this respect he goes beyond what he did in the doctrine of mathematics. He gives a table of principles of the understanding as follows: —

I	II
Axioms of Intuition	Anticipations of Perception
III	IV
Analogies of Experience	Postulates of Empirical Thought in General

The first two classes he calls the mathematical principles and the other two dynamic.

Inasmuch as our experience has the spatial and temporal form and is also founded upon the work of the understanding, we should expect to find the two factors, the sense factor and the rational factor, uniting in our science. The first two divisions given by Kant aim to make mathematics applicable to science, or rather to bring our system of principles under the space and time law so that mathematics can be applied to them. The other two classes relate to the dynamic categories or to the world of power.

For the axioms of intuition Kant lays down the following principle. All phenomena are with reference to their intuition extensive quantities.

Since by hypothesis these phenomena are in space and time, it does not seem very difficult to admit this statement. At the same time Kant gives some rather doubtful reasons in support of them. He says: "I call an extensive quantity that in which the representation of the whole is rendered possible by the representation of its parts, and therefore necessarily preceded by it. I cannot represent to myself any line, however small it may be, without drawing it in thought, that is, without producing all its parts one after the other, starting from a given point, and thus, first of all, drawing its intuition. The same applies to every, even the smallest portion of time. I can only think in it the successive progress from one moment to another, thus producing in the end, by all portions of time and their addition, a definite quantity of time. . . . All phenomena, therefore, when perceived in intuition, are aggregates of previously given parts, which is not the case with every kind of quantities, but with those only which are represented to us and apprehended as extensive." (Page 133.)

If this were taken literally, we should be lost forthwith in the infinite divisibility of space and time, and could never reach any finite quantity whatever. It must, therefore, be taken with allowance. It is much easier to admit directly that spatial and temporal phenomena are extensive quantities admitting of division or increase as a matter of direct insight, than it is to infer the fact from reasoning of this sort.

The anticipations of perception are expressed in the principle that "in all phenomena sensation, and the real which corresponds to it in the object, has an intensive quantity, that is a degree." "All phenomena, therefore, are continuous quantities, whether according to their intuition as extensive or according to mere perception as intensive quantities." This does not tell us very much, but in a way it makes provision for the application of mathematics to the phenomena of experience, whether in the extensions of space and time or in the intensities of natural forces.

The analogies of experience present a problem of greater importance. Here we pass to the metaphysical and dynamic conceptions and come upon problems of greater difficulty. Kant says: "The three modi of time are permanence, succession, and coexistence. There will, therefore, be three rules of all relations of phenomena in time by which the existence of every phenomenon with regard to the unity of time is determined, and these rules will precede all experience, nay, render experience possible. . . .

"These principles have this peculiarity that they do not refer to phenomena and the synthesis of their empirical intuition, but only to the existence of phenomena and their mutual relation with regard to their existence." (Page 144.) In this respect they are different from the mathematical principles which tell us how to produce phenomena according to the rules of a mathematical synthesis, and which therefore might be called constitutive; but "the case is totally different with those modes which are meant to bring the existence of phenomena under rules a priori, for as existence cannot be constructed they can only refer to the relations of existence and become merely regulative principles."

The first analogy is called the principle of permanence, and the principle is given as follows. "All phenomena contain the permanent (substance) as the object itself and the changeable as its determination only, that is, as a mode in which the object exists." It is manifest that Kant here has got out of the realm of phenomenalism into the realm of independent things, for nothing whatever such as is described here is possible in a phenomenal scheme. Kant is really here laying down the foundations of mechanical science as it had existed since the time of Newton. Further Kant reasons very badly for his principle of permanence. He says: "Without something permanent no relation of time is possible. Time by itself, however, cannot be perceived, and it is therefore the permanent in phenomena that forms the substratum for all determination of time, and at the same time the condition of the possibility of all synthetical unity of perceptions, that is, of experience; while with regard to that permanent all existence and all change in time can only be taken as a mode of existence of what is permanent. In all phenomena, therefore, the permanent is the object itself, that is, the substance (phenomenon), while all that changes or can change belongs only to the mode in which substance or substances exist, therefore to their determinations." (Page 150.) "Substances therefore (as phenomena) are the true substrata of all determinations of time. If some substances could arise and others perish, the only condition of the empirical unity of time would be removed, and phenomena would then be referred to two different times in which existence would pass side by side, which is absurd. For there is but one time in which all different times must be placed, not as simultaneous, but as successive.

"Permanence, therefore, is a necessary condition under which alone phenomena, as things or objects, can be determined in a possible experience." (Page 154.)

That in some sense there must be an abiding element to make experience possible, and that change must admit of being gathered up in some fixed expression, is of course perfectly clear, but that question need not be conceived in any such way as Kant here suggests. Neither can the problem of permanence be solved in this crude fashion. On the impersonal plane there is no possibility of combining permanence with change, least of all by a mere analysis of the notion of change. On that plane we cannot reserve anything in the world of change as an abiding element, for as soon as it becomes changeless it no longer explains change, and when it explains change it passes into the changing and changes through and through. The problem here can be solved only as we carry it up to the plane of personality, and find the permanence of experience in the world of meaning and in the self-conscious intelligence which founds and administers the world of meanings under the form of change.

The second analogy Kant calls the principle of production and gives it as follows: "Everything that happens (begins to be) presupposes something on which it follows according to a rule." Under this head Kant discusses the law of causality, and from an altogether different standpoint from that taken in the metaphysical or the transcendental deduction. Kant argues as follows: "The apprehension of the manifold of phenomena is always successive. The representations of the parts follow one upon another. Whether they also follow one upon the other in the object is a second point for reflection, not contained in the former. We may indeed call everything, even every representation, so far as we are conscious of it, an object; but it requires a more profound investigation to discover what this word may mean with regard to phenomena, not in so far as they (as representations) are objects, but in so far as they only signify an object. So far as they, as representations only, are at the same time objects of consciousness, they cannot be distinguished from our apprehension, that is, from their being received in the synthesis of our imagination; and we must therefore say that the manifold of phenomena is always produced in the mind successively. If phenomena were things by themselves, the succession of the representations of their manifold would never enable us to judge how that manifold is connected in the object. We have always to deal with our representations only; how things may be by themselves (without reference to the representations by which they affect us) is completely beyond the sphere of our knowledge. Since, therefore, phenomena are not things by themselves, and are yet the only thing that can be given to us to know, I am asked to say what kind of connection in time belongs to the manifold of the phenomena itself, when the representation of it in our apprehension is always successive. Thus, for instance, the apprehension of the manifold in the phenomenal appearance of a house that stands before me, is successive. The question then arises, whether the manifold of the house itself be successive by itself, which of course no one would admit. Whenever I ask for the transcendental meaning of my concepts of an object, I find that a house is not a thing by itself, but a phenomenon only, that is, a representation, the transcendental object of which is unknown. What, then, can be the meaning of the question, how the manifold in the phenomenon itself (which is not a thing by itself) may be connected." He concludes: "The phenomenon, in contradistinction to the representations of our apprehension, can only be represented as the object different from them, if it is subject to a rule distinguishing it from every other apprehension and necessitating a certain kind of conjunction of the manifold. That which in the phenomenon contains the condition of this necessary rule of apprehension is the object." (Page 155.)

Kant's entire discussion of this subject is hopelessly confused by his doctrine of phenomena which are only representations. He really has, when we take

93

his doctrine at all seriously, many of the difficulties which Hume had in trying to find anything whatever that abides, for phenomena as representations cease with the representing, unless we give to them a species of thinghood which Kant generally forbids, though now and then he comes very close to turning them into things in themselves. He elsewhere speaks of an "affinity of phenomena" which constitutes a kind of rule, and seems to constitute a system of phenomena themselves which have apparently their own nature apart from our apprehension, which nature it is the duty of our apprehension to discover. But in that case phenomena assume a thing-like character and his phenomenalism becomes very much confused; and if we do not take this view, then we are shut up within the solipsistic scheme. We should do better, therefore, to drop Kant's proof of the principle of causation entirely and base the principle upon the insight of reason itself. Since the time of Hume it has been clear that to deny causal connection must end in the abstraction of all experience. This insight, together with the fact that the mind continually affirms such connection by its own authority, is certainly proof enough. At all events it is the only proof we possess, and Kant's alleged proof here is totally inconsequent when taken in connection with his phenomenalism, and is not particularly forcible in any way. This is another case where Kant has given poor reasons for a philosophic truth. The doctrine stands in much clearer evidence when directly looked at than it does when we have these roundabout methods, which after all do not arrive.

Kant's argument for the law of causality is essentially this, that the perception of succession in the orderly world of experience is impossible without the belief in causation. Hence, instead of deducing the law of causation from succession, we must really reverse the process and deduce succession from causality.

This at first sight seems plainly false, for we have a great variety of successions in consciousness without any thought of connecting them causally with each other. For example, we have a succession of feelings or of sensations produced in us we know not how, but we never think in such cases of a causal connection. Again in our external experience we very often trace the temporal order of phenomena without being able to fix any causal order. These obvious facts show that by succession, as Kant is dealing with it here, he means succession in the systematic world of experience, and here it is plain that there is a truth in Kant's view. If we ask how it would be possible to form any articulate conception of the world of succession, it is plain that we could do it only as we further affirm some principle of connection underlying the successions and giving to them that internal connection which Hume meant to deny when he rejected the law of causation. And the chaos [resulting from the denial of this] law of thought shows indirectly the truth of Kant's claim that without this connection of causality there would be no order of experience. In this sense, then, we allow the truth of Kant's claim, but we cannot speak very highly of the argument which he gives. By causality in sequence we commonly understand that the antecedent determines the consequent, that is, produces it or causes it to be. Kant, however, weakens the meaning so as to regard causality as merely succession according to a rule. To be sure he now and then speaks of a necessity in the rule, but seldom. In the argument here Kant seems to be about as much concerned with the proof of objective reality, that is, of the first analogy, as he is with causality, or the second analogy. He points out that we may have a variety of subjective apprehensions, but these are not objects. And the question arises, What is it that turns the subjective apprehensions and their sequences into real objects with real connections among them? The former are not objects because they are in my power. They become objects only when we find uniformity in their connection; that is, when they become independent of our volition and their sequences become, so far as we are concerned, fixed.

As just said, this means the argument for the second analogy runs into that for the first, and indeed, if this argument be allowed, the preceding argument for the first analogy becomes only secondary and really depends upon the argument for the second analogy. There are further difficulties here as to the location of this causality. The necessity of affirming causality somewhere may be admitted, but its nature and location are not thereby determined. For scientific purposes we are really concerned here not with causality but with the rule, that is, with the uniformities of connection among phenomena. The cause itself might not appear in the phenomenal series at all, but might rather be something apart from it, producing the phenomenal series in a fixed order, but yet in such a way that the productive causality would always lie without the series. Thus a musician might produce a series of sounds, or the operator of a stereoscope might cast a series of views upon a screen, but there would really be no causality among the relations of the sounds or views. While the effects in such cases would have to be referred to causality somewhere, they need not by any means be referred to their phenomenal antecedents, but only to their dynamic ground, which consists along with them, but in no way appears within the series of effects. We might, therefore, have a conception of science quite different from that which Kant is setting forth here. We might confine ourselves to the study of the uniformities of coexistence and sequence in the space and time world, without really raising the question of causality at all, and so long as this uniformity was maintained, we should have all the control of phenomena which we now possess and a great deal of knowledge which would practically be very important. It is only, then, in the sense that causality must be affirmed somewhere without deciding as to its nature and location or the form of its manifestation, that we can accept Kant's deduction in any case.

But a very much greater difficulty emerges, arising from Kant's doctrine of phenomena, which at this phase of the discussion is becoming very marked. Causal relations in any case can exist only between realities, veritable substantial things. And if phenomena are, as Kant says, only representations in us, then it becomes quite absurd to speak of their having causal relations to one another. Kant does not succeed in giving his phenomena any true objectivity. When asked what constitutes their objectivity he says, "We find that it consists in nothing but the rendering necessary the connection of representations in a certain way, and subjecting them to a rule; and that, on the other hand, they receive their objective character only because a certain order is necessary in the time relations of our representations." (Page 161.)

Now in this passage phenomena are reduced to our representations, and their objectivity is simply the fact that they are subjected to a rule, but this in no way puts them beyond the mind itself. It leaves them still within the subjective circle of our consciousness, and gives us nothing that can be called an object capable of existing by itself and maintaining causal relations with other things. Here, then, in Kant's doctrine of phenomena we find a really insoluble difficulty. If he would leave the phenomena some kind of thinghood, we then might make a shift to affirm causal relation among them; or if he would regard the system of phenomena as continually produced by a causality beyond them, again we could give to them a certain objectivity and could also find a place for causality in producing their fixed relations; but apart from this we must say that there is really no thoroughfare and that the system here breaks down.

And the same may be said of the third analogy, which relates to the interaction of substances. This

Kant calls the principle of community and states it as follows: "All substances, in so far as they are coexistent, stand in complete community, that is, reciprocity one to another." In the second edition Kant changes this to read as follows: "All substances, so far as they can be perceived as coexistent in space, are always affecting each other reciprocally." Here Kant assumes that the process, by which we become aware of coexistent things in the world of nature, implies the assumption of reciprocal action just as the process, by which we become aware of succession in the world of nature, implies the principle of causality. And here, too, much the same thing can be said as in the previous case. It is manifest that no connected experience of things is possible without this fact of mutual relation, for if we should suppose a world of things to exist in which this reciprocal relation was wanting, it could in no way be known, for nothing whatever that occurred in such a world would ever be any reason for affirming anything beyond the knowing agent himself. There being no interaction he would necessarily be shut up within the solipsistic circle, and could by no possibility reach a world of other things. In such a system nothing whatever that happens in one thing would be any warrant whatever for anything that might happen in other things, and by consequence there could never be any passage from one thing to any other thing whatever. In such a case any event would be an unrelated beginning. The universe would fall asunder into unconnected and uncaused units, and thought would become impossible. We must, then, affirm

some sort of causality and reciprocal action underlying the mutual relations of things as the possibility
of any experience whatever of them.

So much is manifest upon inspection, but here
again the certainty that there is causal interaction
in the case by no means decides where we are to
locate this causality or how we are to conceive it.
For scientific purposes and for all practical purposes
it suffices to affirm an order of concomitant variation
so that the changes of things shall form a system in
accordance with which we can find our way from
any one thing to any other. But the underlying
causality might conceivably be entirely apart from
the system of concomitant changes, not being included in them, but producing them from without
in accordance with a system of uniform rules. In
that case we should have all that science would need
for its purposes, but the metaphysical doctrine would
take on a very different form.

The same difficulty previously pointed out with
reference to Kant's doctrine of causality reappears
here. "Phenomena, as being contained in a possible
experience, must share a communion of apperception, and if the objects are to be represented as
connected in coexistence, they must reciprocally
determine their place in time, and thus constitute
a whole. If this subjective communion is to rest on
an objective ground, or is to refer to phenomena as
substances, then the perception of the one as cause
must render possible the perception of the other, and
vice versa; so that the succession which always exists
in perceptions, as apprehensions, may not be attrib-

uted to the objects, but that the objects should be represented as existing simultaneously. This is a reciprocal influence, that is, a real commercium of substances, without which the empirical relation of coexistence would be impossible in our experience." (Page 174.)

Here again Kant is trying to rest the subjective communion on an objective ground, or to refer to phenomena as substances. Of course this is impossible if by phenomena we mean only our subjective apprehensions, for we cannot regard these as mutually interacting and constituting an objective world. He continues: "By nature (in the empirical sense of the word) we mean the coherence of phenomena in their existence, according to necessary rules, that is, laws. There are therefore certain laws, and they exist a priori, which themselves make nature possible, while the empirical laws exist and are discovered through experience, but in accordance with those original laws which first render experience possible. Our analogies, therefore, represent the unity of nature in the coherence of all phenomena, under certain exponents, which express the relation of time (as comprehending all existence) to the unity of apperception, which apperception can only take place in the synthesis according to rules. The three analogies, therefore, simply say that all phenomena exist in one nature and must so exist because, without such unity a priori, no unity of experience, and therefore no determination of objects in experience, would be possible." (Page 176.)

The matter given by Kant in the "Axioms of

Intuition," the "Anticipations of Perception," and the "Analogies of Experience," constitutes Kant's attempt to explain the possibility of science. As we have already seen, it is of a somewhat doubtful character. The axioms of intuition and the anticipations of perception directly result from the character of objects, as in space and time, but [the matter] given in the analogies of experience is far more doubtful. As we have just pointed out, this whole metaphysical apparatus, while true from the standpoint of metaphysical thought, is very far from deciding what form it shall take on in properly scientific investigation. For scientific purposes we need nothing whatever beyond the uniformities of coexistence and sequence in the space and time world, together with a certain continuity of meaning or logical identity through the spatial and temporal changes. On this basis it is possible for us to get the uniformities of the world of experience and the laws of phenomenal change, and anything beyond this must be handed over to metaphysics and is in no way to be looked upon as necessary to physical science. Kant's conception of physics was essentially that of mathematical physics such as had been inaugurated by Newton in his mechanical philosophy. In the progress of scientific and speculative thought, however, we have come to make a division of labor between science and philosophy which is of real importance to both. Science does not care what we call the factors of experience, whether we call them things or phenomena or unknowable or even nothing. We find in experience itself certain uniformities, the knowledge of which is practically valuable. We also find that by modifying antecedents we can modify consequents. This is a knowledge we need for the practical control of experience and the order of life, and given this knowledge science can go on without any further metaphysical assistance. Accordingly for science the permanence of substance becomes only a certain fixity of quantitative relations among objective phenomena. Causality becomes a certain uniformity of sequence, and interaction becomes an order of concomitant variation among phenomena. Anything beyond this is handed over to metaphysics, where it really belongs. Metaphysics has to decide what substance and causality and identity and the other metaphysical categories really mean, and reflection shows that in any case they cannot be taken in the sense that Kant has given them in this exposition.

The final division in this Analytic of Principles is the "Postulates of Empirical Thought in General." What Kant has to say on this subject is of no particular importance. He lays down the following postulates: —

(1) "What agrees with the formal conditions of experience (in intuition and in concepts) is possible.

(2) "What is connected with the material conditions of experience (sensation) is real.

(3) "That which, in its connection with the real, is determined by universal conditions of experience, is (exists as) necessary."

Kant says: "The principles of modality are nothing but explanations of the concepts of possibility, reality, and necessity, in their empirical employment, confining all categories to an empirical employment only, and prohibiting their transcendental use." The aim, then, seems to be to determine with regard to any conception the way in which we shall regard it, whether as possible, real, or as necessary; and the answer is that only those things should be regarded as possible, of which the concepts agree with the formal conditions of experience, that is, only such things are possible for us. The real for us is that which is connected with the material conditions of experience, and thus is given as actual, and the necessary is that which, as determined by universal conditions of experience, is always given and hence is necessary. This fact is very far from throwing much light on the general subject. The limit of the real to that which is actually given in sensation depends upon Kant's previous limitation of the categories. In a very different sense, however, it is possible to say there may well be realities under and above the range of our experience, sensuous or otherwise. As to necessity, again, there is nothing whatever in the continual presence of a fact in experience to warrant us in calling it necessary. It is simply a uniformity in experience which we find and recognize. Indeed, this notion of necessity is one of the most empty and baseless in human thought when metaphysically taken. The only necessity of which we have any experience is the necessities of thought, and these apply solely to the logical relations of ideas. In concrete experience nothing can be found but uniformity. The ground of this uniformity may be independent of ourselves, and hence the order, so far as we are concerned, may be necessary in the sense of being independent of us; but this will never warrant us in affirming it to be necessary in itself. Moreover, the notion of metaphysical necessity cancels itself. Applied to the world of reality it either brings things to a standstill or else it must itself be subject to change; for there is no way of connecting a rigid necessity with a moving world.

The necessity itself, then, must change, and for this we should need some other necessity, unless we are to fall into the Heraclitic flux; but this new necessity would be in the same condition, and thus we should be on our way to the infinite regress. Finally, possibility is even more doubtful still. As used in popular speech it has a variety of meanings. Thus, that is possible which involves no contradiction. This is logical possibility, and means only conceivability. Or, that is possible which, for all we know, may happen or may have happened. This possibility is only an expression of our ignorance. Or, that is possible which would happen if certain conditions were fulfilled. This merely expresses the order of conditioned events; but so long as the condition is unfulfilled the event is impossible, and when it is fulfilled the event is not only possible but actual. The only clear meaning to possibility is based upon the self-determination of a free agent. Apart from this it is nothing. In reality, then, apart from the sphere of freedom, the only possible is the implications of the actual. Many other things may be conceived, but they are impossible as not founded in the real.

THE PHILOSOPHY OF KANT

If, then, we would know what is concretely or really possible, we must have a complete insight into the nature and implications of reality itself.

In the first edition Kant's critics regarded his work as essentially idealistic. This moved him in the second edition, in connection with this discussion, to produce a disproof of idealism. He lays down the following theorem: "The simple, but empirically determined consciousness of my own existence proves the existence of objects in space outside myself"; and he offers the following proof: "I am conscious of my own existence as determined in time, and all determination in time presupposes something *permanent* in the perception. That *permanent*, however, cannot be an intuition within me, because all the causes which determine my existence, so far as they can be found within me, are representations, and as such require themselves something permanent, different from them, in reference to which their change, and therefore my existence in time in which they change, may be determined. The perception of this permanent, therefore, is possible only through a thing *outside* me, and not through the mere *representation* of a thing outside me, and the determination of my existence in time is, consequently, possible only by the existence of real things, which I perceive outside me. Now, as the consciousness in time is necessarily connected with the consciousness of the possibility of that determination of time, it is also necessarily connected with the existence of things outside me, as the condition of the determination of time. In other words, the consciousness of my own existence is, at the same time, an immediate consciousness of the existence of other things." (Page 779.)

It is not strange that Kant's critics should have regarded this passage as an inconsistency on his part. In the first place, it is not clear what something "permanent in the perception" is to mean other than that experience of whatever kind must have some fixed significance. And since on Kant's own view it is the mind which gives this permanence to experience, it is by no means clear that there must be something permanent outside myself in order to make experience possible. But further Kant here makes a sharp distinction between all internal facts as mere representations, which as such require something permanent beyond them, and the perception of this permanent as possible only through "a thing outside me and not through the mere representation of a thing outside me." It is made possible only through "the existence of real things which I perceive outside me." This seems to give a very substantial character to things and a fairly independent character to space, about as much so as a thoroughgoing realist would desire. If these phrases are to be taken in their obvious significance Kant returns to the good old-fashioned realism; and if they are not to be so taken, then he does not differ from the idealist in his result, but only in his theory of knowledge. Kant and Berkeley, after all, seemed to differ not so much in the idealistic outcome as in their doctrine of knowledge. Certainly Berkeley would not have wished for anything more immaterial than Kant's view becomes when it is consistently and directly interpreted. In fact, Kant's argument here turns entirely upon the nature of self-consciousness, and his conclusion really means only this, that self-consciousness arises [only in connection with the consciousness] of objects, whatever they may be. In other words, there is no abstract self existing apart from and before all of our consciousnesses, but self-consciousness is realized only in and through or in connection with the consciousness of objects nominal or otherwise. This fact may be admitted by any idealist who objects not to the world of experience, as having significance for self-consciousness, but to a world of impersonal things existing apart from all consciousness and simply recognized by us.

It may be objected that in this argument of Kant's the contradiction disappears when we remember his doctrine of the empirical reality of space and its transcendental ideality. In that case we only have the problem before us which has long been threatening to come up, namely, Kant's general doctrine of noumena and the relativity of our forms of thought in general. To this problem we now address ourselves.

V

PHENOMENA AND NOUMENA

BEGINNING with the discussion of space and time
Kant introduces his doctrine of phenomenal knowledge. Things in space are only phenomena, and all
the understanding does in connection with them is
to give these phenomena a substantial form and rational relations by bringing the categories of thought
into the intuitions of sense. But these categories
apply only to phenomena and have no contents in
themselves apart from the phenomena to which they
are applied. This is Kant's theory of phenomenalism.
In opposition to Hume he holds an elaborate mental
activity in the process of knowledge, but he comes
around very close to Hume in the end, by saying
that this knowledge is limited entirely within the
sphere of sense experience. Anything lying beyond
this sphere may possibly be an object of belief, but
can never be properly an object of knowledge.

Strangely enough, Kant nowhere discusses what
the meaning of phenomenon is to be. He seems to
take the conception for granted, and having called
substantial objects phenomenal assumes that the
matter is perfectly plain. In fact, however, this doctrine of phenomenal knowledge is somewhat obscure
in its best estate, and in any case is much more complex than commonly appears. The term itself is
allied to the visual sense or to the facts of vision, and

the explanations of the doctrine and arguments for it are commonly drawn from the field of vision. We are all familiar with the fact that things by no means always look as we have to think of them. In such cases the conception of the distinction between appearance and reality is easily made. In perspective, parallels look like converging lines. The circle when looked at out of the perpendicular seems elliptical. The cube never looks like a cube to the unaided eye. And in general the whole series of visual objects make us familiar with the distinction between things as they appear and things as they are. The eye is perpetually misleading us in this respect, and thought is continually required to dispel the false appearance or to rectify the visual appearance and reduce it to its proper significance. Facts of this kind easily lead to the notion that the objects of knowledge may after all be only appearances, and that the true thing may continually elude us. By keeping these facts of visual experience in mind and then generalizing the problem, we may say we know only appearances and do not know things as they are. And this seems to be the way in which Kant, among the rest, tacitly proceeded. He decided that spatial objects are phenomenal, and being phenomena are to be distinguished from true things, and thus we have the doctrine of phenomenalism.

But all of this is rather hasty, to say the least, and is far enough from founding the doctrine that our knowledge is not of reality but only of appearances. To begin with, in the space world, where this distinction is most at home, we distinguish between the varying appearance due to the laws of perspective and the general laws of vision and a thing as it exists for our non-visual mathematical conceptions and in geometrical relations. We know perfectly well that the converging tracks of the railroad do not really converge, and we understand the reason for the apparent convergences. Similarly we allow for all the other misleading appearances in vision in general. We continually test them by our fixed geometrical conceptions, which give the real nature and relations of the things. There is nothing whatever in such facts to suggest that perhaps our doctrine of the cube or the square or the triangle is only an appearance or point of view. On the contrary, we know very well that our knowledge of these things is absolute so far as it goes.

When from considerations of this kind we next conclude that we cannot tell what things are in themselves, it is manifest that we overlook the fact that space experience is by no means the only way in which we get a knowledge of things. To a very large extent our knowledge of things consists in a knowledge of relations. We get a true knowledge of the relations of space and time phenomena under the geometrical and numerical form. And the knowledge we thus get is not exposed, so far as appears, to any claim of being only a knowledge of appearances. The things in themselves with which we are dealing are spatial and temporal relations; but the knowledge that is given is not a phenomenal knowledge, but a true knowledge of the relations of these things. Thus it would be absurd in the highest degree to say that a geometrical proposition respecting the triangle is true only of the phenomenal triangle and not of the triangle in itself. The phenomenal triangle is the only triangle there is, and our knowledge of that triangle is universally valid for all who know what the term triangle means. Equally absurd would it be to say that the phenomenal time between two dates is of a certain length, but of the real time we can say nothing; for the time between the dates is as real as the dates themselves and the only time there is. Our knowledge, then, of that time is valid for all who understand the problem. Again, numerical knowledge may apply only to phenomena, but the knowledge itself is not phenomenal but valid, that is, real in the only sense in which knowledge can be real.

This suggests to us at the start that the conception of phenomenal knowledge, in so far as it denies real knowledge or knowledge of things, is somewhat obscure. It is manifest that the knowledge of phenomena may be perfectly real in its own field and perfectly valid for all intelligent beings who deal with the phenomena in question. For instance, we might query whether angels are acquainted with our human geometry and the measurements which take place under them. If they are so acquainted they must reach the same results geometrically that we do in any given case. The contents of a solid, the distance between two points, etc., when geometrically given would be the same everywhere and for all. We might decide that space is phenomenal, but our knowledge of space would be valid and universal. These facts suggest that the statement that we know only phenomena is by no means to be identified with the denial of universally valid knowledge, for as yet nothing has been said which forbids our thinking that phenomena themselves may have a universal character. Indeed, as we shall later see, phenomena will have finally to be defined as objects or phases that exist only for intelligence. The conception of phenomena as masks of reality, and hence of phenomenal knowledge as essentially non-knowledge, must be definitely set aside as an illusion. In its place phenomenal knowledge will be defined as the knowledge of phenomena, and phenomena will represent the aspect of reality for intelligence, our own certainly and possibly for all intelligence. In that case phenomenal knowledge will be the only knowledge we could have and the only knowledge worth having, for if we can tell what things must be for intelligence we can cheerfully forego knowing what they are apart from any relation to intelligence. We shall hereafter see that they are nothing in that relation.

Again, the doubt as to our knowledge of reality which is based upon the phenomena of visual sense overlooks the fact that our knowledge of causes does not depend at all upon how they look, but on how they act. The causal relation belongs to the unpicturable ideas of the understanding and can in no way be sensuously perceived. It is, therefore, purely a thought problem, and the solution of it consists entirely in the telling how things act or in finding the laws of their activity. In this way we get our knowledge of the mind, not through any sensuous or spatial intuition of it, but rather by experience of its modes of activity. Thus also we get the laws of heat, gravity, electricity, etc. It never occurs to us to ask how these things look, for we know that they do not look at all. And equally it does not occur to us on this account to doubt that we have a very valuable and valid knowledge of these things when we have discovered the laws of their activity. This fact, then, that we know causes through their effects and the laws of their action, makes it entirely impossible for us to assume a failure of knowledge because of our inability to perceive these objects before the visual sense. We cannot of course see the law of gravity, but the astronomer has no doubt that he has truly formulated its law. Neither can we see mind, and yet we believe that we have a considerable knowledge of it in experience.

Facts of this kind warn us against hastily building up a doctrine of phenomenal knowledge on the basis of visual experience. The facts of vision may serve to suggest to us the possibility that we know only appearances, but then the problem itself is so much larger than the mere visual sense that we need more carefully to analyze it before despairing of knowledge. And, first of all, we must consider some features of knowledge itself.

In general all knowing implies the existence of the object as something independent of the knowing, that is, as something existing apart from the knowing act but as revealed through that act. All the objects of perception, therefore, immediately take on the character of objectivity; that is, of independence of the knowing and in our own case of the knower. They are things to be perceived or they are facts of the inner life, and the function of thought is not to make the facts but to report them. We are not, then, dealing with our subjective states or with appearances, but with things; of course things in their proper sphere. Indeed, this objectivity in the sense of independence of the knowing is inherent in the very nature of the judgment itself. If we ask what the judgment means, we find it always relates itself to some assumed order of facts and relations, which the judgment does not make but finds and reports. Thus a mathematical judgment expresses some fixed relation in mathematical ideas. A physical judgment expresses some fixed relation in the spatial system. A historical judgment expresses some actual occurrence at some date. An ethical judgment expresses something which ought to be in the order of the moral reason, etc. In all of these cases the mind [assumes] spontaneously and necessarily a knowledge [of a system of] reality in some sense, and its aim is to express some fact or relation of that system of reality. And even when we make our objects phenomenal, knowledge is equally objective in its form. The phenomena are not looked upon merely as affections of the individual. They have something objective and universal about them, so that they represent a common to all and not merely a special to me. And even when something is special to me, as when I have a particular feeling, that special to me is regarded as a fact in the psychological world, so that any one making an inventory of that world would have to recognize that fact in its special temporal and psychological context.

This undeniable objectivity in the form of knowledge makes necessary a great deal of reflection in order to bring the distinction between reality and phenomena into harmony with the unquestionable facts of experience. It is not true that the distinction between the knowledge of appearances and the knowledge of reality is obvious either for spontaneous or for reflective thought. Certainly unless we are going to give appearance or phenomenon a much more objective character than Kant does in many passages, the result will be a failure of knowledge rather than any doctrine of phenomenal knowledge. Objects may be phenomena, but they must still be objective and common to all. In many passages Kant reduces phenomena to affections of ourselves and sometimes even to affections of myself, in which case their properly objective character is denied and nothing remains but a play more or less orderly among my representations, and then the system of objective experience becomes a fiction of the individual. Of course this was not Kant's general view, but a great deal of what he said leads up to it, and his attempt to escape it is by no means always successful, although his desire to do so is obvious and at times is precisely affirmed. Evidently our problem is much more complex than at first sight it seems.

Perhaps, however, we shall better reach the Kantian standpoint if we pass at once to his conception of space and time and the phenomenality of all spatial and temporal objects. If this view can be maintained, then the space and time world becomes phenomenal in some sense not yet defined. Conceivably it might mean that the space and time world is only a mask of the real world of power and prevents our knowing it, but it might also mean, in accordance with our previous suggestion, that the space and time world is the form under which the invisible power world manifests itself for intelligence. In that case the subjectivity of space and time would by no means reflect on the validity of knowledge. It would simply limit our spatial and temporal knowledge to the world of space and time experience, without making it the existential thing which the unpicturable world of power is conceived to be.

As already said, Kant's doctrine of the subjectivity of space is very unsatisfactorily deduced. Apart from the ambiguous conception of space as a perception and as a form of perception, Kant's argument for its subjectivity seems largely based on the existence of geometry as a system of undeniable truth. Hence he concludes that space must be the form of our object-ive sense, as otherwise the apodictic certainty of geo-metrical truth could not be maintained. We have already pointed out the unsatisfactory character of this reasoning. A priori space must be understood in the sense that the space intuition involves direct mental insight, but the important feature in the case is the insight and not merely psychological fact of any kind. The pure passivity of empirical doctrine makes geometry impossible, because the mind, hav-ing no insight of its own, can only read off what it has experienced in sense; but the truths of geometry do not admit of being sensuously experienced. The point, the line, and all geometrical figures in general, as they exist for mathematical reasoning, are pure products of intuition. But it is only in this sense that our knowledge is a priori, and in this sense it by no means implies that this knowledge of concepts which the mind possesses of its own right may not be a knowledge of space as it exists for all intelligent beings. And the development of geometrical knowledge implies or agrees with this. We do not need any general theory of knowledge in order to study geometry and be fully convinced of the universality of geometrical truth. We need only a mind capable of forming the fundamental geometrical conceptions and of combining them in due order so as to reach insight into the truth. We cannot, then, conclude from geometry to the subjectivity of space. We can only conclude to the ability of mind to understand the nature of space and some of its implications.

If the subjectivity of space is really to be made out it must be by a different course of reasoning. It must be shown that space, conceived of as an independent and non-mental existence, is something which would commit us to insoluble contradictions and wreck reason altogether. This showing Kant has not given, but it is really the only thing that can make the argument at all acceptable or tenable. The only thing that the existence of space as a principle of mental arrangement does, is to show that the apparent independent existence of space is not necessary to experience. If we confine ourselves simply to reflecting upon our mature experience, it seems evident to us that space is undeniably given as an independent fact which contains things within its extension.

And thus it might seem to us to be so obviously there that no mental process whatever is needed for its apprehension, and that we see things in space for the sufficient reason that they are in space and there is no need to say anything more about it. But if we recur again to what was said about the process of perception, it will be seen that space can exist for us only through a highly complex activity of relation by the mind itself. Space relations do not exist among our sense impressions as affections of the sensibility. As such affections they have no spatial qualities. There may be ideas of bulk, but there are no bulky ideas. There may be ideas of distance, but there are no distances between ideas. The thought life, then, as conscious process has no spatial qualities, and thus the problem arises, How can the ideas of bulk, distance, direction emerge in thought which has no bulk, distance, or direction? We have to deduce spatial [objects] and spatial relations from that which is non-spatial.

This problem is manifestly insoluble unless the mind posits its objects and gives them space relations on its own account. Our objects, then, are spatially real for us because the mind thus relates its objects. And if space were never so real in itself it could not be any fact of experience for us unless the mind did thus relate its objects. The possibility of doing this, even when there is no question of a real space and real objects, is seen in every vivid dream. Dream objects are not in space, but whatever the form of [the objects], the space in which they appear is not anything which contains them. It is rather the form of the dream.

119

In such cases we have a clear illustration of the space-relating activity of thought whereby spatial experience is produced. We need a space to hold things as little as we need a space to dream in.

Thus we see that space is primarily a form of experience. And experience has this form because the mind works under the space law and thus gives its experience a spatial character. But still from this it does not follow that space is only the form of experience. It is still possible that space, in addition to being the form of experience, may also be a something in itself, apart from our experience, and holding things in spatial relations to one another.

But this view upon examination turns out to be impossible. If we take space as an ontological fact and not merely the form of experience, we forthwith fall into insoluble contradictions. The general law of space conceived of as existing would be the mutual externality of every power to every other, and as every power of space is itself spatial we should have to carry the mutual externality down through infinite divisibility to the point in space. Under such a law all existence would be dispersed into infinite otherness and externality through the infinite divisibility implicit in the space law. This in itself serves to show that space is not to be regarded as a fact of itself, but rather as a form of experience only, and in that sense subjective.

But here again we have to guard against hasty conclusions. Let us now say, space is subjective and hence all things in space are subjective and hence phenomenal. These statements would be true in a way, but they could easily be taken so as to be untrue, and therefore we have to determine carefully what our terms are to mean. When we speak of anything as subjective a double meaning is possible. We may mean, and we often do mean, that the thing is subjective to some individual, as when we say the delusions of a fever patient are subjective; that is, they represent no independent objects but merely hallucinations of the disordered mind. Or we may mean by subjective something that exists only in and for intelligence, not something existing apart from mind and independent of all consciousness. This ambiguity is very commonly unsuspected and is the parent of a great deal of confusion in this matter of the subjectivity of space. We may mean that space is something peculiar to the individual mind and that the whole world of spatial objects is within that individual mind, in which case we arrive at solipsism for all objects of experience and agnosticism for whatever lies beyond. But we may say that space is subjective to the human mind, not this, [that, or] the other mind, but the human mind in general. In this case we should have, in the world of objects, a case of human subjectivity only; and we should be shut up within the range of human experience without any possibility of ever transcending our own spatial world. Or again, we might mean that space is subjective in the sense that it has no meaning or existence apart from intelligence somewhere. And it would be compatible with this view to assume a universality of space for all intelligence, so that for all alike the space world would exist for and in intelligence, yet not as something independent of intelligence. Space would then have a true universality and at the same time a universal subjectivity which would give the whole problem a very different aspect from what it has when we limit space merely to human experience. In the former case we have the same universality and validity of space that we have in our traditional view, and at the same time it would lie within the general sphere of intelligence, and the difficulties arising from a supposed ontological space would vanish.

Now, these distinctions escaped Kant. In general he viewed space as a phase of human subjectivity only, and declined to say anything of what might lie beyond. And here he meets a double difficulty. Much of Kant's doctrine is solipsistic in its outcome, but he escapes this conclusion apparently by being ignorant of the fact. Accordingly, he commonly deals with human subjectivity in general and not with individual subjectivity, which is really all his argument admits of. The argument begins with [the latter]. It is carried on, however, on the basis of [the former]. The conclusions are not for the individual mind, but they are for all human minds. But it would puzzle Kant, indeed, to combine this assumption with his general doctrine of phenomenalism. If all my objects are so limited by the categories of my thought that I cannot reach them as they are and must content myself with a set of appearances, then it follows that the neighbors are also only a set of phenomena of my own, concerning whom in reality I must always remain in utter doubt as to whether they exist at all in the form in which I think them; or whether the personal world as well as the spatial world is not simply a form of my own thinking, which does not even adumbrate the world of reality beyond it, but which has such a parallax with that world that I may never say anything about it. In that case both knowledge and life would be in a most forlorn condition. This result Kant escapes by apparently never having suspected it and by the easy fallacy of abstraction which makes the human mind the one subject of human experience. Of course, the reality is always a series of individual minds with a great complexity of individual experiences.

And this brings up another difficulty which Kant has not sufficiently considered. It is necessary in some way, if the object is not to be a mere affection of the individual, to secure some kind of given system in experience in connection with which life and knowledge shall go on; that is, the system of phenomena, if we call it such, must take on an essentially objective character which is no mere affection or product of the individual, but which is given to all, so that from the human side it becomes full of practical purposes, essentially a world of things and persons in various rational relations. Without this we fall back into the solipsistic circle, and with this we have a new order of conception to recognize. This world we may call subjective, yet it must be at the same time objective; that is, it may be subjective in the sense of existing only through and for intelligence, but it must also be objective in the sense of being given to all, at least all human beings. Kant himself recognized the need of something like this in his insistence upon the empirical reality of space. He frequently declares that he maintains the empirical reality of space along with its transcendental ideality. He also speaks of the affinity of phenomena as a condition of our understanding or of a rule among phenomena which determines their essential relations. In this view phenomena begin to be something constituting an objective system, and certainly independent of any individual, however dependent it may be upon intelligence. Now the only way to secure this result is a way which Kant never took, but one which a disciple of Kant must take if he is not to fall into the Kantian agnosticism and skepticism. First, we must define phenomena not as appearances or illusions or masks of any kind, but as something existing only for and through intelligence. And then we must pass behind these phenomena to the intelligence through and for which they exist. In our own case the phenomena of the outer sense are the world of external perception. As phenomenal they exist only through and for intelligence. We apprehend them through our own intelligence, but they do not depend upon our intelligence for their existence; and since they must depend upon intelligence for existence, it only remains that we affirm a backlying intelligence as their cause and presupposition.

So much for Kant's doctrine of phenomena. His doctrine of noumena is no less confused. From the beginning of the work Kant recognizes things beyond ourselves which act upon us and produce the various affections of our sensibility, that is, noumena. If we leave out this conception the doctrine becomes purely solipsistic, and the world is merely a shadow in our thought without any objective cause or ground whatever. So then noumena must be affirmed, but on the other hand, when we consider the passages in which Kant speaks of these noumena, they begin to pass into subjectivity or mere forms of thought without any properly independent character whatever. A few passages respecting phenomena and noumena will indicate the uncertainty of Kant's exposition. Thus, respecting phenomena he says: "All phenomena are not things by themselves, but only the play of our representations, all of which are in the end determinations only of the internal sense." (Page 84.) Here phenomena are in the plainest way declared to be the play of our representations. But in the same passage Kant is looking for some way of connection among phenomena which shall save them from being merely "a play of our representations." Again, "And here we must needs arrive at a clear understanding of what we mean by an object of representations. We said before that phenomena are nothing but sensuous representations, which therefore by themselves must not be taken for objects outside our faculty of representation. What, then, do we mean if we speak of an object corresponding to, and therefore also different from our knowledge?" (Page 86.) Here we find phenomena still affirmed to be "nothing but sensuous representations." At the same time we seem to be looking for an "object corresponding to, and therefore also different from, our knowledge." Kant adds that such an object can only be conceived of as something in general $= x$, and finally decides, as we have before seen, that objectivity is really due to the discovery of the unity of a rule in the synthesis of the manifold, "and the concept of that unity is really the representation of the object $= x$." This rule he next goes on to discover in the transcendental unity of perception. But this as such is subjective and makes no provision for any affinity of phenomena among themselves. In another passage he says: "This objective ground of all association of phenomena I call their affinity, and this can nowhere be found except in the principle of the unity of apperception applied to all knowledge which is to belong to me. According to it all phenomena, without exception, must so enter into the mind or be apprehended as to agree with the unity of apperception." (Page 100.) Here Kant seems to speak of an objective ground of association of phenomena, but in the same sentence he locates it in the unity of perception, which is subjective. Again, "It is clear, also, that as we can only deal with the manifold in our representations, and as the corresponding to them (the object), since it is to be something different from all our representations, is really nothing to us, it is clear, I say, that the unity, necessitated by the object, cannot be anything but the formal unity of our consciousness in the synthesis of the manifold in our representations." (Page 87.) Here both phenomena and the rule which constitutes their objectivity seem to be purely subjective.

Again, "All representations have, as representations, their object, and can themselves in turn become objects of other representations. The only objects which can be given to us immediately are phenomena, and whatever in them refers immediately to the object is called intuition. These phenomena, however, are not things in themselves, but representations only which have their object, but an object that can no longer be seen by us, and may therefore be called the not-empirical, that is, the transcendental object, $= x$.

"The pure concept of such a transcendental object (which in reality in all our knowledge is always the same $= x$) is that which alone can give to all our empirical concepts a relation to an object or objective reality. That concept cannot contain any definite intuition, and can therefore refer to that unity only, which must be found in the manifold of our knowledge, so far as it stands in relation to an object. That relation is nothing else but a necessary unity of consciousness, and therefore also of the synthesis of the manifold, by a common function of the mind which unites it in one representation." (Page 89.)

Here again [Kant's method of expression is confusing, if not self-contradictory. On the one hand, he says that these representations have an object and are objects, and then, on the other hand, that they relate to a transcendental object which is nothing but a necessary unity of consciousness]. "Phenomena are only representations of things, unknown as to what they may be by themselves. As mere representations they are subject to no law of connection, except that which is prescribed by the connecting faculty." (Page 765.) In this last passage, which is from the second edition, phenomena are representations of things which are unknown, and as mere representa-

127

tions are subject to no law or connection except that which is prescribed by the connecting faculty. Here there seems to be no objective affinity or law among the phenomena, and for all we can say the connecting faculty might order them in any way whatever.

So much for phenomena. If we ask what and where phenomena are in the Kantian system, it is fairly hard to tell. They are objects and they are not objects. They are a mere play of representations and they are not such a play. His doctrine of noumena is equally obscure, as appears from the following passages: "All our representations are no doubt referred by the understanding to some sort of object, and as phenomena are nothing but representations, the understanding refers them to a *something*, as the object of our sensuous intuition, this something being, however, the transcendental object only. This means a something equal to x, of which we do not, nay, with the present constitution of our understanding, cannot, know anything, but which can only serve, as a correlatum of the unity of apperception, for the unity of the manifold in sensuous intuition, by means of which the understanding unites the manifold into the concept of an object. This transcendental object cannot be separated from the sensuous data, because in that case nothing would remain by which it could be thought. It is not, therefore, an object of knowledge in itself, but only the representation of phenomena, under the concept of an object in general, which can be defined by the manifold of sensuous intuition." (Page 204.) Here it would seem that the transcendental object is simply an hypos-

128

tasis of phenomena and is nothing in itself; but this conclusion he is not ready to allow, for he continues: "It really follows quite naturally from the concept of a phenomenon in general that something must correspond to it, which in itself is not a phenomenon, because a phenomenon cannot be anything by itself, apart from our mode of representation. Unless, therefore, we are to move in a constant circle we must admit that the very word 'phenomenon' indicates a relation to something, the immediate representation of which is no doubt sensuous, but which nevertheless, even without this qualification of our sensibility (on which the form of our intuition is founded), must be something by itself, that is, an object independent of our sensibility." (Page 205.) Here Kant affirms existence of something independent of our thought and sensibility which he calls "the transcendental object, that is, the entirely indefinite thought of something in general. This cannot be called the noumenon, for I know nothing of what it is by itself and have no conception of it, except as the object of sensuous intuition in general, which is therefore the same for all phenomena." (Page 206.) "The concept of a noumenon is therefore merely limitative, and intended to keep the claims of sensibility within proper bounds, therefore of negative use only. But it is not a mere arbitrary fiction, but closely connected with the limitation of sensibility, though incapable of adding anything positive to the sphere of the senses." (Page 208.) Thus it seems that noumena are only limitative notions and not things in themselves. They are mainly products and have a negative mental function, but are in no sense realities. Apart from the forms of articulate experience all that we can say is, there is something in general which is the reality to which experience relates itself.

And here another ambiguity emerges. When it is declared that we cannot think appearance without reality we might question whether an appearance in which the reality does not truly appear can be called an appearance. If it be said that the notion of appearance implies reality the answer is, it no more implies reality than it implies a reality that really appears. Phrases of this kind really spring from the fact that the term "appearance" is limited to the visual sense, and for vision there can be nothing called an appearance unless there be something that truly appears. Beyond that the notion of an appearance would be some phenomenon objectively founded, but the cause of which is in no respect a part of the appearance. Thus, for instance, we might speak of a luminosity as an appearance of the ether, but that would only mean that the vibrations in the ether produce the appearance of light; in which case, however, it would not occur to any one to regard light as a phenomenon of the ether or as a failure to present to us its true object. As we have before seen, the noumena are not things that are to be judged by the visual sense, but are to be interpreted by the understanding. And in general, if we are to make this doctrine all-inclusive, we shall have to take phenomena as effects and consider their character as effects and determine the realities in the case, not by trying to tell how they would look, but by considering what the effects indi-

cate as to the causes from which they arise. Along
this line it becomes possible to adjust the doctrine
of phenomenal knowledge, so far as it is correct, to
thought itself, without doing violence to our ordinary sense of reality and to good sense in general.
The doctrine of phenomena and noumena, because
of its connection with the Kantian theory of knowledge, is sure to mislead. Phenomenon is supposed
to be something which ought to refer to noumenon,
but instead of so doing it hides and distorts it. The
noumenon, on the other hand, is something trying to
peer through the masking phenomenon, but failing in
the attempt.

Now it is plain that in this sense the apparent or
phenomenal can lead to no insight whatever. The
appearance as affection and illusion can never furnish the premises for valid conclusions respecting
reality. The phenomenal, as masking or distorting
the real, can never give any insight into the real.
There must, then, be a truth in the appearance or
the phenomenon itself, if it is to help us to any knowledge of the real.

The true order of procedure is this. We begin with
experience, which is real and valid in its way. This
is the world of things and persons about us, and the
general order of life. Now in serious thought there
can never be any question as to the validity and truth
of this experience. It must be the contents of life.
It is the platform on which we meet in mutual understanding. It is the field where life and human history
go on, and we need no philosophizing to introduce us
to this field. Life itself is a sufficient introduction.

Where, then, does philosophy come in? In this way. When we come to study this experience, external and internal, we find ourselves compelled by the experience itself to go behind it for its interpretation. Accordingly we find that the sense data, with which we all begin, and which at first seem to all of us to be final, are not properly final. We discover, however, not that they are illusions or unreal, but that they need interpretation. Thus from the phenomena of the visible heavens we infer the astronomic heavens. From the order of our experience of physical change we infer the various doctrines of theoretical science. But in none of these cases do we deny the experience or reject it as false. We rather view it as not final, and we go beyond it for its interpretation. Now experience of this sort is phenomenal; that is, it exists only in and for intelligence. In abstraction from the space of this experience it would have no assignable meaning; but this experience, though thus phenomenal, is not to be looked upon after the analogy of optical illusions as masking and distorting a real which the mind is seeking to perceive. It must rather be looked upon as a veritable order real in and for experience, but not an ontological reality. Neither is it to be viewed as any mask of the real, but rather as a revelation of the same, a revelation, however, as manifesting a hidden causality, a revelation to the understanding and not merely to the visual sense. Looking at the matter in this way we have to make two kinds of reality, which we may call phenomenal reality and ontological or causal reality. They are both real, but they are not real in the same sense.

The phenomena are not causal or substantial, but they are real in the sense that they are no illusions of the individual, but are abiding elements in our common-sense experience. They are not, then, phantasms or errors or hallucinations. They are given to all, at least to all of a normal sensibility, and their truth lies in their being just what they are, certain forms of experience; and when we pass behind them our aim is not to find a supposed reality in them, but rather to find their causal source and ground. It is of the utmost importance for understanding the movement of philosophic thought that these two senses of reality be kept distinct and that both be distinguished from illusion and error.

The possibility of such a view may be illustrated by the established doctrine respecting the sense world. There is universal agreement among both scientists and philosophers that a large part of the sense world has only phenomenal existence. When we inquire into the causality and ontological ground of that world, we are taken behind it to the power world into which only thought can penetrate, and we are told that this is the truly real; but at the same time the phenomenal world remains real in its way. It forms the contents of our objective experience and is the field in which we all meet in mutual understanding. It expresses, then, an element common to all and is no private fiction of the individual. Concerning it the proper question is not, Is it real? but rather, What kind of reality does it have?

In further consideration of Kant's strange doctrine we are led to ask how he came to it. The answer seems to be that Kant began with the naïve conception of a reality external and antithetical to intelligence, the notion with which crude and unreflective common sense always begins. There is a world of things altogether independent, not only of our thought but of all thought, and common sense finds it perfectly easy to know this world, for all we have to do is to look and see. But Kant's theory of the constructive action of the mind in perception at once disposes of this naïve notion of a passive mirroring of things undeniably there, and it becomes clear that the world that we know is primarily and immediately the world that we construct: that is, the known world is our own "construct," considered in its origin. To be sure, we suppose that this world which we "construct" in thought is the world independently existing, but still the "construct" is primarily our product; just as our knowledge of another's thought is primarily our own thought, even if we believe that that thought truly grasps the thought of another mind. By this time it is possible to query whether the object be not simply and only our own "construct" projected in reality. It is clear that with this theory of knowledge nothing whatever can be really known that is entirely outside of intelligence and antithetical to it. It follows at once that that reality which we naïvely assume at the start is unknowable as a matter of course.

But in this we proceed uncritically. In the order of knowledge experience is really first and basal, and things are only the assumptions we make in order to explain our experience. Experience and the things inferred from it are amenable to our thought, and beyond these we have no warrant for saying anything. Spontaneous realism easily mistakes the existence of things apart from our thought for their existence apart from any and all thought. And then their infinity follows as a matter of course. But if all things lie within the thought sphere, if things are the product and expression of some creative thought, they might well, then, be commensurate with our intelligence. In that case there would be as little reason for thinking of an unknowable thing in itself behind the apparent thing we perceive, as there is for thinking of an unknowable thought of itself in our neighbor's mind behind the thought we comprehend. This theistic suggestion in this connection deserves more consideration than it has ever received. If things originate in thought and express thought, there is no difficulty in principle in their reappearing in thought. In that case the objects of experience, being products of thought, are commensurate with our thought, and it is altogether conceivable that our thought should be able to know them as they are. The world itself, though more than a thought, is essentially the expression of thought and hence lies open to our intelligence. And the skeptic, instead of assuming things and proclaiming that they cannot be known, should rather consider whether he has any right to affirm any other than those known things which our thought posits. The skepticism here should attach not to our knowledge of reality but to the skeptic's assumption of an unknowable reality. For a little reflection serves to show that an intelligible experience can never possibly warrant the affirmation of something essentially unrelated to intelligence.

That this is so appears at once when we reflect upon the self-destructive character of the doctrine that denies the applicability of the categories to reality. When no law of thought is allowed to be valid for things, the things themselves become not only unaffirmable but also meaningless and empty of all contents. If all the categories are subjective to us, then the independent reality is neither one nor many, for unity and plurality are categories. It is, then, neither a thing itself nor things in themselves, for either phrase supposes number, which is ruled out by hypothesis. The reality also is neither cause nor effect, for these, too, are categories and hence without application to objective reality. Reality, again, is neither substance nor attribute, neither thing nor quality, for these also are categories. Finally, it is neither real nor unreal, for reality and negation are categories and hence without application. What, then, is it? If these denials are to be taken strictly, it is nothing, neither subjectively nor objectively. It is neither a thing nor a thought. It is only a verbal phrase to which neither reality nor conception corresponds. If we relax the denial sufficiently to bring it under the general head of existence, even then we have no positive thought or thing. We have only the bare category of being suspended *in vacuo* by the imagination. As such it is only the abstract conceptual existence of class terms, and like them is objectively nothing. The unknowable reality, then, vanishes, leaving only verbal phrases in its place. With this result the skepticism based thereon also vanishes, for there being nothing to know we cannot be expected to know it.

To this result every doctrine of unknowability must come which is based upon a denial of the objective validity of the laws of thought. It must finally reject its unknowable as only a form of words, and must reinstate knowledge by leaving experience and its contents as the only reality to be known. The theory, too, in its best estate introduces an incommensurable dualism into philosophy. On the one hand, are things utterly unrelated to thought, and on the other, is thought utterly unrelated to things. Neither accounts for the other, neither can do anything with the other. They stand on opposite sides of an impassable gulf without any means of communication. This Manicheism of philosophy results from uncritically adopting the assumed opposition of thought and thing which rules in spontaneous thought, and making it universal. This produces only the most inconsistent of skepticisms. It must affirm things and can find no reason for so doing. It is equally impossible to give any articulate contents to the things which it affirms; and finally, we can make no use whatever of such an unknowable in the explanation of experience. If this thing cannot be brought into causal connection with experience and its orders of change, it is of no use, and instead of being an absolute existence it is an absolute nothingness. Anything, then, which we can affirm for the explanation of experience must admit of being brought into rational relations to experience so as to form a rational whole with it. Reality, then, must either come within the reach of thought or go out of existence.

It is perfectly plain, then, that if we are to take Kant's subjectivity of the categories in the sense of denying their validity for independent reality, we must deny that reality altogether. If we should take advantage of a statement previously made and make subjectivity itself universal, we might then maintain the subjectivity of the categories without difficulty, because in that case we should deny the existence of anything outside of intelligence, either our own intelligence or cosmic intelligence. But Kant did not have that view in mind when he affirmed the subjectivity of the categories, and then it is plain either that Kant has contradicted himself or else that he did not mean this subjectivity to be taken in absolute literalness. That this is the view he really held seems to appear from his further doctrine concerning the soul and God. Although he would not allow these to be objects of demonstrative knowledge he nevertheless affirms their existence, and in that case it is clear that he must regard them as standing in causal relations to the world of experience, otherwise they would be entirely useless. If it should be replied that Kant only meant to deny that God is an object of demonstrative knowledge, the answer would be that nowadays nobody supposes he is such an object; and in order even to be an object of belief there must be some positive content in our thought of God and his relations to the world, and that can only take on the forms of some of the categories. In some sense, then, whatever we affirm to exist must come under one or more of the categories in order to give it any place whatever in our intellectual system.

It might, however, be said that Kant did not so much mean to deny that these outlying objects may have relations corresponding to the categories, but only that we cannot apply the categories to them in such a way as to get any definite conceptions, or any conceptions which have any hold on reality. Here his doctrine comes in of the formal nature of the categories and their emptiness when not applied to a given material. The sole field of the application of the categories Kant says is experience, and whenever we transcend experience itself the categories become purely conceptual, and we have no means of deciding whether there be any corresponding reality whatever. If we take experience in the largest sense there is an element of truth in this, but Kant took it only in the sense of external experience, and held that the categories apply solely to the phenomena of the external sense, while the inner experience is something which lies beyond them. This limitation is unpermissible, and we have to extend the categories not merely to the presentations of externality, but also to the experience of ourselves and of the inner life. With this extension we may say that the categories have no application apart from the objects of a real or possible experience. This does not imply anything in themselves to which the categories may not be applied, but only that experience real or possible is the field of their fruitful application. Now, with this understanding the Kantian doctrine takes on a permissible form as follows: "The categories in themselves are simply forms of mental arrangement and merely prescribe the form in which experience is to be ordered when it is given. In this respect they are like the rules of grammar, which prescribe how we shall speak if we speak at all, but which in themselves have no concrete contents. Living speech, then, is not merely grammar, but definite meanings expressed according to grammatical rules, and when there is no specific meaning the grammar itself moves in a vacuum. All experience, according to Kant, is real only through some given fact, and apart from such facts is empty. Thus we might talk of sensations of a class we have never experienced, as the sensations of a tenth sense; but it is plain that such talk, however learned it might be, would be formal and empty, as there would be no concrete sensation to give significance or substance to our words. In the case of real sensation, on the contrary, there is an actual experience which gives content to our reflection. Until the actual experience is given there is no security that there is anything whatever corresponding to our formal phrases; but when experience is given we have no longer simple logical concepts, but we have something lived and realized. Now Kant said that the categories are applied only to such sense experience, and otherwise are empty. Here he made the mistake of limiting experience to the physical sensations and did not extend his doctrine to the data of self-consciousness. When this limitation is removed it then becomes strictly true that the categories have simply the function of forming and expressing some matter which is directly experienced or which can be assimilated to experience, and apart from that relation they are formal and empty. They must always be brought into contact with experience in some way in order to acquire reality, or to make sure that they represent any possible object for thought. Thus, if we talk of the categories of being, unity, identity, causality, substance, etc., in abstraction from any given experience, they are utterly vacuous, so that we cannot tell whether there be any corresponding fact or not; and it is only as we find these categories realized in living self-experience that they acquire other than a formal meaning, or pass for anything more than purely verbal counters. They are like grammar when there is no speech, or rules for saying something when there is nothing to be said." [1]

This doctrine springs directly out of the relation of conceptions to experienced objects. The conception alone is empty. Some form of experience is needed to give it content. And hence we may say in general that all class terms as well as categories are formal unless some objects can be found to which they apply or to which they can be assimilated in some way. All conceptions where there are no objects must be rejected as empty, and we have no means therefore of deciding whether they represent any real or possible existence. It further follows that all particular thinking must be done either in terms of sense objects or in terms of inner experience. Those things which cannot be in any way sensuously presented,

[1] Bowne's *Personalism*, p. 100.

141

nor in any way assimilated to the inner life, must be looked upon as only verbal and without any claim whatever to existence. In the case of sensè objects we can merely decide and register their relations in space and time or their uniformities of coexistence and sequence. When we pass to the unpicturable notions of the understanding, that is, the categories in the Kantian sense, we have no security that they are really anything but verbal except in the form which we give them in experience: that is, the categories have to be viewed as functions of conscious intelligence, and when they are not taken in this sense then they are entirely empty and really apprehend no objects whatever. In case the categories acquire an object they are not masks or forms imposed upon something that exists apart from them. They are simply forms of mental activity whereby the intellect builds up experience. They are not something out of which the intellect is built up. They are the forms for the conceptual apprehension of existence, but this conceptual apprehension is empty until it is realized in living experience. Hence the intellect is not to be understood through the categories, but the categories are to be understood through the intellect, and ultimately the intellect grasps itself in its own living experience, which is the logical *prius* of all conceptual understanding.

Things in themselves, then, lying beyond the categories, we reject and equally we reject the subjectivity of the categories unless subjectivity is made universal so that all existence lies within the thought sphere. In that case we can maintain the subjectivity of the categories without loss because there is nothing beyond the thought sphere, and hence nothing to which they could apply. The thought sphere becomes all-embracing, and the categories are rules for forming and expressing experience within this sphere. There is, however, a certain relativity of the categories in relation to experience which can be maintained without passing to the Kantian position. There is a large element in our thinking which is relative to ourselves and which in this sense may be called subjective rather than objective; that is, it expresses merely a point of view and not anything which is universal in the object or in its relations. The practical application of the categories is largely formal only, and relative to our intellectual convenience. The unities and identities and substantialities which appear in our human thought and speech are mostly our own products. They result from the application of the categories of thought to the fluent and unsubstantial manifold of sense, and have only relative validity. Thus the unities we find in experience are mainly formal. This is the case with all spatial and temporal unities, for these can have only conceptual existence. Reality or substantiality also is largely formal or relative in its application. Most of our substantive conceptions present no real thinghood; only processes or phenomena or activities to which the mind has given a substantive form, but which are never to be mistaken for things. Light, heat, electricity, magnetism, and the great number of abstract nouns are illustrations. Identity, too, is more often formal than real. We find very few real identities in experience, where certainly most things are in perpetual change and flow. In all such cases the identity is formally imposed by the mind for its own convenience, and expresses no ontological fact. Our classifications also are largely relative, not representing any eternal ideas or veritable cosmic groupings, but solely conveniences and points of view of our own. Their relativity to our sensibility or to our purposes can lay no claim to be looked upon as any abiding part of the cosmic furniture. They are what Herbart would call "accidental views." In calling attention to this fact, thus shutting off the hasty dogmatism of the pre-Kantian period, Kant has done a great service of lasting value. Hereafter we have to proceed not dogmatically but critically in seeking to eliminate the purely relative and accidental point of view.

A second order of possible relativity may be found with regard to the sense world in general. Our human world, when we look at it carefully, has a large element of relativity. We look upon its contents and rightly view them as objective, that is, as independent of our human laws; but when we inquire into its contents we find that they largely consist of our own sense life put into rational form, yet in such a way that if we should conceive the sense element dropped out it might be exceedingly difficult to tell what would remain. Take away the sense qualities and the resistances and the distances all relative to ourselves, and we find nothing left that could be called a world; and so, however much we may regard this human world of ours as being objectively founded, we must nevertheless query whether it be not after all a certain human world only and of such a sort that we are not able to affirm it to have any existence for beings who might be differently constituted from ourselves in their sensuous nature. The world of ether, for instance, is not adjusted to our senses, and it has therefore only a theoretical existence for us. We cannot make anything out of it for ourselves beyond a somewhat obscure existence [required by] our optical equations; and on the other hand, many of our solid things seem to be practically transparent for various influences which we seem to detect. It is therefore by no means a difficult thought that the things which are solid for us might be vacua for others and the things which are vacua for us might be solid for others.

And this leads to the surmise that there may be widely different systems of reality for beings who are differently constituted or for the same beings in different stages of their development. Being in this world means nothing more than having a certain form and type of experience with certain familiar conditions. Passing out of this world into another would mean simply not a transition through space, but passing into a new form and type of experience differently constituted from the present. And how many of these systems are possible or to what extent this change might go is altogether beyond us. Of course these many systems would all be objectively founded, that is, they would be rooted in the will and purpose of the Creator, and they would also be one in the sense that the creative purpose would comprise them all in one plan; but they would not be one in the sense of being phases or aspects of one absolute reality. They would be stages in God's unfolding plan, but not aspects of the static universe. This static universe is a phantom of abstract thought. The only reality is God and his progressively unfolding plan and purpose and work, and the world of finite spirits. In this case also we should have a relativity but not an illusion, a validity of knowledge within the sphere which finds its ground and warrant in the plan and purpose of the Creator. This system could not be affirmed to exist for all beings. It would therefore be a human world, at least in very many of its aspects. It would be true for the intelligence that comprehends all existence, but it would be non-existent for finite intelligences which are adjusted to another order of experience.

By this time probably we begin to fear that there is not much basis left for objective knowledge, or possibly we may think when so much is made phenomenal and relative that we are not grasping reality at all, and the query arises whether after all we are not living in the midst of illusion, and whether if we knew things as they really are we should not find them altogether different from what we think them to be. This thought springs out of the fancy that there is an absolute system of static reality to which our thoughts ought to correspond in order to be true. This is one of the dogmatic fictions. For us the real can never be anything but the contents of experience and whatever we may infer from them. Back of experience we find no truly real of the noumenal type, but we infer or affirm a cause which is founding and maintaining the order of experience. To ask whether this order be true is really meaningless unless we suppose some absolute static system back of experience, and this notion is baseless. When this is seen the only permissible question becomes this, Does our experience exhaust the possibilities of experience and consciousness? From a theistic standpoint the universe itself is no static existence, but only the divine thought finding realization through the divine will, and that thought for us must find expression in the order of experience. But it is quite credible that our present experience does not exhaust the contents of that thought and so does not exhaust the possibilities of experience. If further possibility should unfold we should not have a truer experience, but a more extensive one. Our present experience is of a certain type with certain contents and limitations, and it is entirely possible that there should be other beings with different types and contents of experience. It is equally possible that we ourselves shall pass into new orders of experience, in which case we should have no right to say that the present order is false, but only that it is not all and final. In like manner the new order would not be rightly described as more true than the present order, but only as perhaps higher and richer in content, giving a fuller and more abundant life. In this sense there may be any number of universes of experience, each of which is relative to its own experience and all of which are embraced in the thought or plan of the infinite mind or will on which they all depend.

By this time we have widely departed from the original Kantian position, yet in such a way as to retain the truth in Kant's view while escaping its essential error. The conception of a world of reality altogether apart from mind and antithetical to it, which is the source of the various agnosticisms, we reject outright. Such a world manifestly can never be known and with equal certainty it can never be affirmed. Kant [assumed] such a reality by taking for granted the crude notions of common sense according to which things just exist apart from mind, and mind has simply the function of knowing them after they are there. Something might be said for this view from the standpoint of our human experience in which we seem to be purely perceptive of a world already existing, but at the utmost all that this makes out is that the world of reality is independent of our thinking and willing, but not that it is independent of all thinking and willing. This independence of our thought superficial common sense takes for independence of all thought, which is a very different matter. When next we join to this affirmation the insight that our minds can know only those things which are related to it, agnosticism follows as a matter of course; but instead of adopting this uncritical view, and then complaining that we cannot know the reality of things, attention should have been rather directed to the inquiry whether we have any warrant for affirming such things. And as soon as this question is raised, the baselessness of the affirmation becomes apparent. For our immediate facts are ourselves and the world of experience. These are the only realities of which we have any immediate knowledge, and any further realities we may affirm must be affirmed for the sake of making this world of persons and personal experience intelligible, and it is clear that the affirmation of no kind of unknowable or impersonal existence will give us the least light upon this subject. Hence we set aside that world of impersonal existence and confine ourselves to the real world of experience, and attempt to discover its uniformities of coexistence and sequence and to spell out its meanings as best we may. But this world is not an illusion. It is the world where we all meet in mutual understanding, the world where life goes on. It is then perfectly real in its way, but when we come to study it we find that some phases of this world of experience compel us to transcend them in order to find their proper causes. In this case we are not looking for noumena or things behind phenomena which the mind ought to know but cannot. We are rather looking for the cause or causes of these facts of experience, and these causes are to be known through their effects. In the nature of the case they can never be brought before our eyes and presented in terms of vision. And this is the case with all causes. They are to be known through their effects. Here, too, we have no unknowable noumenal world forever eluding us; we simply have causes at work, and we seek through studying their effects to form some idea of the nature of those causes. As we have before said, a good part of the Kantian agnosticism rests upon oversight of the fact that in any case causes can be known only by their effects, and that to this problem the antithesis of phenomena and noumena or appearance and reality is inapplicable. The mind is known through its activities, but these activities are not appearances or manifestations in any visual sense. They are known in their proper way in consciousness and the nature of the mind is revealed in them. Similarly the hidden power behind the cosmic order does not appear in any visual sense, but manifests itself in the ongoings of things and is to be known in the same way.

In the beginning of this work we pointed out that knowledge is conditioned, first, by the subject, and secondly, by the object. In common thought the object itself is the only fact considered. It is taken as a matter of course that if things are there we know them as they are, and there seems to be no mystery about it. In opposition to this, Kant set forth the complex mental activity involved in our cognitive operations, and so was led to say that the mind makes nature, that the understanding is the source of natural laws and imposes its forms upon nature, and other things to the same effect. We have seen that this is an important half of the truth in this sense, that if the mind were not a microcosm over against macrocosm there would be no possibility of knowledge; but now it is necessary to emphasize the fact that the mind is conditioned by the nature of the object as well as by its own nature. We cannot impose mental forms upon the world of experience unless that world itself be adapted to those forms. Thus, in the matter of space we cannot see things in any kind of spatial arrangement or vary the arrangement of things at our pleasure. However much the space form may be a mental law it is also a law of the objects to which we have conformed. Similarly with the time order and the causal order and the orders of law in general. Although these orders can be known only by a rational mind, which is led by its own nature to give rational form to things, it is equally plain that the mind can give such form only to things which are already rationally adjusted. If we suppose that the world of things is really a thought world, — that is, it is rooted in thought and expresses thought, — then this harmony of thought and thing can be understood; and on any other supposition we are left to oscillate helplessly between an untenable idealism on the one hand and an equally untenable realism on the other.

Time

As a large part of Kant's phenomenalism rests upon his doctrine of space, we have considered the matter at length without having referred to his teaching concerning time. There is, however, no less in this, and it is now possible to deal with the latter subject more intelligibly than would have been possible without the previous discussion.

Kant's argument for the subjectivity of time is practically the same as that for the subjectivity of space. We have the same confusion between time as a perception and time as a form at the beginning of experience. Also the assumption that the knowledge of time as one and infinite precedes our knowledge of finite times. The objections to the similar claim in the case of space may be understood [to apply] here.

In one point, however, there is a novelty which deserves notice. Space in Kant's psychology is a form of the external sense and is supposed to represent our way of looking at things which are not spatial. Now, so long as we have a real knowledge of the inner life, this view is not entirely unintelligible, and illustrations could be found in the way of making it clear. Thus in dreams we have spatial experience, while of course there is no thought of any spatial reality. Misled by this notion of the external sense and apparently for the sake of symmetry, Kant affirms time to be the form of the internal sense, and this time is supposed to be a kind of veil over reality instead of giving us its truth. But it is difficult to make out just what the internal sense would be other than the fact that we have consciousness of our subjective states in their coexistences and sequences; but this fact in itself does not seem to call for any special sense beyond itself. However, Kant seems to think that there is a veritable mental activity which this internal sense masks, just as the external sense masks the objective fact in external perception. The most careful inspection, however, of our consciousness does not reveal any warrant for an affirmation of this kind. In dealing with the outer world it is possible to think of phenomena which mask reality, but in dealing with the inner world we cannot think in this way. Behind the feelings we feel and behind the successions in consciousness which we experience there certainly are no feelings that we do not feel and no timeless relations that we do not experience. We therefore have to take the life of consciousness as it presents itself and as being perfectly real in its experienced form, and then inquire what this life leads us to affirm respecting its essential nature.

The subjectivity of time is really a more difficult doctrine than that of space. In the latter case we seem to have experience of non-spatial facts, — for instance, consciousness itself, — but we have no experience whatever of any timeless order. The doctrine must, therefore, be established by reflection upon the nature of time itself in connection with the totality of our experience. In this matter Kant takes it all too easily. He refers to an objection to which he gives no adequate answer. He says: "Against this theory which claims empirical, but denies absolute and transcendental reality to time, even intelligent men have protested so unanimously that I suppose that every reader who is unaccustomed to these considerations may naturally be of the same opinion. What they object to is this: Changes, they say, are real (this is proved by the change of our own representations, even if all external phenomena and their changes be denied). Changes, however, are possible in time only, and therefore time must be something real. The answer is easy enough. I grant the whole argument. Time certainly is something real, namely, the real form of our internal intuition. Time, therefore, has subjective reality with regard to internal experience; that is, I really have the representation of time and of my determinations in it. Time therefore is to be considered as real, not so far as it is an object, but so far as it is the representation of myself as an object. If either I myself or any other being

153

could see me without this condition of sensibility, then these selfsame determinations which we now represent to ourselves as changes would give us a kind of knowledge in which the representation of time, and therefore of change also, would have no place. There remains, therefore, the empirical reality of time only, as the condition of all our experience, while absolute reality cannot, according to what has just been shown, be conceded to it. Time is nothing but the form of our internal intuition. Take away the peculiar condition of our sensibility, and the idea of time vanishes, because it is not inherent in the objects, but in the subject only that perceives them." (Page 29.)

Now with regard to this it can be shown, though Kant does not show it, that time considered as a separate existence by itself is full of contradictions. The existing time back of all things and change, which would flow on uniformly if all things were away, is a fiction which could not be allowed without the complete overthrow of reason itself. But while time might not exist as an objective fact, it might yet exist as a law in being itself such that the activities of being are necessarily successive; and in that case time, while not real as thing, remains about as real as ever as a controlling law. To this suggestion, which is embodied in the objection based on the fact of change, Kant gives no answer except to affirm the subjectivity of time, whereas what we really wish to know is whether this subjectivity can be maintained or not. For if change be real there is no possibility, at least on the impersonal plane, of connecting the world of change with any changeless existence so as to make change the effect of the changeless. If it be suggested, as has been done, that the reality is neither changeable nor unchangeable, but simply that which we view under the form of change, the answer must be that this withdraws the problem from all consideration whatever. It would merely introduce an x into the problem which could be brought into no articulate relations with it, and we should have nothing but the speculator's word of honor that it is equal to the demands made upon it.

Let us consider, then, the relation of time to change. We may say that change does not take place in time, but that time is the form of change, and that the temporal relations of things depend upon their relations to one another in the great changing movement. Thus it would seem that time itself is brought back again, in a different form, indeed, from what it has in spontaneous thought, but for all practical purposes in much the same form that it has always had. But here some further difficulties emerge, much more profound than any that Kant refers to. It is first plain from the nature of consciousness that there must be a certain non-temporal element in thought itself, otherwise consciousness becomes impossible; for if we introduce proper succession into thought so that its phases are really mutually external, the earlier coming before the later, and the later arriving only after the earlier has gone, it is clear that consciousness would disappear altogether; so then we have in the consciousness of change itself an element that is unchangeable, and this element cannot possibly be denied without mental disaster.

But here another fact appears, a certain element of relativity in both space and time, which puts a very different aspect on our spatial and temporal experience and profoundly modifies the entire question. Thus, in the case of space the pure geometrical intuition as applied to the world of experience is absolute. Distance as measured in terms of its units is fixed. Direction is equally fixed. Here, then, is something absolute in the spatial experience, but when we come to relate this experience to actuality we find a series of puzzles emerging. Because of the infinite divisibility of space no unitary thing can exist in it. And hence nothing can be located in it except in relation to the other objects of experience. Our space relations, then, from this point on acquire a dynamic character. The "here" of the living person is determined by his immediate activity. Instead of saying, He acts where he is, we must literally reverse the proposition and say, He is where he immediately acts. No other definition of presence or location can be definitely given. In that case our presence or our "here" becomes relative to the range of our immediate action. If we could act as immediately and as effectively on things beyond the sea as we do upon things at arm's length, we should be as present beyond the sea as we are now in our immediate neighborhood; or if our organic activities embraced [the earth, as they do] what we call our body, we should be present to the earth in the same sense as we are now present to the organism. Thus we see that concrete presence is nothing that can be geometrically determined in an absolute space, but is rather a function of our dynamic relations. It is the dynamic relation that determines the space relations. And we also see that presence in space is relative to our dynamic range. Immediate action is presence, immediate action on all things is omnipresence. The ideality of space, therefore, does not permit us to [abolish] space as a form of experience, but it does enable us to dismiss the great phantom of an all-embracing void. Thus space becomes both ideal and actual. It is ideal as not representing an independent thinghood, but it is also actual as representing an order of limitation. In this sense only the Infinite and Absolute Being upon whom all things continually depend can transcend space. The world of experience, then, is spatial in having the space form. It is also spatial in the fact that the space limitation cannot be transcended by us. But it is not spatial in the sense of being an all-embracing void in which all things are stowed and stored. Thus it appears that a large part of our spatial experience is relative to ourselves and to our own dynamic range.

Much the same is to be said of the time judgment. There is a great deal here also that is relative to our human limitations. And for understanding the ideality of time it is necessary to bear this in mind. Time can be interpreted only from the side of experience, and more especially from the standpoint of self-consciousness. Experience cannot be in the present as a separate point of time, but rather the present is in experience. We cannot define the present as a point in independent time. It is only a special relation in consciousness. The person who can grasp only a few things has a small present; one who can grasp many things has a large present; and one who can grasp all things has an all-embracing present.

This bringing of the present with the resulting time judgment into relation to activity greatly modifies the subject. We call those things present which we possess in the certain immediacy of consciousness, and if we possessed all our experiences in a similar immediacy the whole experience would be present in the same sense. There would still be a certain order of arrangement among the factors of experience which could not arbitrarily be modified, but all the members of the series would be equally present to consciousness. If, now, there were a being who could retain all the facts of his experience in the same immediacy, he would have no past. And further, if such a being were also in full possession of himself so as to be under no law of development and possessing no unrealized potentialities, he would also have no future, at least so far as his own existence might be concerned. His present would be all-embracing and his now would be eternal. These considerations modify our judgment of the subjectivity of time very profoundly. Taking up once more the question, Are we in time? we see that it has several meanings and the answers must vary to correspond. If it means, Are things and events in a real time which flows on independently of them? the answer must be, No. If it means, Does our experience have the temporal form? the answer must be, Yes. If we further inquire concerning the possibility of transcending temporal limitations, it is clear that this can be affirmed only of the

Absolute Being, for only in Him do we find that complete self-possession which the transcendence of time would mean. Non-temporality, then, in the concrete sense cannot be reached by passing behind the world of phenomena into the world of noumena, but rather and only by rising above the sphere of the finite into the absolute self-possession of the infinite. These considerations introduce us to an order of complexity which Kant never suspected and which is in no way disposed of by his easy doctrine of the phenomenality of time. And in any case time is not disposed of by making it a phenomenon. For the phenomenon as such might be eternal. The attempt to find what things are in themselves we have definitely set aside, because it is perfectly clear that all we can ever come to know is what things are for intelligence, and any knowing we may ever have will necessarily have our mental nature as one of its coefficients. There is, therefore, not the slightest interest in inquiring what things are in themselves in distinction from asking what they are for intelligence. When we can answer the latter question we have all the knowledge that is valuable, and when the matter is thought out it appears that we know all there is to know. The real fact of the world of experience is ourselves as its subject and the infinite spirit as its ground and creator. That static universe of unclear speculative thought, or that world of things in themselves which thought can never reach, is unknowable for the sufficient reason that it does not exist.

The Æsthetic and Analytic contain the most significant part of Kant's doctrine. We have found in it a great truth; namely, the activity of the mind in knowing, which remains as Kant's permanent and most valuable contribution to speculative thought. The rest of the work is confused in its meaning, unsatisfactory in its reasoning, and very far from consistent in itself. We now pass to the third section of Transcendental Dialectic.

VI

THE TRANSCENDENTAL DIALECTIC

ACCORDING to Kant the great function of the understanding is to raise our sense experience into articulate thought. It does this by applying the categories to the raw material of sense. Beyond this field the categories have no application. However, the understanding, being dogmatic in its tendency and unaware of its own limitations until duly chastened by criticism, seeks to transcend the field of experience, and thus produces a variety of illusions, thus giving rise to what Kant calls the dialectic of the pure reason. This field of illusion he now proceeds to expound.

Kant attributes the dialectical process to what he calls the reason in distinction from sense and understanding. And as the understanding has its categories, the reason has its ideas; and as the categories were deduced from the table of judgments in formal logic, the ideas are to be deduced from the different classes of syllogisms. This deduction is in the highest degree artificial. We have three classes of syllogisms; categorical, hypothetical, and disjunctive. And Kant says: "As many kinds of relation as there are, which the understanding represents to itself by means of the categories, so many pure concepts of the reason we shall find, that is, first, the unconditioned of the categorical synthesis in a subject; secondly, the unconditioned of the hypothetical synthesis of the members

161

of a series; thirdly, the unconditioned of the disjunctive synthesis of the parts of a system. There are exactly as many kinds of syllogisms, each of which tries to advance by means of pro-syllogisms to the unconditioned: the first to the subject, which itself is no longer a predicate; the second to the presupposition, which presupposes nothing else; and the third to an aggregate of the members of a division, which requires nothing else, in order to render the division of the concept complete." (Page 262.) This kind of thing is satisfactory only for those for whom some sort of formal systematic presentation is a condition of mental peace; all others will find it better to pass at once to the transcendental ideas themselves and consider them without reference to their deduction.

"All pure concepts in general aim at a synthetical unity of representations, while concepts of pure reason (transcendental ideas) aim at unconditioned synthetical unity of all conditions. All transcendental ideas, therefore, can be arranged in three classes: the first containing the absolute (unconditioned) unity of the thinking subject; the second the absolute unity of the series of conditions of phenomena; the third the absolute unity of the condition of all objects of thought in general." (Page 271.) By this he means the soul, the world, and the Supreme Being or God. He says, "The thinking subject is the object-matter of psychology, the system of all phenomena (the world) the object-matter of cosmology, and the being which contains the highest condition of the possibility of all that can be thought (the Being of all beings), the object matter of theology." (Page 272.)

These transcendental ideas Kant regards as merely forms of the reason and not as objects of proper speculative knowledge, and this he proceeds to show in his criticism of rational psychology, rational cosmology, and rational theology. He says: —

"Of these dialectical syllogisms of reason there are, therefore, three classes only, that is as many as the ideas to which their conclusions lead. In the syllogism of the first class, I conclude from the transcendental concept of the subject, which contains nothing manifold, the absolute unity of the subject itself, of which, however, I have no concept in this regard. This dialectical syllogism I shall call the transcendental paralogism.

"The second class of the so-called sophistical syllogisms aims at the transcendental concept of an absolute totality in the series of conditions to any given phenomenon; and I conclude from the fact that my concept of the unconditioned synthetical unity of the series is always self-contradictory on one side, the correctness of the opposite unity, of which nevertheless I have no concept either. The state of reason in this class of dialectical syllogisms, I shall call the antimony of pure reason.

"Lastly, according to the third class of sophistical syllogisms, I conclude from the totality of conditions, under which objects in general, so far as they can be given to me, must be thought, the absolute synthetical unity of all conditions of the possibility of things in general; that is to say, I conclude from things which I do not know according to their mere transcendental concept, a Being of all beings, which I know still less

163

through a transcendental concept, and of the unconditioned necessity of which I can form no concept whatever. This dialectical syllogism of reason I shall call the ideal of pure reason." (Page 276.)

According to Kant rational psychology begins with the text "I think," out of which it must evolve all its wisdom. This gives rise to the following table: —

I	II
The Soul is Substance.	As regards its quality, simple.

III	IV
As regards the different times in which it exists, numerically identical, that is unity (not plurality).	It is in relation to possible objects in space.

"All concepts of pure psychology arise from these elements, simply by way of combination, and without the admixture of any other principle. This substance, taken simply as the object of the internal sense, gives us the concept of immateriality; and as simple substance, that of incorruptibility; its identity, as that of an intellectual substance, gives us personality; and all these three together, spirituality; its relation to objects in space gives us the concept of commercium (intercourse) with bodies; the pure psychology thus representing the thinking substance as the principle of life in matter, that is, as soul (anima), and as the ground of animality; which again, as restricted by spirituality, gives us the concept of immortality." (Page 281.)

The discussion of the first paralogism of substantiality differs entirely in the two editions. But there is really not very much difference in the substance of the reasoning, and Kant's conclusion is very far from being established. In the first edition the argument runs as follows: —

"That, the representation of which is the absolute subject of our judgments, and cannot be used therefore as the determination of any other thing, is the substance.

"I, as a thinking being, am the absolute subject of all my possible judgments, and this representation of myself can never be used as the predicate of any other thing.

"Therefore I, as a thinking being (Soul), am Substance." (Page 284.)

This is a false argument, according to Kant, which he proposes to overthrow. Kant reasons as follows: "We showed in the analytical portion of transcendental logic, that pure categories, and among them that of substance, have in themselves no objective meaning, unless they rest on some intuition, and are applied to the manifold of such intuitions as functions of synthetical unity. Without this they are merely functions of a judgment without contents." (Page 284.) He concludes that we have no such intuition with respect to the self, and "have only formed a deduction from the concept of the relation which all thinking has to the I, as the common subject to which it belongs. Nor should we, whatever we did, succeed by any certain observation in proving such permanency. For though the I exists in all thoughts, not the slightest intuition is connected with that represent-

165

ation, by which it might be distinguished from other objects of intuition. We may very well perceive, therefore, that this representation appears again and again in every act of thought, but not that it is a constant and permanent intuition, in which thoughts, as being changeable, come and go."

"Hence it follows that in the first syllogism of transcendental psychology reason imposes upon us an apparent knowledge only, by representing the constant logical subject of thought as the knowledge of the real subject in which that knowledge inheres. Of that subject, however, we have not and cannot have the slightest knowledge. . . . Beside this logical meaning of the I, we have no knowledge of the subject in itself, which forms the substratum and foundation of it and of all our thoughts." (Page 285.)

In this criticism Kant depends on two principles, one the distinction of the percept and the concept, and the other the phenomenality of knowledge. Because of the latter we can have no real knowledge of the self, and therefore no proper percept of it. All we can do, then, is to form logical concepts, and these without the corresponding intuition are empty.

Precisely what Kant would mean by intuition in the case of the self, it would be hard to tell. He tended generally to limit intuitions to the external sense, that is, to spatial phenomena, in which case we have no intuition of the self, of course, as it is nonspatial and formless. But this conception of intuition, as we have before pointed out, is too narrow, and if we are to allow the term "intuition" to stand at all, it must be taken to mean experience and not intuition in a spatial form. In this sense we have self-experience in self-consciousness. We know our feelings, thoughts, etc., as our own, and we know ourselves as thinking and feeling in these several ways. This is not a merely conceptual knowledge which deals in abstractions from experience. It is the real living self-experience, than which there is nothing deeper. Here Kant is simply applying his distinction of perception and conception without noting that this distinction in the nature of the case cannot be made absolute, for there must somewhere be perceptions and conceptions which run together so that neither would be anything without the other, and both are realized in immediate experience, and this is the case with our self-knowledge. Kant's doctrine meets another difficulty here which Kant himself did not consider, but which is none the less important for our thought. We can distinguish with some intelligibility between the knowing subject and objects which it calls phenomena; but the knowing subject can never itself become phenomenon in the sense in which its objects are phenomena. To make it phenomenal in the same sense is to cut loose from reality and from knowledge altogether, and have drifting phenomena, which are expected to have phenomena, or which appear to phenomena or which perceive through phenomena, and by this time all intelligible thought has disappeared. Hence, unless the doctrine is to vanish in sheer absurdity, we must affirm the reality of self-knowledge as far as it goes. Kant himself does not seem to have been satisfied with his reasoning, as appears from the fact just mentioned that in the second edition he gives

THE PHILOSOPHY OF KANT

the argument an entirely different form. He introduces also an additional consideration which is naïve as showing that Kant would perhaps have not been unwilling to admit the substantiality of the soul if it had not been for its bearing upon his doctrine of knowledge. He says: —

"It would be a great, nay, even the only objection to the whole of our critique, if there were a possibility of proving a priori that all thinking beings are by themselves simple substances, that, as such (as a consequence of the same argument), personality is inseparable from them, and that they are conscious of their existence as distinct from all matter. For we should thus have made a step beyond the world of sense and entered into the field of noumena, and after that no one could dare to question our right of advancing further, of settling in it, and, as each of us is favored by luck, taking possession of it. The proposition that every thinking being is, as such, a simple substance, is synthetical a priori, because, first, it goes beyond the concept on which it rests, and adds to act of thinking in general the mode of existence; and secondly, because it adds to that concept a predicate (simplicity) which cannot be given in any experience. Hence synthetical propositions a priori would be not only admissible, as we maintained, in reference to objects of possible experience, and then only as principles of the possibility of that experience, but could be extended to things in general and to things by themselves, a result which would put an end to the whole of our critique, and bid us to leave everything as we found it. However, the danger is not so great, if only we look more closely into the matter.

"In this process of rational psychology there lurks a paralogism, which may be represented by the following syllogism.

"That which cannot be conceived otherwise than as a subject, does not exist otherwise than as a subject, and is therefore a substance.

"A thinking being, considered as such, cannot be conceived otherwise than as a subject.

"Therefore it exists also as such only, that is, as a substance." (Page 795.)

That much of this is verbal or a matter of definition appears from another passage in the discussion of the second edition as follows: "In all judgments I am always the determining subject only of the relation which constitutes the judgment. That I, who think, can be considered in thinking as subject only, and as something not simply inherent in the thinking, as predicate, is an apodictical and even identical proposition; but it does not mean that, as an object, I am a self-dependent being or a substance." (Page 793.)

Here Kant shows that he has a peculiar metaphysical notion of the meaning of substance. The thinking subject is one and identical, but this fact does not mean that as an object he is a self-dependent being or a substance. Here Kant has certainly dropped back into the Cartesian or Spinozistic notion of substance and defined it as self-dependent. For all ordinary purposes and for the whole field of practical life it suffices to define substance as that which can act or be acted upon. If we can produce effects and account for something in the ongoing of events, and if we can be acted upon by things beyond us, then we are substances in a real sense of the term, and we are not made unsubstantial by the declaration that we are not self-existent and self-sufficient. If we take this to be Kant's meaning of substance, then his argument simply amounts to this, that we human beings are not self-dependent; but nobody ever claimed that we are.

Kant further argues against the simplicity of the self, but with equal lack of success. Unity and identity of the subject, he says, does not prove the unity and identity of the substance. He nowhere attempts to show how a [composite substance] can give rise to a unitary consciousness, but he uses an illustration to show how identity of the subject might be combined with [change] of substance. When an elastic ball strikes another of equal mass the former comes to rest and the latter moves on. Kant speaks of this as one body transferring its state to another, and in the same way he suggests a mental substance might transfer its entire consciousness to another. The consciousness being thus passed along from one to another, the subject would remain identical while the substance would be incessantly changing. But this notion of a transmitted consciousness is a piece of picture-thinking which does not admit of being followed out in any way. If there were a conscious subject with its conscious states capable of passing along from one substance to another, it would certainly be able to dispense with the substances altogether, for we need no such substance. This living, thinking self, which is mysterious enough, no doubt, in many phases of its existence, but is nevertheless what all mean when we speak of ourselves, is the only substance we know anything about, and philosophizing can only hope to make progress by assimilating all other objects and processes to just this self-conscious experience. It is, then, this life continuing in self-identification through its various phases that really constitutes what we mean by substance, and any other substance which cannot be assimilated to this is more than unknowable, it is an unaffirmable fiction. Kant says, "That the *Ego* of apperception, and therefore the *Ego* in every act of thought, is a *singular* which cannot be dissolved into a plurality of subjects, and that it therefore signifies a logically simple subject, follows from the very concept of thinking, and is consequently an analytical proposition. But this does not mean that a thinking *Ego* is a simple *substance*, which would indeed be a synthetical proposition." (Page 794.) The reply to all this is that there is no way of conceiving how the thinking subject could be looked upon as a composite of a plurality of subjects, and therefore it is to be regarded as one in experience; and as for that substance over and above this living self of conscious experience, we assume that we know nothing about that, and for the really sufficient reason that there is no such thing to know. We set aside, therefore, Kant's criticism of the "first paralogism of substantiality" and also of the "second paralogism of simplicity," as resting partly upon Kant's determined denial of the possibility of [noumenal] knowledge, and secondly, upon a conception of substance which must be looked upon as outgrown. In the second edition Kant adds

171

a refutation of Mendelssohn's proof of the permanence of the soul, that is, of immortality. The earlier arguments for immortality were based upon the assumption that destruction takes place through decomposition. In physical change there is nowhere any destruction of the substantiality: there is only decomposition and recomposition. This fact applies only to form. The principal reality itself cannot perish by decomposition: it being simple it admits of no such process; hence it is common to regard the physical elements as indestructible at least by any natural process, and hence as eternal. Now, if we apply similar reasoning to the soul conceived of as simple substance we bring it under the head of reality in general, and since as simple substance it admits of no decomposition we may regard it as eternal. To this Kant replies by saying that it is very far from proof, because a simple substance might vanish, not through decomposition but through flickering out. Thus, force or energy of any kind does not admit of division in a spatial sense, but it does come under the head of intensity; and thus intensity may conceivably pass through all degrees down to zero, in which case there would be no energy any longer. Hence the argument for immortality can in no way be looked upon as a demonstration. As a result of all these considerations Kant concludes that the basal propositions of rational psychology concerning the simplicity, unity, identity, and immortality of the soul cannot be looked upon as being properly demonstrated. The argument by which it is sought to prove them turns out, he thinks, upon examination to be sophistical. This view does not disprove the doctrine in question. It simply shows that by dint of great reasoning we can never attain to certain knowledge in this matter. And this Kant regards as really no loss because he thinks these arguments never produce any conviction and their rejection ought never to remove any. In the continual identification of ourselves in conscious experience we have all the proof of unity and identity we need; and in the possibility of acting and producing effects we have equal proof of our reality, and in the demands of our moral nature we have equal practical warrant for the belief in a future life, and this is all that the thought of man in general demands. Anything beyond this he thinks is simply due to pride of the scholastic reasoning, and that is not a matter of much practical importance any way.

In all of this Kant is not entirely off the track. Certainly no one nowadays would seek to demonstrate immortality, or to prove the possibility of our continued existence in incorporeal life, and other things associated with our religious notions. They are to be looked upon in some sense as matters of faith or at least of belief, rather than of demonstration. At the same time Kant's criticism is about equally bad with the argument which he rejects. As we have seen, he holds an impossible notion of substance and then by his [doctrine of] phenomenal knowledge entangles himself in both logical and psychological construction. We should nowadays, as already suggested, give a very different definition of substance from that which Kant gave. With the [conception] of substance as he has given it we are shut up at once to Spinozistic pantheism; but when we regard substantial things as simply those which can act and be acted upon, we find it entirely possible to be ourselves substances. At the same time, since we cannot regard ourselves as absolutely independent, it is plain that our existence is conditioned by something beyond ourselves, and in that something we must really look for the reason for our going into existence, our remaining in existence, or our coming out of existence. No reflection upon ourselves as able to act and be acted upon reveals in any way the immortality of our being. For this belief we must have recourse either to revelation or to some needs or implications of our religious and moral nature. Speculation as such cannot furnish the faith. It will be seen, then, that we agree to some extent with Kant's conclusion, though by no means can we accept the argument by which he reaches it. We may close this discussion by a quotation from Kant himself, in which he sets forth the harmlessness of his results for practical purposes.

"Nothing is lost, however, by this with regard to the right, nay, the necessity of admitting a future life, according to the principles of practical, as connected with the speculative employment of reason. It is known besides, that a purely speculative proof has never been able to exercise any influence on the ordinary reason of men. It stands so entirely upon the point of a hair that even the schools can only keep it from falling so long as they keep it constantly spinning round like a top, so that, even in their own eyes, it yields no permanent foundation upon which anything could be built. The proofs which are useful for the world at large retain their value undiminished, nay, they gain in clearness and natural power, by the surrender of those dogmatical pretensions, placing reason in its own peculiar domain, namely, the system of ends, which is, however, at the same time the system of nature; so that reason, as a practical faculty by itself, without being limited by the conditions of nature, becomes justified in extending the system of ends, and with it, our own existence, beyond the limits of experience and of life. According to the analogy with the nature of living beings in this world, in which reason must necessarily admit the principle that no organ, no faculty, no impulse, can be found, as being either superfluous or disproportionate to its use, and therefore purposeless, but that everything is adequate to its destination in life, man, who alone can contain in himself the highest end of all this, would be the only creature excepted from it. For, his natural dispositions, not only so far as he uses them according to his talents and impulses, but more especially the moral law within him, go so far beyond all that is useful and advantageous in this life that he is taught thereby, in the absence of all advantages, even of the shadowy hope of posthumous fame, to esteem the mere consciousness of righteousness beyond everything else, feeling an inner call, by his conduct in this world and a surrender of many advantages, to render himself fit to become the citizen of a better world, which exists in his idea only. This powerful and incontrovertible proof, accompanied by our constantly increasing recognition of a design pervading all that we see around us, and by a contemplation of the immensity of crea-

tion, and therefore also by the consciousness of an unlimited possibility in the extension of our knowledge,
and a desire commensurate therewith, all this remains
and always will remain, although we must surrender
the hope of ever being able to understand, from the
mere theoretical knowledge of ourselves, the necessary continuance of our existence." (Page 803.) From
this it plainly appears that Kant did not regard his
work as practically destructive. As he says in another place, he disputes knowledge and makes room
for belief. His claim is that the theoretical faculty is
not self-contradictory when it remains within its own
field. It is only limited in itself and falls into contradictions and illusions when it goes beyond the limits
established in its own nature. But inasmuch as man is
not merely speculative but active, not merely theoretical but practical, not merely understanding but will
and conscience, belief may be practically determined
for us by the practical necessities arising out of life
itself, so that what the understanding cannot do because of its own inherent limitations, life itself may
accomplish because of its own practical needs and
moral and religious intuitions. The field outside of
the understanding, however, while it may not be
made a realm for dogmatic affirmation, can also not
be made a realm for dogmatic denial. Accordingly
Kant claims that he has done an important work in
the way of overthrowing all materialistic and atheistic teaching, for this rests upon the dogmatic use of
the understanding in a field to which it has no proper
application. It is possible, then, for the moral and religious nature to see visions and dream dreams with-

out being molested in any way by the old denials of the materialist and the atheist. For religion and conscience have life on their side, and do not therefore float in the air; whereas atheism and materialism have neither life [nor its ideals] on their side, while their reasoning is disposed of by the general results of the critical philosophy.

VII

THE ANTINOMY OF PURE REASON

AFTER discussing the paralogisms of pure reason which deal with rational psychology, Kant next proceeds to the antinomy of pure reason, which has to do with rational cosmology or the general doctrine of the world. In the paralogisms reason falls into arguments which are such only in appearance: in the antinomy it falls into contradiction with itself; hence the case is worse with reason in rational cosmology than it is in rational psychology. In this field of cosmology the reason falls into four contradictions. In its natural play it is led to regard the world as infinite and also as finite. It is also led to affirm causality, and furthermore a conditioned being and an unconditioned being. Thus against each affirmation or thesis, as Kant calls it, it can establish with equal confidence an antithesis, and thus the essential contradiction of reason is revealed. Of the four antinomies thus arising two are concerned with the world in experience and time, and the other two are concerned with the metaphysical ideas of causality and being as conditioned or unconditioned. The first two antinomies Kant calls the mathematical, the second two he calls the dynamic. We consider these now in their order. Kant is by no means so successful in his argument here as he seems to think.

178

THE ANTINOMY OF PURE REASON

FIRST CONFLICT OF THE TRANSCENDENTAL IDEAS

Thesis

The world has a beginning in time, and is limited also with regard to space.

Proof

For if we assumed that the world had no beginning in time, then an eternity must have elapsed up to every given point of time, and therefore an infinite series of successive states of things must have passed in the world. The infinity of a series, however, consists in this, that it never can be completed by means of a successive synthesis. Hence an infinite past series of worlds is impossible, and the beginning of the world a necessary condition of its existence. This was what had to be proved first.

With regard to the second, let us assume again the opposite. In that case the world would be given as an infinite whole of coexisting things. Now, we cannot conceive in any way the extension of a quantum, which is not given within certain limits to every intuition, except through the synthesis of its parts, nor the totality of such a quantum in any way, except through a completed synthesis, or by the repeated addition of unity to itself. In order, therefore, to conceive the world, which fills all space, as a whole, the successive synthesis of the parts of an infinite world would have to be

Antithesis

The world has no beginning and no limits in space, but is infinite, in respect both to time and space.

Proof

For let us assume that it has a beginning. Then, as beginning is an existence which is preceded by a time in which the thing is not, it would follow that antecedently there was a time in which the world was not, that is, an empty time. In an empty time, however, it is impossible that anything should take its beginning, because of such a time no part possesses any condition as to existence rather than non-existence, which condition could distinguish that part from any other (whether produced by itself or through another cause). Hence, though many a series of things may take its beginning in the world, the world itself can have no beginning, and in reference to time past is infinite.

With regard to the second, let us assume again the opposite, namely, that the world is finite and limited in space. In that case the world would exist in an empty space without limits. We should, therefore, have not only a relation of things in space, but also of things to space. As, however, the world is an absolute whole, outside of which no object of intuition, and therefore no correlate of the world can be found, the rela-

179

looked upon as completed; that is, an infinite time would have to be looked upon as elapsed, during the enumeration of all coexisting things. This is impossible. Hence an infinite aggregate of real things cannot be regarded as a given whole, nor, therefore, as given at the same time. Hence it follows that the world is not infinite, as regards extension in space, but enclosed in limits. This was the second that had to be proved.

tion of the world to empty space would be a relation to no object. Such a relation, and with it the limitation of the world by empty space, is nothing, and therefore the world is not limited with regard to space, that is, it is infinite in extension.

(Pages 344–46.)

In the case of this antinomy both the proof and the disproof are unsatisfactory. First, with regard to the limitation of the world in time and space. He says if we assume that the world had no beginning in time, then an eternity must have elapsed up to every given point of time, and therefore an infinite series of successive states of things must have passed in the world. The infinity of a series, however, consists in this, that it never can be completed by means of a successive synthesis; hence an infinite past series of worlds is impossible, and a beginning of the world is a condition of its existence.

With regard to this, the difficulty lies in the notion of the infinite lapsed time, for if we suppose time to be anything that really flows and suppose that this flow is infinite, there would be no difficulty at all in supposing that there should be an infinite series of events as old as the temporal flow itself; and the infinity of past time, supposing time to be anything whatever, seems not to have any special difficulty in it when we reflect upon what that infinity really means. It does not mean that the flow includes all time and admits of no increase. It means only that in the temporal regress we should not come to a beginning in any finite period, as we should come to no end in any finite progress. Kant, then, might have dropped the consideration of the world altogether, unless he includes time itself as a kind of something in the world, and devoted his attention to the conception of infinite time.

The necessary limitation of the world in space is even more unsatisfactory in its proof. He says: "Let us assume again the opposite. In that case the world would be given as an infinite whole of coexisting things. Now we cannot conceive in any way the extension of a quantum, which is not given within certain limits to every intuition, except through the synthesis of its parts, nor the totality of such a quantum in any way except through a completed synthesis, or by the repeated addition of unity to itself. In order, therefore, to conceive the world, which fills all space, as a whole, the successive synthesis of the parts of an infinite world would have to be looked upon as completed; that is, an infinite time would have to be looked upon as elapsed during the enumeration of all coexisting things. This is impossible. Hence an infinite aggregate of real things cannot be regarded as a given whole, nor, therefore, as given at the same time. Hence it follows that the world is not infinite, as regards extension in space, but enclosed in limits."

Here the gist of the argument lies in confusing thinking with picturing. We cannot picture an infinite quantity or infinite number, but we might well conceive that the quantity or the number has no end.

We really do not conceive the infinity of space by any successive movement of the imagination, adding part to part and forever moving on and upward. We rather conceive it by our insight into the space law, which tells us that this law, in the nature of the case, admits of no [exhaustion], that space is to be viewed as infinite if it is to be viewed as anything by itself. The same is true of the numerical series. We certainly do not conceive any large number by adding unit to unit or by paying much attention to any of the particular units. We rather confine ourselves to the numerical law in the case, and by means of our knowledge of this law we are able to deal with large numbers with perfect certainty, although imagination itself would be totally incapable of representing it. The infinitude of number is reached in the same way. We perceive by reflection on the numerical series that it admits of no exhaustion, but may be carried on indefinitely and forever. And this we express by saying that number is infinite. No given number, of course, can be infinite, and we have only to add one to that given number to increase it by a unit; but a numerical object in its essential exhaustible character is such that we affirm the infinitude of number.

In the antithesis Kant claims to prove that the world has no beginning and no limits in space, but is infinite both in respect to time and to space. The proof runs: "For let us assume that it has a beginning. Then, as beginning is an existence which is preceded by a time in which the thing is not, it would follow that antecedently there was a time in which the world was not, that is, an empty time. In an empty time, however, it is impossible that anything should take its beginning, because of such a time no part possesses any condition as to existence rather than non-existence, which condition could distinguish that part from any other (whether produced by itself, or through another cause). Hence, though many a series of things may take its beginning in the world, the world itself can have no beginning, and in reference to time past is infinite."

Here Kant assumes that the world equals all existence, conditioned and unconditioned alike, and all that he gives us is a rather operose statement of the fact that something must have always existed, for if there ever was a time when nothing existed that void would have remained unfilled forevermore; but supposing the existence of some unconditioned being, say God, it is entirely conceivable that the world, that is, the cosmic system or the system of finite things, might have had a beginning in time, not through some potency of impotent time, but through the causal power of the infinite.

The infinitude of the world with respect to space is proved by an argument bordering closely on sophistry. He says: "Let us assume again the opposite, namely, that the world is finite and limited in space. In that case the world would exist in an empty space without limits. We should therefore have not only a relation of things in space, but also of things to space. As, however, the world is an absolute whole, outside of which no object of intuition, and therefore no correlate of the world can be found, the relation of the world to empty space would be a relation to no object. Such a relation, and with it the limitation of the world by empty space, is nothing, and therefore the world is not limited with regard to space, that is, it is infinite in extension." In criticism of this argument, suppose we have a sphere three feet in diameter, and can also conceive [that all things] outside of this sphere should fall away. In that case the sphere would have nothing beyond it but empty space, which is nothing and can limit nothing, hence the sphere would become unlimited, yet all the while its diameter would remain three feet. There certainly would be nothing in the passing of other things to make this three-foot sphere infinite in the positive sense of the word.

We now pass to the second autinomy, which has to do with the composition or simplicity of things in the world.

THE ANTINOMY OF PURE REASON

SECOND CONFLICT OF THE TRANSCENDENTAL IDEAS

Thesis	*Antithesis*
Every compound substance in the world consists of simple parts, and nothing exists anywhere but the simple, or what is composed of it.	No compound thing in the world consists of simple parts, and there exists nowhere in the world anything simple.

Proof	*Proof*
For let us assume that compound substances did not consist of simple parts, then, if all composition is removed in thought, there would be no compound part, and (as no simple parts are admitted) no simple part either, that is, there would remain nothing, and there would therefore be no	Assume that a compound thing, a substance, consists of simple parts. Then, as all external relation, and therefore all composition of substances also, is possible in space only, it follows that space must consist of as many parts as the parts of the compound that occupies the space. Space, how-

substance at all. Either, therefore, it is impossible to remove all composition in thought, or, after its removal, there must remain something that exists without composition, that is, the simple. In the former case the compound could not itself consist of substances (because with them composition is only an accidental relation of substances, which substances, as permanent beings, must subsist without it). As this contradicts the supposition, there remains only the second view, namely, that the substantial compounds in the world consist of simple parts.

It follows as an immediate consequence that all the things in the world are simple beings, that their composition is only an external condition, and that, though we are unable to remove these elementary substances from their state of composition and isolate them, reason must conceive them as the first subjects of all composition, and therefore, antecedently to it, as simple beings.

ever, does not consist of simple parts, but of spaces. Every part of a compound, therefore, must occupy a space. Now the absolutely primary parts of every compound are simple. It follows, therefore, that the simple occupies a space. But as everything real which occupies a space contains a manifold, the parts of which are by the side of each other, and which therefore is compounded, and, as a real compound, compounded not of accidents (for these could not exist by the side of each other, without a substance), but of substances, it would follow that the simple is a substantial compound, which is self-contradictory.

The second proposition of the antithesis, that there exists nowhere in the world anything simple, is not intended to mean more than that the existence of the absolutely simple cannot be proved from any experience or perception, whether external or internal, and that the absolutely simple is a mere idea, the objective reality of which can never be shown in any possible experience, so that in the explanation of phenomena it is without any application or object. For, if we assumed that an object of this transcendental idea might be found in experience, the empirical intuition of some one object would have to be such as to contain absolutely nothing manifold by the side of each other, and combined to a unity. But as, from our not being conscious of such a manifold we cannot form any valid conclusion as to the entire impossibility of it in any objective intuition, and as without this no absolute simplicity can be established, it follows that such simplicity cannot be inferred from any perception whatsoever. As, therefore, an absolutely simple object can never be given in any possible experience, while the world of sense must be looked upon as the sum total of all possible experience, it follows that nothing simple exists in it.

This second part of the antithesis goes far beyond the first, which only banished the simple from the intuition of the composite, while the second drives it out of the whole of nature. Hence we could not attempt to prove it out of the concept of any given object of external intuition (of the compound) but from its relation to a possible experience in general.

(Page 352.)

Here the argument for the thesis, namely, that every compound substance in the world consists of simple parts, is valid, for compounds exist only in the components just as number exists only in the component units. If, then, there be real compounds, there must equally be uncompounded components, otherwise we are committed to the infinite regress and thus can reach no stopping-place. We conclude, then, with Kant, "It follows as an immediate consequence that all the things in the world are simple beings, that their composition is only an external condition, and that, though we are unable to remove these elementary substances from their state of composition and isolate them, reason must conceive them as the first subjects of all composition, and therefore, antecedently to it, as simple beings." The only escape from this conclusion would be to say that things are neither compounded nor simple, which may possibly be the case with phenomena in general, but so long as we regard them as real things there is no escape from passing from a world of experience to a world of simple components.

The proof of the antithesis, namely, that no compound in the world consists of simple parts, and that [there exists] nowhere in the world anything simple, rests on the nature of space and the infinite divisibility in the notion of existence in extension. The infinite divisibility of space forbids that any part should be viewed as ultimate, for so long as we can suppose any two components we can conceive a plane to be passed between them and thus a division produced. And anything that exists in extension is subject to the same law. It is therefore impossible to find in the extended any ultimate unities, for in any such unities we can distinguish components, and therefore these components are mutually external and admit of further division. But this is really not so much a contradiction of the previous argument as it is an argument for the phenomenality of space.

These two antinomies refer to the world as existing in space and time, and Kant's solution of the difficulty consists in affirming the phenomenality of space and time, from which he concludes that both the thesis and the antithesis disappear. We cannot say that the world must be finite or infinite in space and time. We can only say that experience gives us no completed finitude and no realized infinitude, and hence we are compelled to accept experience as not deciding the question, and we are left entirely free to leave the question undecided, since we see that the spatial and temporal laws leave the question forever open. If space and time were truly existential facts, then all existence would be subject to them, and the laws of space and time, with their infinite divisibility and their infinite extent, would apply to all reality and would disperse in complete illusion. But when we see that space and time are only laws of phenomena or are forms of experience, we escape this difficulty.

THE ANTINOMY OF PURE REASON

THIRD CONFLICT OF THE TRANSCENDENTAL IDEAS

Thesis

Causality, according to the laws of nature, is not the only causality from which all the phenomena of the world can be deduced. In order to account for these phenomena it is necessary also to admit another causality, that of freedom.

Proof

Let us assume that there is no other causality but that according to the laws of nature. In that case everything that takes place presupposes an anterior state, on which it follows inevitably according to a rule. But that anterior state must itself be something which has taken place (which has come to be in time, and did not exist before), because, if it

Antithesis

There is no freedon, but everything in the world takes place according to the laws of nature.

Proof

If we admit that there is freedom, in the transcendental sense, as a particular kind of causality, according to which the events in the world could take place, that is, a faculty of absolutely originating a state, and with it a series of consequences, it would follow that not only a series would have its absolute beginning through this spontaneity, but the determination of had always existed, its effect, too, would not have only just arisen, but have existed always. The causality, therefore, of a cause, through which something takes place, is itself an event, which again, according to the law of nature, presupposes an anterior state and its causality, and this again an anterior state, and so on. If, therefore, everything takes place according to mere laws of nature there will always be a secondary only, but never a primary beginning, and therefore no completeness of the series, on the side of successive causes. But the law of nature consists in this, that nothing takes place without a cause sufficiently determined a priori. Therefore the proposition, that all causality is possible according to the laws of nature only, contradicts itself, if taken in unlimited generality, and it is impossible, therefore, to admit that causality as the only one.

We must, therefore, admit another causality, through which something takes place, without its cause being further determined, according to necessary laws by a preceding cause, that is, an absolute spontaneity of causes, by which a series of phenomena, proceeding according to natural laws, begins by itself; we must consequently admit transcendental freedom, without which, even in the course of nature, the series of phenomena on the side of causes, can never be perfect.

that spontaneity itself to produce the series, that is, the causality, would have an absolute beginning, nothing preceding it by which this act is determined according to permanent laws. Every beginning of an act, however, presupposes a state in which the cause is not yet active, and a dynamically primary beginning of an act presupposes a state which has no causal connection with the preceding state of that cause, that is, in no wise follows from it. Transcendental freedom is, therefore, opposed to the law of causality, and represents such a connection of successive states of effective causes that no unity of experience is possible with it. It is, therefore, an empty fiction of the mind, and not to be met with in any experience.

We have, therefore, nothing but nature, in which we must try to find the connection and order of cosmical events. Freedom (independence) from the laws of nature is no doubt a deliverance from restraint, but also from the guidance of all rules. For we cannot say that, instead of the laws of nature, laws of freedom may enter into the causality of the course of the world, because, if determined by laws, it would not be freedom, but nothing else but nature. Nature, therefore, and transcendental freedom differ from each other like legality and lawlessness. The former, no doubt, imposes upon the understanding the difficult task of looking higher and higher for the origin of events in the series of causes, because their causality

is always conditioned. In return
for this, however, it promises a
complete and well-ordered unity
of experience; while, on the other
side, the fiction of freedom promises, no doubt, to the inquiring
mind, rest in the chain of causes,
leading him up to an unconditioned causality, which begins to
act by itself, but which, as it is
blind itself, tears the thread of
rules by which alone a complete
and coherent experience is possible.

(Page 362.)

This antinomy and the next concern our more
metaphysical ideas of causation and the fundamental
reality. [The present one] deals with causality, and
the thesis is that, in addition to causality according to
the laws of nature, another causality of freedom must
be admitted. The proof is valid. It consists in saying
that causality of the mechanical type only contradicts the law of causation itself. It is like suspending
a chain by adding links to the upper end, without,
however, providing any hook by which the whole may
be supported. Either, then, there must be a reality
which refers us to nothing behind it, that is, a causality of freedom, or causality itself disappears.

The proof of the antithesis, namely, that there is
no freedom, but everything in the world takes place
entirely according to the laws of nature, is arbitrary
and fictitious. Kant says, "Transcendental freedom
is, therefore, opposed to the law of causality, and represents such a connection of successive states of
effective causes that no unity of experience is possi-

190

ble with it. It is, therefore, an empty fiction of the mind, and not to be met with in any experience. . . . Freedom (independence) from the laws of nature is no doubt a deliverance from restraint, but also from the' guidance of all rules. For we cannot say that, instead of the laws of nature, laws of freedom may enter into the causality of the course of the world, because, if determined by laws, it would not be freedom, but nothing else but nature. Nature, therefore, and transcendental freedom differ from each other like legality and lawlessness. The former, no doubt, imposes upon the understanding the difficult task of looking higher and higher for the origin of events in the series of causes, because their causality is always conditioned. In return for this, however, it promises a complete and well-ordered unity of experience; while, on the other side, the fiction of freedom promises, no doubt, to the inquiring mind, rest in the chain of causes leading him up to an unconditioned causality, which begins to act by itself, but which, as it is blind itself, tears the thread of rules by which alone a complete and coherent experience is possible."

Kant adds some observations on this antithesis as follows: —

"He who stands up for the omnipotence of nature (transcendental physiocracy) in opposition to the doctrine of freedom, would defend his position against the sophistical conclusions of that doctrine in the following manner. If you do not admit something mathematically the first in the world with reference to time, there is no necessity why you should look for something dynamically the first with reference to causality. Who has told you to invent an absolutely first state of the world, and with it an absolute beginning of the gradually progressing series of phenomena, and to set limits to unlimited nature in order to give to your imagination something to rest on? As substances have always existed in the world, or as the unity of experience renders at least such a supposition necessary, there is no difficulty in assuming that a change of their states, that is, a series of their changes, has always existed also, so that there is no necessity for looking for a first beginning either mathematically or dynamically." (Page 365.) —

And then he further adds:

"For by the side of such a lawless faculty of freedom, nature could hardly be conceived any longer because the laws of the latter would be constantly changed through the influence of the former, and the play of phenomena which, according to nature, is regular and uniform, would become confused and incoherent." (Page 369.)

There is vast confusion arising through this proof of the antithesis. To begin with, the statement that freedom is "opposed to the law of causality and represents such a connection of successive states of effective causes that no unity of experience is possible with it," is sheer extravagance. It is a purely abstract and fictitious conception of what freedom means. The same is to be said of the further utterance, that freedom is a deliverance from the guidance of all rules, and that nature and freedom differ like legality and lawlessness. Now, all that is necessary for experience and science is simply a certain uniformity within experience itself. This uniformity as such is altogether independent of the metaphysics of its possibility. If we suppose it to rest on necessity or to rest upon freedom, science and experience are equally possible. We find as a matter of fact that there are certain uniformities of experience, and science states these so far as it can, and by means of the knowledge thus gained seeks to control life. But, as said, the question of freedom or necessity is entirely independent of this uniformity. Freedom violates no law of nature and no law of mind. The believer in freedom would be as good a psychologist or physicist as the believer in necessity. It is only as we pass from this practical science to some kind of basal doctrine which regards the universe as something absolutely determined from everlasting to everlasting, and seeks to bind all events together in one scheme of necessity, that any difficulty arises; but this notion is a sheer fiction of the dogmatic intelligence. We do not know the world to be any such scheme, and Kant himself held that the world was no such scheme. We simply know that there are certain uniformities on which we can practically rely for the guidance of life within the range of experience. Anything beyond this is dogmatic assertion or some species of fate.

Kant's further suggestion, that if we do not admit something mathematically the first in the world with reference to time there is no necessity for admitting something dynamically the first with reference to causality, is equally unsatisfactory. In this argument Kant seems to have no difficulty in believing in a temporal infinitude, [against] which he argues in the first antinomy. There he seemed to think an infinite series of past changes altogether impossible, but here he proceeds to bring up this argument against what he calls sophistical conclusions of the doctrine of freedom, and argues that with infinite past time there might well have been an infinite series of changes. In this Kant is not only inconsistent with himself, but he also mistakes the doctrine of causality. On the first point there is implicit here, though Kant does not seem to have seen it, an argument for the ideality of time. For if there be no temporal first there is likewise no temporal second, and the whole ordinal system of time becomes purely relative to ourselves, that is, to experience; but in the great temporal continuum of time there would be neither first nor second nor any other date. On the second point, the misunderstanding of causality, Kant proceeds on the supposition that the causality itself is through the temporal series and that the original cause must be sought at the beginning of that series; and if the series had no beginning, then the original cause cannot be found at all. The result of this fact is to cancel the law of causality altogether. In truth, the cause is not to be found at the beginning any more than at any successive point in the causal movement. The cause in its dynamic efficiency is contemporaneous with its effect, and any act of causation, no matter how many previous acts may have gone before, is a truly dynamic first. Thus, if we were considering the causality in the production of a piece of music, we should not expect to find

194

a causality in the first notes and from them floating on through the latter notes. We should rather see that each note is specially produced, owing its production not to antecedent notes or antecedent events of any kind, but solely to the causal properties present and productive through the series. In the same way, metaphysics shows, we have to think of the causality of the cosmos. It was not condensed in an unattainable first moment, since [when] it has done nothing but slide along the temporal groove. It is rather the continuous productivity, by which the things that were and the things that are alike have been produced; which worked and works and will work forevermore.

As to Kant's notion that the denial of freedom would help us in this matter, nothing can well be more fictitious. The thing that would be fatal would be caprice and groundless arbitrariness, or simply an order of kaleidoscopic change in the ongoing of the world. Now necessity secures this regularity not at all in its character of necessity, but purely and only because the necessity, if there be such, is shut up by its nature to a certain order of movement to the exclusion of all others; but we have no insight into the necessity supposed to rule in nature that will assure us that the present order will continue another day. The existing order is compatible with change, and how much change is involved in the order is entirely beyond us. We are in the midst, then, of a changing world, and what changes the future may bring is something that only a crass dogmatist will attempt to decide. So far, then, as a ground of confidence in the natural order is concerned, we certainly have far more reason for trust if we trace this order to the uniform administration of free intelligence. Such intelligence can choose ends to be reached and the means for reaching them, and can direct itself to their realization. It is, therefore, in the highest degree mistaken to declare that there could be no orderly system and no unity of experience if we grant the notion of freedom.

Kant's solution of this antinomy consists in distinguishing between man as phenomenon and as noumenon. Nature in general, including man himself as an empirical being, is subject to necessity, but beyond nature, at least in man, is a realm of freedom to which the law of causal necessity does not apply. The way in which Kant puts this matter is very far from satisfactory. And the thing which he is after admits of being reached in a much simpler way. It should be noticed first of all that we have here a departure from Kant's doctrine of the categories as purely subjective. He breaks through his subjectivity and affirms a transcendental causality of freedom for man considered as noumenon, that is, as lying beyond the phenomenal realm. Of course, if the subjectivity of the categories is to be taken strictly, as we have before pointed out, this introduces a hopeless contradiction into Kant's system. But that subjectivity is not to be taken too seriously. Kant proceeds in this antinomy and in the next one to introduce a solution of the difficulty by bringing in a transcendental world where freedom and the unconditioned reality have their seat.

But the reconciliation he seeks to reach is possible in a much simpler way. Nature is not the seat of necessity in any conceivable sense, because necessity itself is only a negative notion without any positive contents. It cannot be found in experience or in any way demonstrated in the outer world. There are really two worlds with which we have to do. First, the space and time world of phenomena, and second, the invisible power world where phenomena have their cause and source. Now, nature belongs to the former world altogether, and in that world we are seeking not for necessity but simply the uniformities of experience, and we use the knowledge of these uniformities for the control and [practical guidance] of life. This is the field of science, and into this field as such freedom does not enter. We simply ask for the order in which things are united in the space and time world in an order of law, and in this inquiry we are not permitted to transcend the space and time world at all. When we are unable to connect spatial and temporal events according to a scheme of law, then we must simply leave the events as something common and something which we cannot further classify or relate in space and time forms. In this field science has absolute right of way, and it must report its findings throughout in spatial and temporal terms. For this field, then, we should accept all that Kant says about the unpermissibility of transcending the spatial and temporal order.

But on the other hand, it must be noticed that this space and time order as such has no causality in it, and no direction or guidance. And this again carries us over into the power world and the world of meanings. When we have found the uniformities of coexistence and sequence in the space and time world, the question as to the power world and the world of meanings remains absolutely untouched. Where now shall we look for the causality and how shall we define the meaning of the spatial and temporal movement? This question applies to philosophy, and the answer to it is in no way in opposition to the space and time world. It is simply and only an interpretation of it, an attempt to form some conception of what the space and time world may mean. Now, this power world, as before suggested, does not lie behind the space and time world at its beginning, but rather comprehends that world at all times and in all places, being the ever present ground of it. And when we come to examine the notion of power or causality from this point of view, it turns out that it can be expressed only in terms of intelligent and volitional activity. All mechanical causality loses itself in the infinite regress and denies causality altogether. The only thing that really meets the demand for causality is the conception of a living, active intelligence which is imminent in all its deeds, and which is equally present to all of them, to the last as well as the first. With this understanding we see the Kantian antinomy disappearing.

And as for the unity of experience and all that, it also must be finally found in the unity and consistency of reason itself. No ground for it can be discovered in any experience of nature. No necessity for it can be found in any speculation. Our confidence in the order of things rests at last, not upon any demonstration of the speculative reason, but on the living confidence of the mind that we are in a rational world, the continuous deed of the ever-living will upon which all things depend, and which in its rational character can be trusted to maintain harmony and consistency in its activities. This is the source of what we call the uniformity of nature, and our faith in this uniformity is at bottom essentially of an ethical kind. We pass now to the fourth antinomy.

THE ANTINOMY OF PURE REASON

FOURTH CONFLICT OF THE TRANSCENDENTAL IDEAS

Thesis

There exists an absolutely necessary Being belonging to the world, either as a part or as a cause of it.

Proof

The world of sense, as the sum total of all phenomena, contains a series of changes without which even the representation of a series of time, which forms the condition of the possibility of the world of sense, would not be given us. But every change has its condition which precedes it in time, and renders it necessary. Now everything that is given as conditional presupposes, with regard to its existence, a complete series of conditions, leading up to that which is entirely unconditioned, and alone absolutely necessary. Something absolutely necessary, therefore, must exist, if there exists a change as its consequence. And this abso-

Antithesis

There nowhere exists an absolutely necessary Being, either within or without the world, as the cause of it.

Proof

If we supposed that the world itself is a necessary being, or that a necessary being exists in it, there would then be in the series of changes either a beginning, unconditionally necessary, and therefore without a cause, which contradicts the dynamical law of the determination of all phenomena in time; or the series itself would be without any beginning, and though contingent and conditioned in all its parts, yet entirely necessary and unconditioned as a whole. This would be self-contradictory, because the existence of a multitude cannot be necessary if no single part of it possesses necessary existence.

lutely necessary belongs itself to the world of sense. For if we supposed that it existed outside that world, then the series of changes in the world would derive its origin from it, while the necessary cause itself would not belong to the world of sense. But this is impossible. For as the beginning of a temporal series can be determined only by that which precedes it in time, it follows that the highest condition of the beginning of a series of changes must exist in the time when that series was not yet (because the beginning is an existence, preceded by a time in which the thing which begins was not yet). Hence the causality of the necessary cause of changes and that cause itself belong to time and therefore to phenomena (in which alone time, as their form, is possible), and it cannot, therefore, be conceived as separated from the world of sense, as the sum total of all phenomena. It follows, therefore, that something absolutely necessary is contained in the world, whether it be the whole cosmical series itself, or only a part of it.

If we supposed, on the contrary, that there exists an absolutely necessary cause of the world, outside the world, then that cause, as the highest member in the series of causes of cosmical changes, would begin the existence of the latter and their series. In that case, however, that cause would have to begin to act, and its causality would belong to time, and therefore to the sum total of phenomena. It would belong to the world, and would therefore not be outside the world, which is contrary to our supposition. Therefore, neither in the world, nor outside the world (yet in causal connection with it), does there exist anywhere an absolutely necessary Being.

(Page 370.)

Here both the proof and the disproof are very unsatisfactory. To begin with, it is by no means clear what a necessary being would mean. The common argument on this subject is from the fact of conditioned being to unconditioned being, which is then decided to be absolutely necessary. Only half of this conclusion is valid. If there be conditioned things, there must be something which conditions them, and in that sense the thought of the conditioned implies the thought of the unconditioned. But when we next pass to declare that the unconditioned being is necessary, it is impossible to follow the conclusion by the way of logic and even to tell what the conclusion really means. The thing which is necessary in the logic is the affirmation of an unconditioned being, but there is a difference between the necessity of an affirmation and the affirmation of a necessity. Manifestly all that the existence of given facts can warrant is the affirmation of some unconditioned fact on which they depend, but to call this being necessary is something which logic does not warrant, neither can we tell what necessity would mean in the case. We simply come down to a being self-dependent and self-sufficient, that is, not needing any other being for its existence or for its conception.

Kant further argues that this absolutely necessary being belongs itself to the world of sense. "For if we supposed that it existed outside that world, then the series of changes in the world would derive its origin from it, while the necessary cause itself would not belong to the world of sense. But this is impossible. For as the beginning of a temporal series can be determined only by that which precedes it in time, it follows that the highest condition of the beginning of a series of changes must exist in the time when that series was not yet. Hence, the causality of the necessary cause of changes and that cause itself belong to time and therefore to phenomena, and it cannot, therefore, be conceived as separated from the world of sense, as the sum total of all phenomena." But this also is unsatisfactory. The distinction we have just made between the space and time world and the power world forbids us to find this unconditioned being anywhere in the space and time world, least of all at the beginning of a temporal series which it precedes in time. The unconditioned existence is altogether independent of the question of a beginning or non-beginning of the temporal series, and the only precedence we can certainly affirm is a logical precedence. The cause logically precedes the effect, but the effect may still coexist with the cause; for there is nothing whatever in the conception of an unconditioned cause to forbid the thought that it máy have always been causal and therefore coexistent with its effects.

The proof of the antithesis is no more satisfactory. It says: "If we supposed that the world itself is a necessary being, or that a necessary being exists in it, there would then be in the series of changes either a beginning, unconditionally necessary, and therefore without a cause, which contradicts the dynamical law of the determination of all phenomena in time; or the series itself would be without any beginning, and though contingent and conditioned in all its parts, yet entirely necessary and unconditioned as a whole. This would be self-contradictory, because the existence of a multitude cannot be necessary if no single part of it possesses necessary existence."

Here we have the assumption that free activity is causeless and contradicts the dynamic law of the determination of all phenomena in time. This assumption we have seen to be false. Free activity does not deny causality. It is simply activity that is self-directed toward ends, which is the mark of all intelligent causality. It is then extravagance, and indeed mere assumption, to repeat that freedom means causelessness. It means simply and only the causality of intelligence directing itself toward ends which lie before. Kant continues: "If we supposed, on the contrary, that there exists an absolutely necessary cause of the world, outside the world, then that cause, as the highest member in the series of causes of cosmical changes, would begin the existence of the latter and their series. In that case, however, that cause would have to begin to act, and its causality would belong to time, and therefore to the sum total of phenomena. It would belong to the world, and would therefore not be outside the world, which is contrary to our supposition."

Much the same criticism may be made of this argument as of the preceding one. It manifestly rests on the supposition of the reality of time and that the unconditioned cause must temporarily precede its effect. If, however, the precedence is logical only and the cause may coexist with its effects, this argument loses its force. If the world is really in time, then the causality of the unconditioned being must also be in time, as otherwise there would be no connection between cause and effect. It is therefore no objection to say its activity must begin in time. If, on the other hand, the world is not really in time, but only seems so to us, then the causality of the unconditioned being is also not really in time, and objections drawn from the temporality of the world need not be considered.

Kant adds some observations in the way of

strengthening these conclusions. These are: "If, however, we once begin our proof cosmologically, taking for our foundation the series of phenomena, and the regressus in it, according to the empirical laws of causality, we cannot afterwards suddenly leave this line of argument and pass over to something which does not belong as a member to this series. For the condition must be taken in the same meaning in which the relation of the condition to that condition was taken in the series which, by continuous progress, was to lead to that highest condition. If, therefore, that relation is sensuous and intended for a possible empirical use of the understanding, the highest condition or cause can close the regressus according to the laws of sensibility only, and therefore as belonging to that temporal series itself. The necessary Being must therefore be regarded as the highest member of the cosmical series." (Page 374.) All that this means is that by mere temporal realities we [cannot reach the unconditioned], but when it comes to causality, it is equally true that the infinite regress denies causality altogether.

Kant finds the solution of this antinomy also in his doctrine of phenomenalism. So far as experience of phenomena goes we have simply conditioned things and events. Thus, "All things of the world of sense might be entirely contingent, and have therefore an empirically conditioned existence only"; and yet he says, "There might nevertheless be a non-empirical condition of the whole series, that is, an unconditionally necessary being. For this, as an intelligible condition, would not belong to the series as a link of it (not even as the highest link), nor would it render any link of that series empirically unconditioned, but would leave the whole world of sense, in all its members, in its empirically conditioned existence. This manner of admitting an unconditioned existence as the ground of phenomena would differ from the empirically unconditioned causality (freedom), treated of in the preceding article, because, with respect to freedom, the thing itself, as cause, belonged to the series of conditions, and its causality only was represented as intelligible, while here, on the contrary, the necessary being has to be conceived as lying outside the series of the world of sense, and as purely intelligible, by which alone it could be guarded against itself becoming subject to the law of contingency and dependence applying to all phenomena." (Page 453.) "What is shown by this is simply this, that the complete contingency of all things in nature and of all their (empirical) conditions, may well coexist with the arbitrary presupposition of a necessary, though purely intelligible condition, and that, as there is no real contradiction between these two views, they may well both be true. . . . The world of sense contains nothing but phenomena, and these are mere representations which are always sensuously conditioned. As our objects are never things by themselves, we need not be surprised that we are never justified in making a jump from any member of the several empirical series, beyond the connection of sensibility, as if they were things by themselves, existing apart from their transcendental ground, and which we might leave behind in order to seek for the cause of their existence outside them. . . . To conceive, however, an intelligible ground of phenomena, that is, of the world of sense, and to conceive it as freed from the contingency of the latter, does not run counter either to the unlimited empirical regressus in the series of phenomena, nor to their general contingency. And this is really the only thing which we had to do in order to remove this apparent antinomy, and which could be done in this wise only." (Page 455.) "The empirical use of reason is not affected by the admission of a purely intelligible being, but ascends, according to the principle of a general contingency, from empirical conditions to higher ones, which again are empirical. This regulative principle, however, does not exclude the admission of an intelligible cause not comprehended in the series, when we come to the pure use of reason (with reference to ends or aims). For in this case an intelligible cause only means the transcendental, and, to us, unknown ground of the possibility of the sensuous series in general, and the existence of this, independent of all conditions of the sensuous series, and, in reference to it, unconditionally, necessary, is by no means opposed to the unlimited contingency of the former, nor to the never-ending regressus in the series of empirical conditions." (Page 456.)

Here again we see Kant departing from the strict subjectivity of the categories. Even if we grant that we cannot in strictness affirm that such unconditioned being could be demonstrated to exist, the possibility of its existence is not merely allowed, but the existence of the being itself is admitted. Of course if the categories of thought did not apply to it in any sense which is conceivable, the admission would be entirely empty, for that of whose nature we can form no conception whatever is for us strictly nothing. We are, then, passing here from the strict denial which Kant's subjectivism would imply to a position of faith, and affirming for practical reasons the existence of something which speculatively we cannot demonstrate. Undoubtedly, as said before, if we should proceed by rigorous logic, this involves contradiction on Kant's part; but when we consider the general drift of his thought and also remember the moral aim of his system, we must interpret his subjectivism in harmony with these assumptions rather than rule out these assumptions as an [unconscious] yielding to popular religious faith. The latter view has been held by many critics, but Kant would not seem to have been a man lacking in courage or candor, and therefore we must relax the subjectivity and retain the belief in those things the existence of which could not be demonstrated.

This brings us to consider the final section of the transcendental dialectic, which he discusses under the head of the ideal of pure reason. This section concerns itself with the arguments for the existence of God, and the conclusion is drawn that from a purely speculative standpoint the conception of God represents an Ideal of Reason rather than something that can be strictly demonstrated. The arguments carefully considered turn out to fall short of demonstration.

In this general conclusion everybody would agree nowadays. Matters of fact do not admit of demonstration in any case. Demonstration attaches only to the formal sciences like mathematics, which deal with the relation of ideas. Whenever we come to consider concrete reality there is always an element of assumption in any so-called demonstration. Nowadays in dealing with the arguments for the existence of God we should generally treat them, not as the demonstrations of a theorem, but rather as the solution of a problem which our experience of the world and life presents. When we consider the order of the world, its rational character, the way in which things work together in the organic world apparently for the production of ends, the nature of human history also and its gradual progress, we find in these facts a problem for which our reason demands a solution, and the theistic solution is the only one that gives our mind any insight or satisfaction. This is what we call the proof of the Divine Existence. It does not claim to be a demonstration, but it does furnish the only solution of the world problem in which the mind can rest. In Kant's time these proofs were more highly estimated than they are to-day. They were considered to be demonstrations, and there was the further thought that if the demonstration were not rigorous, faith itself was likely to be overthrown. Hence, when Kant proceeded to show that the arguments are not demonstrations, many persons found this an exceedingly dangerous performance and felt that the foundations were being taken away. Probably every practiced thinker to-day would admit Kant's conclusions in advance, and we have become so used to recognizing the practical and volitional basis of most of our beliefs that no one would be at present disturbed by anything that Kant has said. Thought has become pragmatic, especially in ethical and religious fields, and we are very little concerned at speculative inadequacy, provided a doctrine works well in practice and enriches and furthers life.

Kant groups the arguments for the being of God in three classes, — the ontological, the cosmological, and what he calls the physico-theological, that is, the design argument. In the first argument the inference is from our conception of the perfect Being to the existence of that Being. In the second argument we infer from the contingency of the order of the world the existence of a necessary being on whom it depends. In the third argument we infer, from the evidences of design in the world about us, the existence of an intelligent Creator. Now none of these arguments, Kant says, can be looked upon as really demonstrative. First of all, the ontological argument is entirely without logical cogency. In its common form it rests upon the idea of the perfect Being. The idea of the perfect necessarily includes the idea of existence and would be a contradiction without it; for if we should form a conception of a perfect Being that had only conceptual existence, and should then affirm the conception of another perfect Being that really existed, it is manifest that the latter being would be far superior to the former, hence the former would not really have been perfect. Thus the thought of the perfect Being includes the thought of its existence, and hence it has been inferred that the perfect exists; but there is not the shadow of cogency in this reasoning. It only points out that the idea of the perfect must include the idea of existence in order to make it consistent with itself, but it by no means follows that the self-consistent idea represents a real existence. As Kant said, the thought of a hundred thalers contains logically all the meaning of a hundred real thalers, but there is nevertheless a great difference in point of fact between them. Descartes sought to supplement the argument by showing that only the perfect can be the source of the idea, but this does not mend the matter. It made the idea really an effect in us, and concluded from this effect to an adequate cause by the principle that only the perfect could produce an idea of the perfect; but in this form it would be hard to find any force in the reasoning, and we can only say with Kant that the perfect represents primarily an ideal of the human mind and no fact of human experience. Neither is it anything that can be proved or be demonstrated by the facts of human experience. The argument is really nothing but the expression of the æsthetic and ethical conviction that the true, the beautiful, and the good, which alone have value in the universe, cannot be foreign to the universe. The ontological argument owes all its force to this immediate faith of reason in its own ideals. Its technical expression is due to the desire to give this faith [the form of] demonstration. The result is to weaken rather than to strengthen it.

And yet this argument, as Kant points out, gives all their value to the other theistic arguments. The cosmological argument concludes from the contingency of the world to us to an unconditioned and absolute cause. But this is very far from giving us a conception of God which would have any moral or religious value. There is no possibility of equating the notion of God with the notion of the unconditioned being; and when, then, we ask how we pass from the faith in a first cause or unconditioned being to the perfect ideal which transforms this non-religious speculative abstraction into the idea of God, the answer must be, it is just the presence of that ideal of the perfect Being immanent in the mind which makes the transition. And the same is to be said of the design argument. If we should take this in logical strictness and proceed with fidelity to the canons of inductive science, we should at best not be able to affirm anything more than a being adequate to the production of the rather commonplace world of experience, but this world is very far from being perfectly transparent in its wisdom or goodness. A purely inductive attitude [of mind] which would take account of all the phases of apparent evil and meaninglessness, and strike the average between the good and the evil, the wisdom and unwisdom in life, would find itself very far from the faith in God which the perfect religion demands. Here again, if we ask, How do we pass from these finite and conflicting data to the conception of a perfect Being, supreme in reason, righteousness, and goodness? the answer must be that we pass by the ideal of the perfect implicit in the human mind. So then, logically, we are in this condition, the ontological argument is itself inadequate, but the other two arguments get their force from it and hence they share in its inadequacy; and hence we must say that so far as demonstration in this field is concerned no demonstration is possible.

However, we need not be too much disturbed at this, for equally no disproof is possible. The various arguments for atheism are readily seen in their superficiality upon very brief critical reflection. The real conclusion is that by way of pure speculation we cannot attain to certain conviction in this matter. Conviction must be reached in life itself, and this has always with scantiest exception led the race to theistic faith, not indeed as something which can be speculatively demonstrated or against which any cavil or objection is impossible, but something which represents the line of least resistance for human thought. The intelligent world points to an intelligent author, the moral world to a moral author, the rational world to a rational author. This is the conclusion which the race has drawn and the conclusion in which it increasingly rests, the conclusion which it holds with more and more confidence as the ground of all its hope and the security of all its efforts, whether in the field of science and cognition or of morality and religion.

In this general result we have the original source of pragmatism, so far as it has an intellectual root. According to Kant man is not merely intellect. He is also will and conscience and he is religious, and these facts also have to be taken into account in considering our human life. The intellect, considered by itself as a purely speculative faculty, is not contradictory, but it is limited, and it is not able to reach a great many of those truths in which nevertheless we steadfastly believe. But while it cannot positively reach them, it can overturn the arguments against them, and thus, as Kant said, it may at once destroy knowledge and make room for rational belief. Now, assuming the legitimacy of life and of our human instincts, we may ask ourselves what life implicitly implies; and Kant says it implies God, freedom, and immortality, as postulates without which the mind would fall into discord with itself and life would lose itself in inner contradiction. We may, then, hold these postulates, not as something given by the speculative reason, but as something rooted in life; and then we may work them out into the great and ever-growing conquest of science and into the progress of humanity in civilization and morals and religion.

PART II

THE PHILOSOPHY OF SPENCER

THE PHILOSOPHY OF SPENCER

INTRODUCTION

MR. SPENCER's philosophy had great vogue in the generation just passed. Mr. Spencer himself was called, by some of his more devoted disciples, the "Modern Aristotle"; and his teachings became a kind of orthodoxy for naturalistic science, which if any man kept not whole and entire, he was a candidate for the outer darkness. All this has changed. Mr. Spencer has little standing to-day with trained philosophers, although he has still a large following among hearsay speculators of the cruder sort. For the philosophical student, however, there is an interest in the study of the system, as it sums up so many of the principles and doctrines of the now decadent mechanical naturalism.

For the popularity of the philosophy there were several leading reasons. First, it had an air of conciliation. It seemed to make a place for views which had hitherto been regarded as contradictory. Mr. Spencer says, As there is a soul of good in things evil, so there is also a soul of truth in things erroneous. He set himself, therefore, to seek out the good, even in opposing views, in the hope of uniting them in some higher insight. This appeared especially in his treatment of

217

religion and philosophy. It had been quite common to regard religion as baseless, a manifest product of ignorance and superstition, and something to be unconditionally cast out. But Mr. Spencer, on the contrary, set forth that it is quite impossible to say that so universal and potent a factor in human life as religion has been, can be regarded as totally baseless. Accordingly he maintained that religion must be allowed a place in human life. This was a relief from the open denial of many previous thinkers of the positivistic type, and for a time many religious people looked upon Mr. Spencer's system as a kind of ally of religion. Protests, indeed, were not wanting from the more clearsighted religious thinkers, but they were shrewdly suspected of the *odium theologicum.* Science, the beautiful but rather scornful young heathen, was not, indeed, to be baptized, but she was to be instructed that religion also has inalienable rights. Only recently a work of some pretensions has been published by a conservative house, in which a theologian maintains that Spencer's philosophy, with slight modifications, is the truly religious one.

Again, in the philosophical field there was an outstanding debate between the empirical and the rational schools, and there seemed to be no way of reconciliation. The rationalist held that, while all knowledge is through experience, not all knowledge is from experience, but depends to some extent upon the nature of the mind itself, which nature is not a product of experience, but rather its presupposition, that which the mind brings with it to make experience possible. The empiricist, on the other hand, had held

218

that the mind with all its furniture is the outcome of experience. But this experience was supposed to be the experience of the individual, and the philosophers of this school were much at a loss to furnish a young child with a full set of mental faculties in the few years of childhood. On this account the doctrine was in a somewhat bad way. Sir William Hamilton and Dr. Whewell and others had so belabored it that the view was about going into the hands of a receiver, when Mr. Spencer appeared with the saving proposition that the rational view is correct from the standpoint of the individual, while the empirical view is correct from the standpoint of the race. There are, he says, a great many things in the experience of the individual of to-day which cannot be explained by his own scanty experience. The facts of mental heredity in themselves make such a supposition impossible. But that which the experience of the individual cannot do, the experience of the race may do; and hence we have only to substitute a race experience for that of the individual, to unite the two schools in one.

These are illustrations of the reconciling and comprehensive character of Mr. Spencer's philosophy as it seemed when it first appeared. The value of these reconciliations will be discussed later on.

But the leading ground for the popularity of Mr. Spencer's philosophy is found in its relation to physical science. The last generation witnessed an enormous growth in the scientific field; great discoveries were made, vast and far-reaching generalizations were reached, like those of the correlation of forces, the conservation of energy, the evolution of species, and finally the extension of the doctrine of evolution to the entire cosmos itself. Spencer's view fell in with this movement very happily and was quite a prominent factor in it. It spoke the language of science and acquired some of its prestige. In this way Spencer almost became the official philosopher of the scientific world, and in his great formula of evolution he sought to give a comprehensive interpretation to the whole cosmic movement in its organic and inorganic forms, and also in mind and society and history.

On all these accounts the system had for a time great popularity. It impressed by its size and apparent completeness. It was more than human and terrestrial in its sweep; it was cosmic and universal. This grandiosity agreed with the temper of the time and was an additional attraction. In the self-confidence and the historical and critical ignorance of the time, all things were supposed to have been made new, and the last word in philosophy had been spoken. The "Synthetic Philosophy" had come.

Our aim in these lectures is to consider the philosophical and logical basis of the system. Of course, in so extensive a scheme by so able a man as Spencer we should expect to find a great deal of value in the way of detached observations and special reflections, etc.; and all of this would be compatible with essential weakness in the basal ideas and the systematic construction. Locke's philosophy is incredibly inconsistent, but his great "Essay" is a storehouse of valuable material. Spencer's philosophy may be found equally wanting, but his works may still point to a master mind as their author. A system, however,

220

depends only on its logic. An incoherent system is none. In the history of philosophy nothing abides but those ideas which are established in the nature of reason itself. All other things, sooner or later, go to pieces, serving possibly as the raw material for later construction, but really amounting to little in the great thought movement whereby reason seeks to master itself and its experience.

Mr. Spencer's system is set forth in a large number of volumes: "First Principles," one volume; "Principles of Biology," two volumes; "Principles of Psychology," two volumes; "Principles of Sociology," four volumes; and several works on Ethics. Of these, the "First Principles" and the "Principles of Psychology" contain the gist of his philosophy and are the works we purpose to consider. The others have nothing of marked speculative importance. The discussion will deal in order with Mr. Spencer's "Agnosticism," his "Doctrine of Science," his "Definition of Evolution," his "Doctrine of Life and Mind," and his "Empirical Theory of Knowledge." If we master his teaching on these points we shall be in a position to estimate the philosophic value of the system.

The first three points are treated in the volume on "First Principles." This work has been run through six editions. The first edition differs considerably from the later ones, but only in matters of detail. It is interesting to compare it with the later works, and especially with the last edition, as showing the changes Mr. Spencer made, partly as the result of his own reflection and partly as the result of criticism, but they reveal no essential change in the point of view and in the general argument. The matter is redistributed, the exposition is condensed, some illustrations are omitted and others introduced, but no essential change is made. Unless otherwise stated, our quotations will be from the last edition.

I

MR. SPENCER'S AGNOSTICISM

THIS feature of Mr. Spencer's philosophy is set forth in "First Principles." This book falls into two parts, one section entitled "The Unknowable," and one entitled " The Knowable." The former contains both a theory of knowledge and a doctrine of religion. The latter, which is much the larger, contains his doctrine of science and his general theory of evolution. The first section expounds his Agnosticism.

Mr. Spencer's Agnosticism is largely a borrowed product. In the original "Prospectus for the Publication of a New System of Philosophy," he speaks of "Part I, The Unknowable," as " carrying a step farther the doctrine put into shape by Hamilton and Mansel; pointing out the various directions in which Science leads to the same conclusions; and showing that in this united belief in an Absolute that transcends not only human knowledge, but human conception, lies the only possible reconciliation of Science and Religion." Mr. Spencer adds some arguments of his own, but the larger part of his discussion is based upon arguments quoted from the authors named. They are the immediate sources of his doctrine; but in its general character it finds its roots in the Kantian philosophy, of which, however, Mr. Spencer seems to have had little if any direct knowledge and not much knowledge of any kind. The doctrine of Phenomenalism, which appears here and there in his theory, of course, runs back to Kant, possibly through Comte.

The doctrine itself is vaguely conceived, and is hardly defined at all, except in conclusions from arguments. The claim in general is that we have no proper knowledge of essential reality; that in both religion and science we are unable to reach the truly real, and must content ourselves with the knowledge of appearance or phenomena. There is, however, a fundamental reality back of all appearance which we must affirm, though we cannot know it, as it transcends all knowledge and even all conception. Here, then, is a realm of mystery, and in this realm religion has its seat. But the world of phenomena, that is, the world of daily experience, is open to us, and its coexistences and sequences are open to observation, discovery, and registration. This is the field of science.

How much this doctrine needs in order to bring it out in clearness and firmly to establish it is plain to the practiced reader. But this matter will come up farther on. We shall do better to begin with Mr. Spencer's arguments and work our way into his doctrine from this point.

The argument in brief outline is this: Mr. Spencer examines our fundamental ideas in both religion and science and declares them to be impossible because contradictory and self-destructive. Thus the contents of knowledge vanish. He next examines the process of knowledge, in a chapter called "The Relativity of all Knowledge," and here he claims to find that the knowing process upon critical investigation shows itself to be incapable of absolute knowledge. We are then shut up by this fact to the field of the relative or the apparent, and can lay no claim to a knowledge of the truly real. Such is the agnostic argument in outline.

The two parts of this argument do not seem to be perfectly consistent. If the first contention, that our fundamental ideas are self-destructive, could be made out, the result would be overwhelming skepticism which would swallow up, not merely absolute knowledge, but phenomenal knowledge as well. If, then, we regard the first contention as established, the second claim would be disposed of in advance. No system of phenomenal knowledge can be based on a doctrine of general skepticism. It presupposes some real knowledge and some rational insight whereby the reason is able to discern and fix its own limits, and that in such a way as not to cast any general discredit upon its own operations; otherwise, as said, the outcome is universal skepticism and no doctrine of knowledge at all. As Kant did not sufficiently consider this problem, Mr. Spencer also failed to give it attention, — in fact, he cannot be said to have considered it at all. But we leave these general remarks and proceed to Mr. Spencer's specific arguments.

Ultimate Religious Ideas

Mr. Spencer opens the discussion of religious ideas by some remarks on what he calls "symbolic knowledge" or "symbolic conceptions." Most things, he says, are not truly conceived in themselves, but only through conceptions which we form of them and which are a kind of shorthand expression for the fact, rather than any true apprehension of it. In this respect they are somewhat like the symbols of algebra, which stand for things without, however, truly reproducing the nature of the things in any way. He concludes from these considerations as follows: "When our symbolic conceptions are such that no cumulative or indirect processes of thought can enable us to ascertain that there are corresponding actualities, nor any fulfilled predictions be assigned in justification of them, then they are altogether vicious and illusive and in no way distinguishable from pure fictions." (Paragraph 9, p. 24.) This doctrine is true, but exceedingly vague. It really contends only that all conceptions must admit of being verified in some way, either in direct experience or in inferences which can be tested by experience. When our conceptions cannot be presented in experience or assimilated to it or justified by it, then of course they are at best only formal, and can lay no claim to being real. But the importance of all this consists in the use made of it.

Mr. Spencer next proceeds to examine existing notions about the origin of the universe. He says: "Respecting the origin of the universe three verbally intelligible suppositions may be made. We may assert that it is self-existent, or that it is self-created; or that it is created by an external agency." These views are identified respectively with Atheism, Pantheism, and Theism. Now, concerning these he says they are all really inconceivable in the true sense of the word, and Theism is as much so as either of the other two. Those two assume that something is self-existent, while Theism, in addition to the assumption of self-existence, also assumes the additional inconceivability of creation. He says: "Did there exist nothing but an immeasurable void, explanation would be needed as much as it is now. There would still arise the question — how came it so? If the theory of creation by external agency were an adequate one, it would supply an answer; and its answer would be — space was made in the same manner that matter was made. But the impossibility of conceiving this is so manifest that no one dares to assert it. For if space was created it must have been previously non-existent. The non-existence of space cannot, however, by any mental effort be imagined. . . . Lastly, even supposing that the genesis of the Universe could really be represented in thought as due to an external agency, the mystery would be as great as ever; for there would still arise the question — how came there to be an external agency? To account for this only the same three hypotheses are possible — self-existence, self-creation, and creation by external agency. Of these, the last is useless: it commits us to an infinite series of such agencies, and even then leaves us where we were." "Thus these three different suppositions, verbally intelligible though they are, and severally seeming to their respective adherents quite rational, turn out, when critically examined, to be literally unthinkable. It is not a question of probability, or credibility, but of conceivability. . . . Differing so widely as they seem to do, the atheistic, the pantheistic, and the theistic hypotheses contain the same ultimate element. It is impossible to avoid making the assumption of self-existence somewhere; and whether that assumption be made nakedly or under complicated disguises, it is equally vicious, equally unthinkable. Be it a fragment of matter, or some fancied potential form of matter, or some more remote and still less imaginable mode of being, our conception of its self-existence can be framed only by joining with it the notion of unlimited duration through past time. And as unlimited duration is inconceivable all those formal ideas into which it enters are inconceivable."(Paragraph 11, p. 28.) Hence our fundamental ideas of the origin of the universe are inconceivable, and any theory whatever of this origin, religious or irreligious alike, is seen to shatter on this inconceivability.

Before commenting on this argument we must point out a great lack of precision in Mr. Spencer's use of these terms, "unknowable," "inconceivable," and "unthinkable," against which the student must be on his guard. They are frequently used as synonyms, which is far from being the case; and the same word often has a variety of meanings. Thus, by "inconceivable" we may mean something of which the mind can form no conception whatever, either because no attributes are given or because the attributes are incompatible. The void would be a case of the former kind. Nothing is inconceivable because nothing has no attributes, and when we attempt to think of nothing, only a mental vacuum results. Again, contradictions are inconceivable, because the attributes are incompatible. Hence all those things are inconceivable which distinctly violate the laws of thought. Thus we cannot think of space and time as finite, supposing them to be real things; for as soon as we assume a limit, the thought of space and time beyond the limit emerges. Further, we cannot view 4 plus 3 as equal to 9, because the laws of numerical thinking forbid it; and we cannot think of two straight lines as inclosing space, for the laws of geometrical thinking forbid it. All these inconceivables violate the laws of thought itself.

Again, "inconceivable" sometimes means that which cannot be pictured or imagined. In this sense a spirit is inconceivable. Only corporeality or extended things or limited extension can be pictured, and in this sense conceived; but then those things which cannot be pictured may nevertheless very well be conceived, because they are experienced, as in the case of our inner life. Picturing is limited to the spatial imagination. We know a good deal about thought and feeling, however, although these things are in the strictest sense unpicturable. Consciousness itself is unpicturable, but it is not inconceivable on that account. And in general, the unpicturable notions of the understanding are quite inconceivable in one sense, but very definite objects of knowledge nevertheless.

Another use of "inconceivable" makes it equivalent to "incredible." A great many things are said to be inconceivable when we really mean only that they are incredible. Thus, in the case of the antipodes, there was not the slightest difficulty in picturing the proposition that the antipodes existed, but there were no facts in experience which made credible such a notion. Similarly with ice; to a native of the tropics who had never seen it, it would be inconceivable, because his experience with water would be such that he could not, apart from a new experience, believe it capable of taking on the solid form. There are also a great many things of which we cannot give the rationale, but which are manifest facts nevertheless; and many things may be inconceivable in that sense which are everything but incredible. In addition to these meanings, Mr. Spencer, in the general discussion, but especially in his treatment of the relativity of knowledge, assumes another inconceivability adopted from Sir William Hamilton. This is the inconceivability of all ultimate facts, of which he says they cannot be subsumed under any higher class and are therefore inconceivable. This is next identified with "unknowable," giving the result that we must look upon all those general truths which underlie knowledge, and of which we are most certain, as inconceivable, which is supposed to mean unknowable.

The term "unknowable," also, is one of uncertain meaning. It might mean something unrelated to our faculties, and therefore beyond their range. The contents of a new sense would be unknowable, as there is nothing in our present experience to suggest what they would be like. Again, a thing might be unknowable because, while we could easily conceive the fact, we have no evidence of its existence. The landscape of the opposite side of the moon would be a case of this kind. As that side is forever turned away from the earth, we have no means of knowing anything about it. And sometimes by "unknowable"

we merely mean that the subject does not admit of
demonstration, but remains an object of belief in
distinction from knowledge. In this sense the great
bulk of our convictions belong to the unknowable.

Thus it is manifest that the terms we have been discussing are far from univocal in themselves, and still
farther from being synonymous with one another.
This uncertainty continually appears in Mr. Spencer's
use of them, provoking most justly critical impatience
if not wrath.

We return now to Mr. Spencer's argument against
all ideas of the origin of things. And first, we call
attention to the extraordinary misreading of the law
of causation involved in the statement, "Did there
exist nothing but an immeasurable void, explanation
would be needed as much as it is now. There would
still arise the question, — how came it so?" Mr.
Spencer apparently thought that the law of causation
commits us to the infinite regress, so that we must
forever explain the explanation — which is the same
as explaining nothing. One sometimes finds this
notion with children who ask, Who made God? But
apart from these infantile philosophers, it would be
difficult to find it outside of Mr. Spencer's pages. In
fact, the demand for causation arises only in connection with the changing and dependent.

The fatal objection to our ideas of the origin of
things, according to Mr. Spencer, is that they all
imply existence through infinite time, and the infinitude is the point of difficulty. Some question may
arise about this position. As Mr. Mill has pointed
out, "The Infinite" may perhaps be an impossible

notion, but infinitude, when applied to matter of which we have some experience, seems by no means to be so fatal. We shall later consider this "Infinite" and find that, instead of being a veritable thought, it is rather "a symbolic conception of the illegitimate order." But when we are dealing with the infinite as an attribute instead of a reality, the matter is not so clear. Suppose we apply it to space, time, power, goodness, and so on. These ideas do not become absurd and impossible because of the infinitude which may be attributed to them. We know somewhat of space, its geometric properties, and so forth. We can measure it and determine various relations about it. The results thus reached are real knowledge, and they would not disappear if this space were declared to be unlimited. In that case we should simply have the knowledge we now possess, with the additional knowledge that this space extends in all directions without limit. Similarly with time and number. We measure time by number and have some idea of these temporal and numerical relations, and these again would not vanish if it were said that the temporal and numerical series are unlimited. Geometry and arithmetic would not be overthrown by bringing the attributes of infinitude into the subjects of which we now have some knowledge. Similarly with power and goodness. The positive content of these ideas would in no way be affected if we conceived that there is a power to which no limit can be set and a goodness which is perfect and complete. If to this we objected that even so we remain within the limits of the finite and do not apprehend the infinite as such, the answer would be that even then we should remain within the field of knowledge, in spite of the finitude of our apprehension.

But leaving this doubt, Mr. Spencer's argument rests on the assumption that to conceive infinite time we must image it, and of course the infinite cannot be imaged by the finite mind. But this assumption is distinctly false and rests upon confounding pure thought with the imagination. Mr. Mill, in his examination of Sir William Hamilton, has criticized this view very clearly and decisively. Speaking of Hamilton he says, "Sir William Hamilton argues that we cannot conceive infinite space because we should require infinite time to do it in."[1] This is clearly the same argument as that of Mr. Spencer, and Mr. Mill's criticism applies equally. He says: "It would of course require infinite time to carry our thoughts in succession over every part of infinite space. But on how many of our finite conceptions do we think it necessary to perform such an operation? Let us try the doctrine upon a complex whole, short of infinite; such as the number 695,788. Sir William Hamilton would not, I suppose, have maintained that this number is inconceivable. How long did he think it would take to go over every separate unit of this whole, so as to obtain a perfect knowledge of that exact sum, as different from all other sums, either greater or less? Would he have said that we could have no conception of the sum until this process had been gone through? We could not, indeed, have an adequate conception. Accordingly, we never have an adequate conception

---

[1] J. S. Mill, *Examination of Sir William Hamilton's Philosophy*, p. 105.

of any real thing. But we have a real conception of an object if we conceive it by any of its attributes that are sufficient to distinguish it from all other things." [1] In other words, we have a conception of a thing when we know what we mean and when the conception is distinguished from all other conceptions, keeping its own place and significance; and it is not necessary in order to this conception that it should be complete or that it should be picturable. Of course we cannot imagine infinite time or space, as it would require infinite time to do it, and moreover the idea itself is a contradiction, for when we imagine a thing we do it only through the establishment of limits; but it is still conceivable that we should have the thought of infinite space or infinite time, supposing either of them to be anything real, through the insight that no limit can be set. In which case our thought would not be negative, but would have the positive content of extension and duration with the added insight that there is no end and no beginning to either.

Thus, Mr. Spencer's first application of his doctrine of symbolic conceptions turns out to be an unlucky one. Moreover, Spencer very soon contradicts himself when he passes into the section on the Knowable, for there he affirms a fundamental reality which certainly seems to be self-existent in the sense that it does not depend on anything else, and also seems to be eternal. And not only the fundamental reality is thus complicated with infinite time, past and future, but the fundamental doctrines of the persistence of force and the indestructibility of matter seem to be in

[1] Mill, op. cit., p. 106.

the same condemnation. These doctrines apparently imply existence through infinite time, past and future; and these doctrines are set up as a priori truths of the first evidence, so much so that to question them is set down as a mark of belated intelligence. Certainly no one would suspect, when reading this section, that the fundamental reality or even matter and force begin or end. But clearly if these doctrines are to be maintained, in spite of the infinitude of time which they imply, there seems to be no reason why the same infinitude should be fatal to the religious ideas, which certainly no more imply them. It would be unpermissible partiality to rule out the religious ideas because they imply infinite time, and to maintain these scientific doctrines although they imply the same infinitude. If it should be said that the infinite implied in these doctrines is a symbolic infinitude and not to be literally taken, that would simply empty the doctrine of all meaning.

Mr. Spencer now leaves the origin of the universe and turns to its nature and finds similar difficulties and inconceivabilities emerging. He says: "Certain conclusions respecting the nature of the universe thus seem unavoidable. In our search after causes, we discover no resting-place until we arrive at a First Cause; and we have no alternative but to regard this First Cause as Infinite and Absolute. These are inferences forced on us by arguments from which there appears no escape. Nevertheless, neither arguments nor inferences have more than nominal values." (Page 32.) But instead of showing this by his own arguments, Mr. Spencer prefers to adopt an argument from Mr. Mansel, which he quotes at length as follows: "But these three conceptions, the Cause, the Absolute, the Infinite, all equally indispensable, do they not imply contradiction to each other, when viewed in conjunction, as attributes of one and the same Being? A Cause cannot, as such, be absolute: the Absolute cannot, as such, be a cause. The cause, as such, exists only in relation to its effect; the cause is a cause of the effect; the effect is an effect of the cause. On the other hand, the conception of the Absolute implies a possible existence out of all relation. We attempt to escape from this apparent contradiction, by introducing the idea of succession in time. The Absolute exists first by itself, and afterwards becomes a Cause. But here we are checked by the third conception, that of the Infinite. How can the Infinite become that which it was not from the first? If Causation is a possible mode of existence, that which exists without causing is not infinite; that which becomes a cause has passed beyond its former limits." (Page 33.)

This argument is little more than a play on words. It is rather etymologizing than philosophizing, and fails to notice the true character of the ideas in question. The first cause is of course related to the effect. A cause out of all relation to an effect is no cause. There could be no reason for affirming it and no use could be made of it if it were affirmed. Hence the first cause is related, and hence it is said it cannot be absolute. But the real absolute is not unrelated, for if it were, it too would be altogether worthless. The real absolute is reached in the following way. We find the things of experience of such a kind that no one has its existence in itself, but each thing refers us to other things as at least its partial ground. Now, such things, because they exist only in relation, we call relative, and their relatedness extends to their very existence. But by the necessity of thought we are unable to rest in such things as final and are driven on to affirm some other being which is self-centred and self-sufficient, which needs nothing else therefore for its existence. This being we call the absolute, and it is the only real absolute. But this absolute is not out of relation, but out of restrictive relation. Its relations are freely posited and maintained by itself and are not imposed upon it from without, and this absolute can be a cause without any injury to its absoluteness.

Likewise, the infinite conceived of as the All is a mere conception, and it is easy to show that such an infinite cannot coexist with anything beyond itself; for in that case there would be something beyond the All, and this would be absurd. But the real infinite is not the All, but rather the independent ground of the finite. We are forced to affirm it from observing the limitations of things in experience, and we affirm it not as something which includes and swallows up or annihilates all other things, but rather as their independent and, in that sense, unlimited source. But the first cause, the absolute, and the infinite in this sense, so far from being contradictory ideas, really imply one another. Neither the absolute nor the infinite would be anything were it not a cause, and the first cause would not be such if it were not both absolute and infinite in the sense we have mentioned. We have, then, simply to keep to the philosophical meaning of these terms in order to dismiss entirely the argument which Mr. Spencer quotes from Mr. Mansel. Mr. Mill, in his "Examination of Sir William Hamilton," referring to the verbal character of this argument, says that it is hard to believe its author "serious."

So much for ultimate religious ideas. Mr. Spencer claims to have shown that they are impossible and self-destructive. He next proceeds to make the same showing for ultimate scientific ideas.

Ultimate Scientific Ideas

In this chapter Mr. Spencer gives a somewhat miscellaneous collection of difficulties and contradictions in the basal ideas of science; space, time, matter, motion, force, and conscious mind are reflected upon and divers inconceivabilities and impossibilities are pointed out. In this work Mr. Spencer is not very strong. His analysis of space and time is superficial and the difficulties he urges are not weighty. Similarly in the case of motion. The difficulties in matter turn largely on its space relations, its divisibility or indivisibility, its extension or its punctual character. The conception of force likewise is convicted of various inconceivabilities, and finally the notion of consciousness is shown to be also impossible. In the first edition of "First Principles" Mr. Spencer declared that resisting matter is a contradiction, since force must vary as the inverse square of the distance. This was changed in the third edition, he having come to see the physical absurdity of the alleged scheme. The notion of consciousness is declared to be unthinkable or inconceivable, because we cannot think of consciousness as finite nor yet as infinite. We cannot view the conscious chain as infinite and we cannot say it is finite; for we have no direct knowledge of either of its ends. "Go back in memory as far as we may, we are wholly unable to identify our first states of consciousness. Similarly at the other extreme. We infer a termination to the series at a future time, but cannot directly know it; and we cannot really lay hold of that temporary termination reached at the present moment. For the state of consciousness recognized by us as our last, is not truly our last. . . . Now to represent the termination of consciousness as occurring in ourselves, is to think of ourselves as contemplating the cessation of the last state of consciousness; and this implies a supposed continuance of consciousness after its last state, which is absurd.

"Hence, while we are unable either to believe or to conceive the duration of consciousness is infinite, we are equally unable either to know it as finite, or to conceive it as finite." (Page 52.)

It would be hard to tell in what sense "know" and "conceive" are used in this passage. There is certainly no difficulty in conceiving and knowing that our consciousness is not infinite. The argument, such as it is, all turns upon the fact that we cannot be conscious of the beginning or the end of consciousness as such, for to be conscious of the end of consciousness is to be conscious after consciousness, which is absurd. But to conclude from this that we may not have the very best reason for saying and believing that consciousness may begin and may end is in the highest degree grotesque. Thus, if I say, I believe I was not alive in the year 1800 and I shall not be alive in the year 2000, [it is clear that this] is very different from saying that [I am] conscious of myself as not alive in the year 1800 and the year 2000. If the statement meant this, it would be to think of myself as living and dead at the same time, and this is what Mr. Spencer's argument assumes it to mean. Of course I could not consciously realize myself as dead, that is, as unconscious at any time; but there appears to be no difficulty in the notion that I might have the best of reasons for believing that I was not conscious at some particular time and that I will not be conscious at some other particular time. It is certainly very different, to think of a fact as true at a certain date, and to be present and conscious of the fact as actually occurring at that date. Such argument hardly rises to the dignity of a sophism. It would equally prove that I cannot believe or know or conceive that I shall go to sleep to-night, because to do that I must be conscious of my being unconscious in sleep. It would appear almost a good a priori argument for immortality, and would show those people who have doubts about life after death that they really do not think when they express such doubts, for when they think they see that the conception of death is impossible.

Mr. Spencer adds to this a further contradiction in the notion of self-consciousness. He says, "The personality of which each is conscious, and the existence of which is to each a fact beyond all others the most certain, is yet a thing which cannot be known at all, in the strict sense of the word." (Page 55.) And the reason for this is found in the fact that all consciousness involves the distinction of subject and object. Where there is no subject and where there is no object there is equally no consciousness. In self-consciousness, then, if the object perceived is self, what is the subject that perceives? or if it is the true self which thinks, what other self can it be that is thought of? Clearly a true cognition of self implies a state in which the knowing and the known are one, in which subject and object are identified, and this is held to be the annihilation of both.

The answer to all this is that it mistakes the dual form of consciousness for a metaphysical distinction. All consciousness does take place under the form of subject and object, but it does not imply that the subject and object must be different things. The subject and the object in self-consciousness are the same. The thinking self thinks of itself, and thus it is at once subject and object. Of course there is no telling how this is possible. But at the same time it is the most manifest fact of experience or the most certain idea of knowledge. Facts may be known as facts which we cannot further construe, and indeed this must be the case with all ultimate facts, and yet they may remain, though unconstruable, among the most undeniable items of knowledge.

Thus, by analysis of our ideas, both religious and scientific, Mr. Spencer claims to show their self-destructive character. He next proceeds by analysis of the process of knowledge itself to prove that the human mind by its very nature is absolutely incapable

241

of other than purely phenomenal knowledge. This doctrine he discusses under the name of the "Relativity of all Knowledge."

The Relativity of all Knowledge

This doctrine, or rather this phrase, is a very vague thing and admits of a great variety of meanings. Mr. Mill says of it: "In one of its senses, it stands for a proposition respecting the nature and limits of our knowledge, in my judgment true, fundamental, and full of important consequences in philosophy. From this amplitude of meaning, its significance shades down through a number of gradations, successively more thin and unsubstantial, until it fades into a truism leading to no consequences, and hardly worth enunciating in words. When, therefore, a philosopher lays great stress upon the relativity of our knowledge, it is necessary to cross-examine his writings, and compel them to disclose in which of its many degrees of meaning he understands the phrase."[1] There are really only two meanings of much significance. The doctrine may mean that all knowledge is relative to our faculties. In this sense it is a truism. If there be anything whatever that is strictly unrelated to our faculties, say the objects of a new sense, it is clear that we cannot know them. But the doctrine in this sense is so obvious as to call for no statement. Again, the doctrine may mean that our faculties are such that in some way they mask or transform reality, so that it cannot be known to us in its true character. This is the meaning the doctrine generally has in all the views

[1] *Examination of Sir William Hamilton's Philosophy*, p. 13.

of relativity which have sprung from the Kantian system. Mr. Spencer himself does not define the doctrine, and we have to ascertain its meaning from the argument he gives for it and the uses he makes of it. In general he understands it in the second sense given. We cannot know the real as it is. We can know it only as it appears to us, and this appearance never truly represents the fact.

Mr. Spencer opens the discussion by showing that all explanation consists in referring a fact to some more general class. When a new fact is presented to us it remains isolated and strange until we are able to classify it as a case of a kind. In this sense all cognition involves recognition. That is, the cognitive act is not complete until the new fact is assimilated to other facts. When this can be done, we view the fact as explained. Any further explanation of the fact would consist in explaining this class in the same way, that is, by referring it also to some other class still more general. From this Mr. Spencer draws the conclusion that the ultimate fact must be inexplicable and unknowable.

The argument here given is a case of the confusion mentioned in the previous paragraph, that is, the confounding of something which cannot be subsumed under a higher term with something unknowable. This is a misleading use, as we have seen, of the term "conceivable." It is a use which Hamilton bequeathed to us and which Mr. Spencer has adopted, but it is a misuse nevertheless. And in any case, what this process gives us is simply a set of facts which cannot be further classified or deduced from other facts beyond them. Whether they shall be knowable or not depends upon their own character and not upon the impossibility of further classification. If the original facts are mysterious and are simply grouped in a common mystery, then they remain mysterious in their ultimate nature after classification. But if the mysterious facts are grouped in a class, into whose nature we have insight or which we perceive to be a reality which can be known and described, then the mystery of the original facts disappears. We find illustration of the former case in gravitation. We explain the fall or floating of bodies by referring them to the force of gravity, but this explanation leaves gravity as mysterious as ever; and no amount of reference of such facts to gravity makes their inner nature in any respect less mysterious. The advantage of such explanation is one of mental convenience rather than of insight. We lump certain mysteries in a common mystery and then they are more conveniently managed as belonging together. But if we should find a reason for thinking that the force of gravity is really the volitional causality of an all-embracing intellect, then the classification would give us some real insight. We could perceive both that the facts belong together in a common class and we should assimilate that class to our own volitional action. In other cases classification remains entirely within the limits of knowledge. When we classify mathematical truths, for instance, under simple principles, or refer them to axioms and intuitions, we may gain very real insight as they are seen to be implications of familiar truths. In that case our first principles which support them all are not unknowable because they cannot be further referred or deduced, for they stand in their own right and are seen by direct insight. Squares, rectangles, parallelograms are classified as quadrilaterals, and we may go on to include triangles and polygons and circles and elipses as plane figures. Here there is inclusion of classes within higher classes, but there is no movement toward any ultimately unknowable fact. Such facts are inexplicable only in the sense of not being explained by something else. They are incomprehensible in the sense of not being comprehended by something else, and they are not unknowable at all.

This rather confused and inconsequent argument Mr. Spencer uses to prove the impossibility of our knowledge of the real existence of the Absolute, the Infinite, the Unconditioned, etc. He says: "If the successively deeper interpretations of Nature which constitute advancing knowledge, are merely successive inclusions of special truths in general truths, and of general truths in truths still more general; it follows that the most general truth, not admitting of inclusion in any other, does not admit of interpretation. Of necessity, therefore, explanation must eventually bring us down to the inexplicable. Comprehension must become something other than comprehension before the ultimate fact can be comprehended." (Page 61.) In this quotation we see again the oscillation between the inexplicable and incomprehensible and the unknowable, a continual substitution of synonyms, which are not quite synonyms, to reach his result.

After thus opening the argument, Mr. Spencer

quotes again Sir William Hamilton and Mansel with approval in support of his conclusion. Thus Mr. Mansel is quoted as saying: "The very conception of consciousness, in whatever mode it may be manifested, necessarily implies distinction between one object and another. To be conscious, we must be conscious of something; and that something can only be known, as that which it is, by being distinguished from that which it is not. But distinction is necessarily limitation; for, if one object is to be distinguished from another, it must possess some form of existence which the other has not, or it must not possess some form which the other has. . . . If all thought is limitation;— if whatever we conceive, is by the very act of conception regarded as finite, — the *infinite*, from a human point of view, is merely a name for the absence of those conditions under which thought is possible. . . . A second characteristic of Consciousness is, that it is only possible in the form of a *relation*. There must be a Subject, or person conscious, and an Object, or thing of which he is conscious. . . . The subject is a subject, only in so far as it is conscious of an object: the object is an object, only in so far as it is apprehended by a subject: and the destruction of either is the destruction of consciousness itself. It is thus manifest that a consciousness of the Absolute is equally self-contradictory with that of the Infinite." (Page 64.) Mr. Spencer further supports this conclusion by an additional argument of his own. He points out that knowledge involves, besides distinction and relation, also likeness. Cognition involves recognition. To know a thing is to know it as such or such, and if there were anything which could not be classified with other things under some element of likeness, it would necessarily lie beyond our knowledge. From this he concludes as follows: "A cognition of the Real, as distinguished from the Phenomenal, must, if it exists, conform to this law of cognition in general. The First Cause, the Infinite, the Absolute, to be known at all, must be classed. To be positively thought of, it must be thought of as such or such, — as of this or that kind. Can it be like in kind to anything of which we have experience? Obviously not." (Page 67.) That is, the first cause, the infinite, and the absolute, by their nature, cannot be classed with anything. There cannot be more than one first cause, he says, neither can there be more than one infinite or one absolute. Hence he concludes: "The Unconditioned therefore, as classable neither with any form of the conditioned nor with any other Unconditioned, cannot be classed at all. And to admit that it cannot be known as such or such kind, is to admit that it is unknowable.

"Thus, from the very nature of thought the relativity of our knowledge is inferable in three ways. As we find by analyzing it, and as we see it objectively displayed in every proposition, a thought involves relation, difference, likeness. Whatever does not present each of these does not admit of cognition. And hence we may say that the Unconditioned, as presenting none of them, is trebly unthinkable." (Page 68.)

This argument also rests on etymologizing rather than on philosophizing, that is, it rests upon that false conception of the Infinite as the All and of the

Absolute as unrelated, and it really has no application whatever to the real infinite, absolute, and first cause. It is true that all knowledge involves relation of some kind and a strictly unrelated object could not be known. But it is equally true that this fundamental reality is related and may be known as such. The infinite is distinguished, it is related, it is classed, as cause, being, power, etc. When Mr. Spencer says there can be only one first cause, and therefore it cannot be classed, his remark would apply equally to the first wheelbarrow: there is only one first wheelbarrow, and yet the first wheelbarrow might be classed with other wheelbarrows although it is unique in being first. The first cause would be classed in the same way with other causes and other beings in spite of its uniqueness as first cause. Similarly with the absolute, it would be classed with other things as existing, as having various attributes, etc., and its own self-existence would not forbid its classification. We admit, then, the premises of Hamilton, Mansel, and Spencer, but deny their conclusion, and for the obvious reason that their conclusion rests upon sheer verbalism which ignores the essential character of the facts.

But now begins a regress. Hamilton and Mansel made the infinite and absolute simply negations. They held that they did not represent any positive thought, but rather the absence of the conditions of thinking. In that case all knowledge is of course shut up within the sphere of the finite, and anything beyond that must be looked upon as pure vacuity, a vacuum in which no flight is possible because there would be no resisting air. But Spencer, although

quoting with approval all their argument based upon
the negative character of the notions, is unwilling to
accept their results, and hence he begins to move
toward the opposite extreme of making the fundamental reality the most positive element of thought
instead of a mere negation. It is interesting to note
that Hamilton himself drew back from his own conclusion in a peculiar way. He says: "By a wonderful revelation, we are thus, in the very consciousness
of our inability to conceive aught above the relative
and finite, inspired with a belief in the existence of
something unconditioned beyond the sphere of all
comprehensible reality." (Page 63.) Mansel also
says: "The Absolute, on the other hand, is a term
expressing no object of thought, but only a denial of
the relation by which thought is constituted." (Page
65.) But Mr. Mansel, too, was not willing to hand
the absolute over to sheer non-existence, but regarded
it, in spite of utterances like that just given, as something altogether real. Hence Mr. Spencer is not out
of their line when he proceeds to save the fundamental reality from the mere negation to which the argument that has been given would consign it. And he
proceeds to claim that, besides the definite consciousness to which the laws of thought apply and where
the conclusions reached would be absolutely valid,
there is another indefinite consciousness which cannot
be formulated, and he holds that we have this indefinite consciousness of the absolute. He says all of the
argument presupposes that the absolute is actual,
that it is a reality, and adds: "Clearly, then, the very
demonstration that a definite consciousness of the

Absolute is impossible to us, unavoidably presupposes an indefinite consciousness of it." (Page 75.)

This doctrine of an indefinite consciousness is constructed purely *ad hoc* to save his argument from its own consequences. It represents no actual facts of consciousness whatever. A consciousness without some definite elements is something which in no way admits of being experienced. When Mr. Spencer says that when all attributes have been abstracted there still remains a sense of something, we have really only the bare conception of subject without the conditions of its meaning anything to us. Thus, if I take an object and abstract from it its experienced properties, I may say the object still remains after the products are withdrawn, but in truth nothing remains. When I am dealing with some objective thing I may possibly fancy that at least objectivity remains, but in truth nothing but the shadow without content remains, the ghost of an object, in short. I have the same experience when I take a conceptual object, say a triangle, and lay aside the various attributes of area, triangularity, three-sidedness, etc., but plainly it would be absurd to suppose that any triangle remained in that case. And the same thing is to be said of Hamilton's "wonderful faith," by means of which we are made sure of existence of which we can form no conception. This wonderful faith has the same function of saving the argument from its own consequences. And here also it is plain that when we affirm a subject of which no conception whatever can be formed, of which every conception we form is declared to be a mere negation, the affirmation of such subject is entirely empty. We seem to say something, but really say nothing. Every doctrine of unknowability meets this difficulty. The unknowable must to some extent be brought into knowledge or else compelled to go out of existence. This is the case with the doctrine of Kant, who was the originator of this sort of thing. Kant maintained that the categories of thought are relative to ourselves and do not apply to reality proper; but it is clear that with this result the reality vanishes altogether. If all the categories are relative to us, then the independent reality is neither one nor many, neither substance nor attribute, neither cause nor effect, neither real nor unreal, for all of these things are categories and hence do not apply to the thing in itself. What, then, is this truly real? If these denials are to be taken strictly it is nothing, either subjective or objective. It is neither a thing nor a thought; it is only a verbal phrase to which neither reality nor conception corresponds. If we relax the denial sufficiently to bring it under the general head of existence, even then no positive thought or thing remains. We have only the pure category of being "sustained *in vacuo* by the imagination." As such it has only the abstract conceptual existence of class terms, and, like them, is objectively nothing. The unknowable reality, then, vanishes, leaving only verbal phrases in its place.

The Unknowable, then, taken absolutely as that of which no positive conception can be formed, is strictly nothing, and moreover no one has ever succeeded in so taking it. Thus Kant had no doubt that it existed, that it was the ground of phenomena, and apparently no doubt of its unity. This is still more the case with Spencer, who declares this absolute to be one, to be a power, to be eternal, to be a reality, and in all of these categories he seems to have great faith; indeed, he goes so far in this direction as to give it about all the attributes of God except the personal and intellectual ones. Inconsistency of this kind is necessary in the nature of the case. One looks in vain for anything in Mr. Spencer's argument to prove some of these attributes. Thus, the unknowability of the real, supposing it made out, in no way proves that the real is one. I might say that my neighbors are essentially unknowable, that there is a background of mystery in each case which prevents any absolute knowledge of them. But this fact would not warrant me in saying that my neighbors are one. Similarly we might find a mystery in material things and might affirm that we should never be able to penetrate that mystery, but that would not warrant us in saying that all material things have a common ground. In this monistic affirmation, however, Mr. Spencer takes sides against all pluralistic systems and makes a very important affirmation, without, however, giving any adequate reasons, if, indeed, he gives any reasons at all. Similarly, as against the positivists or mere phenomenalists, he declares this being to be a reality and a power. He calls it "the infinite and eternal energy on which all things depend and from which all things forever proceed." Here certainly is a piece of important information respecting the hidden ground of things, and one in which he by no means agrees with all philosophic speculators.

That it is eternal and without beginning and end appears from many a passage after he gets clear of the Unknowable.

Moreover, this Unknowable is introduced as the cause of phenomena. They forever depend upon it and proceed from it, and the changes, successions, and likenesses among appearances point to corresponding changes, successions, and likenesses among the unknown realities or within the Unknowable itself. In that case we bring the unconditioned being into fixed relation with the system of experience, subject it to time and change, and are in a fair way to get what Mr. Mill called "a prodigious amount of knowledge respecting the Unknowable." This necessity of bringing the Unknowable into these causal relations makes an especial difficulty for every system of this kind. If the Unknowable is not brought into such relations, it is of absolutely no use in explaining the world of time and change; but if it be brought into such relations, then we necessarily get some information respecting it from the order of relations which it founds and maintains.

This matter of the Unknowable has been so confused ever since the time of Kant that it seems worth while, even at the expense of some repetition, to point out once more the emptiness of every such doctrine. All philosophizing must begin with the facts of experience. From these it must proceed as its foundation and to these it must return for its justification. The essential aim of philosophy is to give an account of experience, that is, to rationalize and organize experience so that our reason may get some insight into it. From this it is plain that we never can affirm anything whatever unrelated to the system of experience. For if we should do so it would thereby become worthless for its proper function. As soon, then, as we find ourselves affirming something which cannot be rationally apprehended and understood, we are going beyond our premises and affirming something essentially without any meaning. Again, as soon as we affirm something that cannot be brought into relation with experience as its dynamic and rational explanation, it is manifest that that something loses all reason for existence. It matters not what we call this being or these beings; we must observe that whatever we call them their function is to make experience intelligible. And when they will not do this, instead of being unknowable they are rather unaffirmable. The application of this principle to this subject would rule out the whole family of absolutes, unconditioneds, and infinities which have wrought such confusion in this field. They can only be regarded as abstract fictions resulting from uncritical thought. When, then, we are asked if the absolute can be a cause, the reply is, Any absolute that is not a cause is fictitious. When we are asked, Can the infinite coexist with the finite? the reply is, Any infinite that cannot coexist with the finite must be dismissed as a fiction. The thing which must go in all such cases is the verbal abstraction of the speculator.

The same general principle has a bearing upon the question of the Unknowable from another point of view. It is commonly said that we know only phenomena, and it is assumed that these phenomena are simply appearances which do not rightly represent the real. In all of this there is a tacit reference to the appearances of vision. It is a familiar experience that visual phenomena are somewhat irregular and often distort the object. Thus a straight stick standing in the water looks bent. A pair of colored glasses lends its own color to the object. If one looks at his face in the bowl of a spoon it is lengthened out portentously. If he looks at his face in the back of a spoon it is correspondingly broadened. Facts of this kind, all of which are connected with the visual sense, suggest the thought that all phenomena may in the same way fail to give a correct view of things. But all of this overlooks the fact that the chief way of knowing things is not through their appearances, but through their effects. In such cases there is no question of looking at things, but rather one of finding the nature of things through their products and activities. Thus the soul is not known by the way it looks, for it does not look at all. It is rather the invisible personality living, experiencing itself in various ways and putting forth various activities, and in and through these the soul is known. In the same way the forces of nature, supposing them to exist, would be known through the forms and laws of their activity. Gravitation would be known in this way, and also chemical affinity, electricity, etc.; and, as we before said, no agnostic has ever succeeded in separating his unknowable from the order of experience to this extent, because as soon as it is thus separated it becomes entirely worthless. Kant could not keep his things-in-themselves entirely free from experience, and Mr. Spencer, likewise, in Part Second at last tells us that the coexistences and sequences in experience point to coexistences and sequences in the fundamental reality, thus giving a basis for Mr. Mill's remark, before quoted, that in this way we seem likely to get a "prodigious amount of knowledge respecting the Unknowable."

Thus the doctrine of the Unknowable appears as doubly useless. We see that when all predication is rejected we no longer have any conception whatever. Nothing remains but the ghost of a vanished subject, which, with Spencer, we may call an indefinite consciousness, or, with Hamilton, the revelation of a wonderful faith. And when we attempt to use our Unknowable as an explanation of the world of experience, it at once becomes worthless unless we are permitted to bring it into definite relations which reveal to some extent its nature and character.

It is plain that Mr. Spencer's doctrine of the Unknowable leaves us in great uncertainty. What is the Unknowable? It is "the real as distinguished from the phenomenal." It is the "actual," in opposition to the "apparent." It is the "fundamental reality," it is noumena in whatever realm. He affirms that the ideas of first cause, absolute, the infinite, space, time, matter, motion, force, and conscious mind, are all unthinkable. Then theology, physics, and psychology are all impossible. Even mathematics, the science of pure space, time, and motion, is also impossible. This is pure skepticism, and we are curious to see what Spencer is going to make of it. He insists upon the full conclusion with reference to religion. We are not to think of God at all except as the omnipresent mystery. We are not to affirm reason, consciousness, intelligence, least of all personality, of it. Mr. Mansel had insisted upon a regulative theology. We cannot conceive God, he said, to be personal and intelligent, but we must think of Him as such. This notion Spencer repudiates with some warmth, and declares that if there be truth in the argument it is not our duty to say anything about God. But we must add, it is equally not our duty to say anything about reality at all, because not merely religious realities, but also scientific realities are remanded to the realm of impenetrable mystery where no thought whatever is possible. But Spencer has a plan for rehabilitating science, and it is interesting to note how it is done. By the logic of his argument science has no real apprehension of objective reality, and nothing remains but positivistic registration of the orders of coexistence and sequence among phenomena. However, Mr. Spencer was not a positivist, and regarded phenomenalism as inadequate, if not erroneous. Accordingly, he proceeds to make a place for science as something more than such mere description and registration of the phenomenal order. The first move is to postulate an indefinite consciousness of the absolute and to declare that it is the most positive factor of thought. We can only know of the real, that it is. All other knowledge is of appearance. But these appearances force us to admit a reality back of them as their cause. We can even, by means of these appearances, get some insight into the realities themselves, for the changes and successions and likenesses among appearances point to changes, likenesses, etc., among reality. This we get at by common sense, and are next helped by a new notion, which appears early in the doctrine of the knowable, that of relative realities. These relative realities are simply things in the common-sense meaning. They are declared to be constant effects of the unconditioned cause and to stand in indissoluble connection with it, and being equally persistent with it are equally real. Thus the common-sense view of things is fairly being reinstated, but with a drawback; reality is defined to be persistence in consciousness. So, then, first, nothing is knowable except appearances; second, appearances suggest realities; third, changes in appearances point to corresponding changes in reality; fourth, suddenly reality becomes double, absolute and relative, and these two are in constant relation; and fifth, reality changes its character and is declared to be persistence in consciousness. If his reasoning be sound, then we have only a regulative physics. In the discussion of the Unknowable he declares space, time, matter, motion, and force to be impossible ideas, but in the discussion of the knowable we have the same ideas made the basis of his system, and we are told that our ideas on these same subjects stand in indissoluble connection with reality and are just as good and real as the real itself. But if this process is possible with the impossible ideas of science, it seems it might be equally possible with the no more impossible ideas of religion. If a valid physics is possible in spite of our ignorance of the Unknowable, why is not a valid theology equally possible? Let us grant that our knowledge is all symbolic; still the question arises, How do we know that mechanical and material symbols better represent the fact than spiritual and intellectual symbols? If it be said that none of our symbols at all represent the fact, then physical science is a pure delusion; but if it be allowed that thought symbols more or less well represent the fact, then we must know which does it best. Shall we be further from the fact when we think of the Unknowable as a blind mechanical force or as a conscious and free spirit? Here is the dilemma. If the Unknowable be strictly unknowable, so that it cannot in any way be symbolized, then we must all keep the peace; but if the scientist may build up a valid physics on the basis of symbolical knowledge, there is no reason why the theologian also should not be allowed to speak. Pressed by these difficulties many of Spencer's friends have claimed that by Unknowable he does not mean strictly unknowable, but only incomprehensible. We reply, first, that this would make it a mere truism without the slightest importance and consequence. When dealing with the theologians he tells what he means by the Unknowable by forbidding any attribution whatever, and any other view he regards as showing the impiety of the pious. Nevertheless, as already pointed out, he makes many attributions. For example, it is one and not many, thus denying all dualistic and pluralistic theories. It is the real as opposed to the apparent, thus cutting off phenomenalism. It is a power and the fundamental cause. It is persistent and indestructible. It is omnipresent in space and time. Surely here is an embarrassing richness of affirmation about that of which we are forbidden to affirm anything. If we are allowed to say so much, there seems no reason why we should not be allowed to go one step further and affirm even intelligence if the facts call for it.

We shall return to this matter later when discussing the Knowable, but here it suffices to point out that the Unknowable is a very uncertain quantity in Mr. Spencer's thinking, and moreover is full of contradiction.

Doctrine of Religion

The last chapter of the discussion of the Unknowable is the reconciliation of science and religion, and the conclusion to which Mr. Spencer comes is this: A permanent peace between the two will be reached when science becomes convinced that its explanations are approximate and relative, while religion becomes fully convinced that the mystery it contemplates is ultimate and absolute. There is, then, a field of knowledge and this belongs to science, and there is a realm of mystery and this belongs to religion. The shortcoming of religion has been that it has sought to bring the absolute into the forms of finite thought, and the shortcoming of science is that it has failed to recognize that its explanations remain on the surface, while a great depth of mystery must forever underlie it. Mr. Spencer rebukes Mr. Mansel for having held that it is our duty to think of God as personal and to believe that He is infinite. He also says that "volumes might be written upon the impiety of the pious." This impiety consists essentially in trying to think of God under the forms of our thought, instead rather of recognizing the limitations of our faculties and remaining in utter silence and emptiness of thought before it. In a single passage, however, he seems almost to recognize the necessity of something like Mr. Mansel's regulative theology. He says: "Very likely there will ever remain a need to give shape to that indefinite sense of an Ultimate Existence, which forms the basis of our intelligence. We shall always be under the necessity of contemplating it as some mode of being; that is, of representing it to ourselves in some form of thought, however vague. And we shall not err in doing this so long as we treat every notion we thus frame as merely a symbol." (Page 96.) Here we seem permitted to form conceptions which, while inadequate, are nevertheless useful, playing their part in the life both of the individual and of the community. At the same time we are to recognize that these conceptions are not merely inadequate, but strictly unthinkable when carried out into their implications. The conception of God as having plans and purposes in nature and as creating is rejected with some contempt, and we are recommended to cultivate reverence by refraining from affirmation of this kind. He says: "The attitude thus assumed can be fitly represented only by further developing a simile long current in theological controversies — the simile of the watch. If, for a moment, we made the grotesque supposition that the tickings and other movements of a watch constituted a kind of consciousness; and that a watch, possessed of such a consciousness, insisted on regarding the watchmaker's actions as determined like its own by springs and escapements; we should simply complete a parallel of which religious teachers think much. And were we to suppose that a watch not only formulated the cause of its existence in these mechanical terms, but held that watches were bound out of reverence so to formulate this cause, and even vituperated, as atheistic watches, any that did not venture so to formulate it; we should merely illustrate the presumption of theologians by carrying their own argument a step further." (Page 94.) It seems sufficient to say in reply to this that no religious person really ever thinks of his own conceptions of God as adequate, or as being other than symbolic or as adumbrations of the truth. We should quite agree with Mr. Spencer that a spiritual anthropomorphism easily passes into irreverence and is to be avoided; but it is equally plain that if we are to think at all we must think in terms which our own experience makes possible. All terms are in some sense symbolic, but yet there may be a choice among symbols. The personal and spiritual symbols may bring us nearer the truth than the material and mechanical symbols. Mr. Spencer says there may well be existence as far beyond mind and intellect as these are beyond matter and mechanism, and seems to suggest that the alternative is not between mind and something lower, but rather between mind and something higher. But it is plain that this something higher is only a form of words without any positive content. All that results is the exhortation not to take our symbols of whatever kind in too hard and fast a way, yet plainly we shall do our best when we think in terms of the highest symbols and not in terms of the lowest. And as to the watch referred to, it is curious that Mr. Spencer should have failed to see how much better logic the watch ticked out than he himself has done; for the argument from the watch is from intelligible purpose in the watch to intelligence in its maker, not to springs and escapements, wheels and levers in its maker, but to thought and purpose. If, then, the watch had concluded not to wheels and levers, but to an intelligent maker, it would seem to have been quite as near the truth as it would if, having taken a course in the Unknowable, it had decided that the thought of an intelligent maker was irreverent and impious, and that its true ground was an unknowable something beyond all thought and understanding.

In general, Mr. Spencer seeks to base religion on pure and utter mystery. Religion is to say nothing and think nothing beyond the recognition of mystery, pure and impenetrable. This is really one of the most extraordinary utterances in the history of philosophy. That there must be an element of mystery in religion is of course beyond all question, but religion with no element of knowledge whatever is impossible to any intelligent being. A famous controversy between Mr. Spencer and Frederic Harrison on this topic broke out in the "Nineteenth Century" in 1884. "To make a religion out of the Unknowable," Mr. Harrison said, "is far more extravagant than to make it out of the Equator, for we know something of the Equator. It means much for sailors, geographers, astronomers, and has great significance for tropical life; but respecting the Unknowable our minds are a blank. We can only stare in empty wonder." This criticism is clearly correct. If we take our agnosticism seriously, the Unknowable is for our thought pure mystery and negation. At best it is an infinite, at which we can only stare. The only religion possible on this basis is the recognition of mystery and perhaps some emotion of wonder, a relation that would be entirely possible with the law of gravitation. Actual religion has always implied more than mere mystery. It has rooted permanently in our sense of need and dependence, as Schleiermacher pointed out, and also in the needs and aspirations of our entire humanity. It has been our good refuge against the shortcomings of the present life and our great source of inspiration and aspiration. It has issued in great systems of belief, worship, and conduct, and no actual religion is without these. Now, the religion of the Unknowable has none of these. The creed is very short: I believe that nothing can be known about the fundamental reality. It has no worship, for how can one worship a mental vacuum? It has no relation to conduct. We cannot connect it with life in any way for our guidance or inspiration. It furnishes no bond for social union and essential aims. Alike for the individual and society it is empty and barren. We might trust in the Lord, but who could trust in the Unknowable or pray to it or worship it, or be grateful to it or desire to be conformed to it? As Mr. Harrison says, "A religion which could not make any one any better, which would leave the human heart and human society just as it found them, which left no foothold for devotion and none for faith; which could have no creed,

no doctrines, no temples, no priests, no teachers, no
rites, no morality, no beauty, no hope, no consola-
tion; which is summed up in one dogma, — the Unknowable is everywhere and Evolution is its prophet
— this is indeed to 'defecate religion to a pure trans-
parency.' . . . A religion without anything to be
known, with nothing to teach, with no moral power,
with some rags of religious sentiment surviving,
mainly in a consciousness of mystery, — this is indeed the mockery of religion."

These points are well taken. The worship at the
altar of the Unknowable would certainly have to be
mainly of the silent sort. It is a matter of psychological curiosity to know how such a view ever became
acceptable to any one. In the case of its author there
would seem to have been an atrophy of the spiritual
nature or an original lack of religious insight and
interest. He says in his "Autobiography": "Memory
does not tell me the extent of my divergence from
current beliefs. There had not taken place any pronounced rejection of them, but they were slowly losing their hold. Their hold had, indeed, never been
very decided: 'the creed of Christendom' being evidently alien to my nature, both emotional and intellectual. To many, and apparently to most, religious
worship yields a species of pleasure. To me it never
did so; unless, indeed, I count as such the emotion
produced by sacred music. A sense of combined
grandeur and sweetness excited by an anthem, with
organ and cathedral architecture to suggest the idea
of power, was then, and always has been, strong in me
— as strong, probably, as in most — stronger than in

many. But the expressions of adoration of a personal being, the utterance of laudations, and the humble professions of obedience, never found in me any echoes. Hence, when left to myself, as at Worcester and previously in London, I spent my Sundays either in reading or in country walks." (Vol. i, p. 171.) In the case of his more religious disciples the acceptance of this view seems due to carelessness and lack of thought, because of which religious sounding phrases were taken for religious sense. When therefore they hear religion accorded the high merit of dimly discerning from the beginning the ultimate verity, and never ceasing to insist upon it, they suppose it means religion in their sense and not the blank negation of Mr. Spencer's system. In this respect they are like the disciples of Spinoza, who were led by Spinoza's use of terminology to overlook the fact that when he said God he meant nature.

The Unknowable, then, as the subject of religion, can do nothing for us so long as we keep our thought tolerably clear. We might make a shift to get along without any religion, but we are not willing to be mocked with the ghost of religion.

Mr. Spencer seems to have been of a rather cheerful opinion as to the value of his advanced thought until the end, then some doubts began to invade. The following paragraph in his "Autobiography" shows a suspicion that religion is a more important matter practically and socially than he had originally suspected. He says: —

"Less marked, perhaps, though still sufficiently marked, is a modification in my ideas about religious institutions, which, indicated in my later books, has continued to grow more decided. While the current creed was slowly losing its hold on me, the sole question seemed to be the truth or untruth of the particular doctrines I had been taught. But gradually, and especially of late years, I have become aware that this is not the sole question.

"Partly, the wider knowledge obtained of human societies has caused this. Many have, I believe, recognized the fact that a cult of some sort, with its social embodiment, is a constituent in every society which has made any progress; and this has led to the conclusion that the control exercised over men's conduct by theological beliefs and priestly agency, has been indispensable. The masses of evidence classified and arranged in the *Descriptive Sociology* have forced this belief upon me independently: if not against my will, still without any desire to entertain it. So conspicuous are the proofs that among unallied races in different parts of the globe, progress in civilization has gone along with development of a religious system, absolute in its dogmas and terrible in its threatened penalties, administered by a powerful priesthood, that there seems no escape from the inference that the maintenance of social subordination has peremptorily required the aid of some such agency." (Vol. II, p. 544.)

Throughout the chapter on the reconciliation of science and religion Mr. Spencer often seems to be on the point of recognizing a relative religion and even a relative theology, that is, the doctrines which are inadequate to the reality, but yet are more or less valuable symbols or adumbrations of the same. In the passage just quoted, religion and even theology seem to be recognized as important elements in the development of society. It would certainly be strange to introduce a factor of distinct error into social progress as something necessary to it. But in other parts of the same chapter Mr. Spencer, as we have seen, was very strenuous against any affirmation whatever respecting the unknown cause. Had he retained and developed the former position he would have been in close harmony with all Christian theologies of the better class, who have always maintained that our conceptions of the divine order are inadequate, and while they have affirmed an element of knowledge have also affirmed an element of mystery. God's ways are not as our ways nor his thoughts as our thoughts; for as the heavens are high above the earth, so are his ways higher than our ways and his thoughts than our thoughts. But Mr. Spencer did not hold this possible view with any certainty or consistency, but in the main gave the impression that when thought was perfectly clear there is nothing left but mystery. This has certainly been the understanding of the great majority of his critics, and moreover it seems to be the view to which he himself came toward the end. In a little work published the last of all, entitled "Facts and Comments," there is a chapter, "What Should the Skeptic Say to Believers?" Here it appears that the truth as it is in Agnosticism is a dangerous drug which is not rashly to be administered. "The prospect of heaven makes life tolerable to many who would else find it intolerable. In some whose shattered constitutions and perpetual pains, caused perhaps by undue efforts for the benefit of dependents, the daily thought of a compensating future is the sole assuaging consciousness. . . . And there are many who stagger on under the exhausting burden of daily duties, fulfilled without thanks and without sympathy, who are enabled to bear their ills by the conviction that after this life will come a life free from pains and weariness. Nothing but evil can follow a change in the creed of such; and unless cruelly thoughtless the Agnostic will carefully shun discussion of religious subjects with them." (Pages 285–86.)

This quotation shows a deeper insight than appears in much of Mr. Spencer's writings. It also shows the embarrassment and helplessness of religious agnosticism in the face of life's tragedies and woes. No one would have the heart to say to these sufferers and burden-bearers, Think on the Unknowable, lift your hearts to the "great enigma," cast your burdens on the inscrutable. No! They must be left to the cruder notions of Moses and the Prophets and the Man of Nazareth. And seeing that these notions, also according to Mr. Spencer, have been wrought out in us by the Unknown Cause, we feel justified in holding on to them until we find something better. That something we do not find in the religion of the Unknowable.

A single paragraph at the close of this chapter is interesting in many ways. Mr. Spencer has pointed out that some form of religious conception is likely long to be necessary for those who need it, and that this form may very possibly be better adjusted to them than the higher interest which he aims to reach. This leads him to raise the question whether in that case we should not leave these believers to their own view, instead of disturbing them by the reflections which come from a more profound criticism. He concludes, however, that the advanced thinker who is possessed of the highest truth should not fail to express his views. He says: "It is not for nothing that he has in him these sympathies with some principles and repugnance to others. He, with all his capacities, and aspirations, and beliefs, is not an accident but a product of the time. While he is a descendant of the past, he is a parent of the future: and his thoughts are as children born to him which he may not carelessly let die. Like every other man he may properly consider himself as one of the myriad agencies through whom works the Unknown Cause; and when the Unknown Cause produces in him a certain belief, he is thereby authorized to profess and act out that belief." (Page 105.) This seems clear and convincing and comforting. Mr. Spencer has before recognized the needs of those who are on lower planes of thought, but here he also vindicates the rights of the highest and most advanced thinkers. The rights of free thought are vindicated and are set on high beyond all cavil; and yet the utterance is a little confusing when we remember that Mr. Spencer expressly includes all other men and all other beliefs in the same relation, and gives to them all the same sanction and authorization of the Unknown Cause. Forthwith we begin to grope, for it is not the advanced thinker only who stands in this august relation and has this supreme sanction, but "every other man" also "may truly consider himself as one of the myriad agencies through whom works the Unknown Cause; and when the Unknown Cause produces in him a certain belief, he is thereby authorized to profess and act out that belief." But it is plain that every other man is a somewhat numerous personage, and his beliefs and acts, produced and authorized by the Unknown Cause, are a rather heterogeneous and unsavory collection, for it includes all the superstitions, absurdities, and imbecilities which have ever been believed and all the horrors and atrocities which have ever been perpetrated. All of these are the products of the Unknown Cause, and the believers are of course authorized to profess, and act out their beliefs, for all these are "as children born to them which they may not carelessly let die."

But what is truth in such a system? The Unknown Cause seems to have not one opinion, but many, and does not abide in any one for long. For a disciple of this view it must be a very grave circumstance that the Unknown Cause has produced a great many false opinions for one true one, that along with a little truth there has been a most overwhelming production of error. The Unknown Cause has shown a grotesque tendency to revel in low and unsavory views, fetishisms, anthropomorphisms, theologies, whims, infatuations, obstinacies, instead of tending to the sun-clear truths of a synthetic philosophy. This fact has so impressed many critics of a pessimistic turn that they have not hesitated to think meanly of the Unknown Cause and all its works. In any case, it is clear that up to date the Unknown Cause has not advanced beyond an indefinite, incoherent heterogeneity of opinions, every one of which has the same source and sanction as any other. Who would have thought that so much absurdity lay concealed in Mr. Spencer's encouragement of the advanced thinker! If we adopt this view clearly, as already suggested, we may retain our Christian theology without being ashamed of our faith, for that theology has been wrought out in us by the Unknown Cause and we are thereby authorized to profess and act it out. Nothing has a higher sanction than this.

It is plain that Mr. Spencer's doctrine of Agnosticism has much inconsistency in it. His more thoughtful disciples long ago found fault with it and were rather desirous of repudiating it. Mr. Spencer himself, in the last edition of his "First Principles," seeks to reply to his critics in a general way, especially to the claim that a strictly Unknowable cannot be affirmed. The reply consists, in effect, in reëmphasizing the notion of an indefinite consciousness which we must affirm, but which we cannot further define. This notion has already been considered. If this indefinite consciousness eluded all affirmation, it would equally elude all existence. When affirmation is emptied out of a thought-state, there is really nothing left, definite or indefinite.

But a more instructive admission is the declaration that the doctrine set forth in Part First has no bearing upon the doctrine next to be unfolded in Part Second or in his "Doctrine of Science." He says, "But now let it be understood that the reader is not called on to judge respecting any of the arguments or conclusions contained in the foregoing five chapters and in the above paragraphs. The subjects on which we are about to enter are independent of the subjects thus far discussed; and he may reject any or all of that which has gone before, while leaving himself free to accept any or all of that which is now to come." (Page 109.)

It seems, then, that according to Mr. Spencer this opening discussion has nothing to do with the doctrine of science, to which he now proceeds. He says: "An account of the Transformation of Things, given in the pages which follow, is simply an orderly presentation of facts; and the interpretation of the facts is nothing more than a statement of the ultimate uniformities they present — the laws to which they conform. Is the reader an atheist? The exposition of these facts and these laws will neither yield support to his belief nor destroy it. Is he a pantheist? The phenomena and the inferences as now to be set forth will not force on him any incongruous implication. Does he think that God is immanent throughout all things, from concentrating nebulæ to the thoughts of poets? Then the theory to be put before him contains no disproof of that view. Does he believe in a Deity who has given unchanging laws to the Universe? Then he will find nothing at variance with his belief in an exposition of those laws and an account of the results." (Page 110.)

However, it will appear that the two parts of the work are by no means so independent as Mr. Spencer here affirms. On the contrary, we shall find the Unknowable reappearing again and again in confusing ways, and much use made of principles he is supposed to have established. In particular we shall find the

Unknowable invoked to repel the charge of atheism and materialism. Of course we shall also find considerable contradiction between the conceptions of science in Part First and those set up in Part Second. Mr. Spencer's admission is not strictly correct, but it is interesting as a recognition that all is not well with the logic of the system.

II

MR. SPENCER'S DOCTRINE OF SCIENCE

ASSUMING the correctness of Mr. Spencer's reasoning in the previous discussion, the drift of his logic is to make science, as a knowledge of reality, impossible. If, then, science exists at all, it can only be as a knowledge of phenomena. In strictness, however, even this is doubtful, for, as was pointed out, the conclusion of the first part of the argument is pure Pyrrhonism or skepticism. The mind is convicted of being essentially contradictory in its operations as shown in its products, and hence it must be essentially untrustworthy. But the second half of his argument is for a relativity of knowledge, that is, a knowledge relative to ourselves, or of phenomena only. In this phenomenal field it is assumed that the mind can be trusted. But these two results cannot be put together without difficulty. If we assume that the mind is essentially untrustworthy in its normal operations, there seems to be no good ground for trusting it at all. This difficulty is one that Mr. Spencer seems never to have suspected.

But leaving this out of account, it is plain that on the previous reasoning, all that science can be is a positivistic observation and registration of the coexistences and sequences of phenomena. It cannot even read the past or predict the future with any logical right. To do this it must assume the system of phenomena with its fixed laws and also a considerable measure of insight on our part. Apart from this assumption we have only psychological expectation, which we never can turn into a logical warrant. Had Mr. Spencer contented himself with this humble position for science, there would have been a certain consistency in developing a doctrine of science after the possibility of real science had been disproved. But he was not thus content, and set out to make a foundation for science which should be something more solid than positivism, and at the same time should completely ignore the positions taken in Part First. In Part Second, which we now consider, science often seems to forsake the humble ways of phenomenalism and to take the high a priori road, talking confidently of indestructible substances and energies without beginning or end, and of laws without variableness or shadow of turning. And all this sounds strange from an empirical science that knows only phenomena and eschews all knowledge of the real. Certainly it is an interesting problem to know how all these things occur.

We recall that in discussing the Unknowable, Mr. Spencer examined the ideas of First Cause, Absolute, Infinite, Space, Time, Matter, Motion, Force, and Conscious Mind, and found them all unthinkable and contradictory. Thus theology, physics, mathematics, and psychology as real sciences were made impossible at a stroke. Mr. Spencer was well content to leave theology in this outcast condition, but physics he proceeds to rescue as a foundation for science. All the more must we scrutinize the process and make sure of our goings. Again, Mr. Spencer was neither a materialist nor an atheist in intention. The charge of materialism he repelled with warmth, and as for atheism he held that the choice is not between personality and mechanism, but between personality and something that may be higher. Nevertheless Evolution is defined in terms of matter and motion, and the formula is held to include all the phenomena of life, mind, and society. Now, it is plain that if matter and motion are to be taken in the usual sense, this is pure materialism and smacks pretty strongly of atheism. Mr. Spencer meets such suggestions by pointing out that matter and motion are only symbols of the inscrutable power behind phenomena. There is, then, a double problem for Mr. Spencer. First, he must rescue science from the skeptical conclusions of his agnostic argument, and, secondly, he must set forth a doctrine of phenomena and phenomenal knowledge which will at once make a foundation for science and also save his system from lapsing into vulgar materialism and atheism. In both respects Mr. Spencer's success is very meagre.

On the first point Mr. Spencer's method is to recall the notions of space, time, matter, motion, and force which were cashiered and discredited before, and reinstate them as the cornerstones of science. He says, "That skeptical state of mind which the criticisms of Philosophy usually produce, is, in great measure, caused by the misinterpretation of words." In consequence, "there results more or less of that dreamlike illusion which is so incongruous with our instinctive convictions." This sense of illusion Mr. Spencer proceeds to dispel by a better definition of real and reality. The peasant, he says, makes appearance and reality one and the same thing. But "the metaphysician, while his words imply belief in a reality, sees that consciousness cannot embrace it, but only the appearance of it; and so he transfers the appearance into consciousness and leaves the reality outside. This reality left outside, he continues to think of much in the same way that the peasant thinks of the appearance. The *realness* ascribed to it is constantly spoken of as though it were known apart from all acts of consciousness." For the peasant there is nothing but the real thing, and that is outside. For the metaphysician there is a distinction between the thing and the appearance, the thing being outside and the appearance inside. Hence illusions arise when the peasant and the metaphysician get together. The remedy for this is a new definition of reality: "By reality we mean *persistence* in consciousness. . . . The real, as we conceive it, is distinguished solely by the test of persistence; for by this test we separate it from what we call the unreal. . . . How truly persistence is what we mean by reality, is shown in the fact that when, after criticism has proved that the real as presented in perception is not the objectively real, the vague consciousness which we retain of the objectively real, is of something which persists absolutely, under all changes of mode, form, or appearance. And the fact that we cannot form even an indefinite notion of the absolutely real, except as the absolutely persistent, implies that persistence is our ultimate test of the real."

These quotations are taken from chapter III of the

MR. SPENCER'S DOCTRINE OF SCIENCE

sixth edition of the "First Principles," pages 141–43. It can hardly be said that they will do much to remove "that skeptical state of mind," or "that dreamlike illusion," "which the criticisms of philosophy usually produce." The metaphysician is rebuked for leaving the reality outside, as the peasant does; whereas "by reality we mean persistence in consciousness," in which case everything is inside. But in the next sentence persistence in consciousness is shortened into persistence, and we are left in further uncertainty whether persistence is the *meaning* or the *mark* of reality. Yet, as a result of these and similar considerations, Mr. Spencer concludes: "Thus, then, we may resume, with entire confidence, those realistic conceptions which Philosophy at first sight seems to dissipate." (Page 144.) Thus space, time, matter, motion, and force are restored to us as "relative realities." They stand in indissoluble relation with their absolute cause, and for us are equally real. We may, therefore, build up our science upon them with all confidence, only referring now and then, for form's sake, to the absolute reality, lest we forget.

Now the friendliest critic could not fail to see that for all this we have little more than Mr. Spencer's assurance. We are merely told that they are relative realities, and that we may safely build upon them. But when we insist on walking by sight rather than faith we find this doctrine in the highest degree obscure even in its meaning. This brings us to the second point mentioned, Mr. Spencer's doctrine of phenomena, their place and nature.

What and where are these relative realities? What

is their relation to us and to the unconditioned reality? On this point Mr. Spencer is very unclear. Indeed, except in the vaguest way, he does not seem to have thought of it at all. At times the relative realities seem to be only effects in us, as in the following: "If, under certain conditions furnished by our constitutions, some Power of which the nature is beyond conception, always produces a certain mode of consciousness, — if this mode of consciousness is as persistent as would be this Power were it in consciousness; the reality will be to consciousness as complete in the one case as in the other." (Page 144.) Here the relative reality appears to be only a "mode of consciousness" wrought in us by the absolute reality. But in speaking of space and matter, Mr. Spencer inclines to regard the relative realities as corresponding to absolute modes in the Unknowable. "Our conception of Space is produced by some mode of the Unknowable." Again, of matter he says: "Such being our cognition of the relative reality, what are we to say of the absolute reality? We can only say that it is some mode of the Unknowable, related to the Matter we know as cause to effect." (Page 149.) Similarly of motion: "That this relative reality answers to some absolute reality, it is needful only for form's sake to assert. What has been said above, respecting the Unknown Cause which produces in us the effects called Matter, Space, and Time, will apply, on simply changing the terms, to Motion." (Page 151.) Thus space, time, matter, motion, and force appear to be merely effects in us, or modes of consciousness produced in us. Apart from them there would seem to be at times only the unknowable, or the fundamental reality, and then again there seems to be this absolute being *plus* some absolute modes, each of which corresponds to some one of the relative realities and causes the appropriate effect in us.

This result gives rise to a long series of puzzles. If space, time, matter, motion, and force are only effects in us, then all that is described in these terms, including, of course, the whole process of evolution, is purely subjective to us and nothing objective whatever. If we were away they would also be away, and we should not be very far from what Mr. Spencer calls "the insanities of idealism." But this was certainly not Mr. Spencer's view. He had not the least doubt that evolution, as "an integration of matter and concomitant dissipation of motion," was going on long before we arrived and would keep on if we should depart. All the more are we puzzled to know what and where these relative realities are. If they are only effects in us, evolution is merely a mirage of human notions. The same is true of science in general. It has nothing objective in it. We must in some way make these relative realities independent of us if we are to have a real evolution.

There is one sense in which we can find a meaning for this term relative reality, but it is not one that would meet the demands of Mr. Spencer's system. In the Berkeleian Philosophy the system of nature is no substantial fact, but rather an order of experience which is continuously maintained in us by God. In some sense, then, we might say that this system is unreal and in another sense that it is real. It would be

281

a relative reality, something which we do not produce, something which is common for all human beings, something which in its origin is independent of us, something also on which we can practically depend, something, finally, with its established relations and orders of coexistence and sequence. For all practical purposes, then, this system would be real. It would be real in experience and for experience, and moreover it would perfectly meet Mr. Spencer's test of reality in that it would be persistent in consciousness. But this reality would not be accepted by Mr. Spencer. It would be [a case of] what he calls the "insanities of idealism," and of which he says, "If Idealism be true, Evolution is a dream." But this is the only sense in which we can give the phrase, "relative reality," any certain meaning. We are quite unable to tell what this relative reality that is more than this is relative to, and in what its relativity consists.

What is the relation of these relative realities to the Unknowable, according to Mr. Spencer? In the exposition already given, we seem to have at least three distinctions: first, the Unknowable, or the fundamental reality; second, modes of the Unknowable; third, relative realities, which are also spoken of as manifestations of the Unknowable. Now, what shall we make of all this?

In the phrase, "modes of the Unknowable," we go back to the earlier philosophical notion of fundamental being as substance and modes. This conception finds its classical expression in Spinoza's doctrine of the one substance and its modes. But in order to clear up our doubts respecting Spencer's doctrine, we should need to know if this Unknowable is distinct from the modes, so that it could exist apart from them, or whether the modes exhaust the reality in the case, while the Unknowable is some principle of unity of them. For instance, if we speak of bricks as modes of clay, it is clear that the clay would not be anything apart from the bricks; so that while they are modes of clay the clay is expressed and exhausted in the bricks. If this were Mr. Spencer's conception of the relation of the fundamental reality to its modes, we could in practice dispense with the fundamental reality altogether except for form's sake, and deal only with the concrete modes. In general, however, Mr. Spencer conceives the relation between the fundamental reality and the relative reality as dynamic, not as rigid, static, or modal; and the modes, except in occasional expressions, drop out of sight. So, then, we have the fundamental reality, and the static realities, and here again the question comes up, What is the relation of the former to the latter? Is it expressed in them so as to be nothing apart from them? In that case, matter, etc., would be the only realities, just as the bricks made out of clay are the only realities in the case. Or does the fundamental reality produce these relative realities as something separate from itself and endowed with such properties that they are able to go on and conduct the cosmic order without any further aid from the fundamental reality, or would these relative realities be anything but the form under which the one and only fundamental reality founds and conducts the cosmos? Mr. Spencer's language would harmonize with the latter view, but in general these questions lay beyond his horizon, so that he never even came in sight of them, to say nothing of settling them.

In further exposition of his doctrine, the question arises, What would there be in existence if we were away? The fundamental reality would exist, but would it be doing anything in the evolution line under spatial, temporal, and material forms? If Yes, these relative realities are more than effects in us. If No, the system collapses into a subjective mirage. Without suspecting it Mr. Spencer was here in the presence of a double difficulty. The first is one that has haunted all systems of phenomenalism since the time of Kant. Such systems make phenomena subjective only, and then we are puzzled to find an objective meaning for knowledge. Phenomena are not things; and they are not *thinks*. They are not subjective in the sense of belonging to the individual, and they are not objective in the sense of being substantial realities existing apart from mind. The only way out of this puzzle lies through theistic idealism. A system of phenomena which is common-to-all, if it is only a set of individual dreams, is a contradiction unless a Supreme Mind be affirmed as its abiding seat and absolute condition.

The second difficulty lies in determining the relation of these phenomena to the Unknowable reality. If that Unknowable did nothing and remained rigidly one and changeless, there would be no assignable connection between it and the world of manifold and changing phenomena, and thus it would become useless and fictitious. And if the Unknowable acted only in transcendental ways, it would be equally worthless;

for in that case our laws of thought would be foreign to the Unknowable Reality, and there would be no way of telling how they arise or how they could be imposed upon the Unknowable, which is incommensurable with them. There is here an impassable gulf between the two factors of the system; but if we make the changes, successions, and likenesses among appearances point to corresponding changes, successions, and likenesses in the unknown reality itself, we subject the Unconditioned itself to time and change, and are in a fair way to get Mr. Mill's "prodigious amount of knowledge respecting the Unknowable." But these difficulties lay beyond Mr. Spencer's horizon. He picked up the terminology of phenomenalism as it lay at his hand and called matter and force relative realities, and forthwith they became real enough for mechanical naturalism. The deeper questions were not so much ignored as unsuspected, although they are really vital to the system. If, then, we ask what Matter, Motion, Force are, we learn that they are "symbols," "appearances," "phenomena," "relative realities"; but when we seek to determine what the terms mean, or what the relations of the things are to ourselves, on the one hand, and to the Fundamental Reality, on the other, we get no consistent information.

Having thus secured to his own satisfaction the basal ideas of physical science, Mr. Spencer proceeds to deduce its fundamental doctrines. These are the indestructibility of matter, the continuity of motion, and the persistence of force. We consider them in their order.

THE PHILOSOPHY OF SPENCER

The Indestructibility of Matter

Mr. Spencer introduces the discussion as follows: "Not because the truth is unfamiliar, is it needful here to assert the indestructibility of Matter; but partly because the symmetry of our argument demands enunciation of this truth, and partly because the evidence on which it is accepted must be examined. Could it be shown, or could it with reason be supposed, that Matter, either in its aggregates or in its units, ever becomes non-existent, it would be needful either to ascertain under what conditions it becomes non-existent, or else to confess that Science and Philosophy are impossible. For if, instead of having to deal with fixed quantities and weights, we had to deal with quantities and weights which are apt, wholly or in part, to be annihilated, there would be introduced an incalculable element, fatal to all positive conclusions. Clearly, therefore, the proposition that matter is indestructible must be deliberately considered." (Page 153.)

"Science and Philosophy" of a certain sort might be impossible in that case, but the sane and sober science that understands itself might still be possible for practical purposes. For such science a certain quantitative constancy in physical change is all that is necessary for phenomenal science, and is indeed all that we possess. Anything beyond this is simple dogmatism and can be reached only by dogmatic affirmation. In the first edition of "First Principles" the argument from experience was much fuller and Mr. Spencer had more confidence in it. He seemed then to think that experiment itself pretty solidly establishes the truth of the doctrine. In the last edition, however, while he refers to the experimental argument, he admits that the argument itself is really a begging of the question. He says: "It must be added that no experimental verification of the truth that Matter is indestructible, is possible without a tacit assumption of it. For all such verification implies weighing, and weighing assumes that the matter forming the weight remains the same." (Page 158.) He might have added that even the weighing would give different results if we changed distances from the earth. A pound at the earth's surface would only weigh four ounces four thousand miles up in the air. Manifestly, weighing gives a certain fixity of quantitative relations and has no application to the idea of substance whatever.

However, Mr. Spencer thinks that we have a higher warrant for this fundamental belief than the warrant of conscious induction, and he proceeds to develop this higher warrant by showing the doctrine to be a necessity of thought. He says: "What is termed the ultimate incompressibility of Matter, is an admitted law of thought. However small the bulk to which we conceive a piece of matter reduced, it is impossible to conceive it reduced into nothing. While we can represent to ourselves its parts as approximated, we cannot represent to ourselves the quantity of matter as made less. To do this would be to imagine some of the parts compressed into nothing; which is no more possible than to imagine compression of the whole into nothing." (Page 157.) The appeal here is to the static imagination, and seems to be successful, but if we should look at the matter dynamically, as we have to do, there seems to be no reason why matter might not disappear, not through compression of it into nothing, but at least through the weakening of its existence force, which, for all we can see, might approximate indefinitely to zero, in which case there would be something which we could represent as a vanishing of matter.

Mr. Spencer's great reliance in this matter is an a priori argument which appears in all the editions: "Our inability to conceive Matter becoming non-existent, is consequent on the nature of thought. Thought consists in the establishment of relations. There can be no relation established, and therefore no thought framed, when one of the related terms is absent from consciousness. Hence it is impossible to think of something becoming nothing, for the same reason that it is impossible to think of nothing becoming something,—the reason, namely, that nothing cannot become an object of consciousness. The annihilation of Matter is unthinkable for the same reason that the creation of matter is unthinkable." (Page 158.)

This argument has uncommon interest. If valid, it proves that everything, substances, qualities, states, acts, is eternal. To think of any one of them as beginning or ending is to compare its existence with its non-existence, which is impossible. For "thought exists in the establishment of relations," and "there can be no relation established and therefore no thought framed when one of the real terms is absent

288

from consciousness." It is also interesting as a distinct contradiction of the argument for the impossibility of religious ideas. They were found unthinkable and "pseud," because they all involve the conception of unbegun existence or existence through infinite past time. This objection was fatal in Part First; but now it turns out in Part Second, according to this argument, that only unbegun existence is conceivable. It seems, too, that we have nothing but this argument to rest upon; for Mr. Spencer adds, as already said, that no experimental verification is possible.

And after all, we are still left in the dark as to what is indestructible; for "by the indestructibility of Matter we really mean the indestructibility of the *force* with which Matter affects us." The same is said of the continuity of motion. We can easily conceive the change of position to cease, but "that which defies suppression in thought (disciplined thought, of course) is the force which the motion indicates." (Page 168.) So far as the exposition goes, matter and motion are manifestations of force, ultimately of the fundamental reality, and the argument at best gives us only the indestructibility of this fundamental force. But there is nothing to assure us that the matter and motion manifestations of this force are constant quantities; for all that appears, it is possible that force might go out of the matter and motion line altogether and yet persist in self-equality, and thus meet all Mr. Spencer's demands upon it. A firm might invest its capital in various lines and change from one to another without diminishing its capital, but the fixity of the capital does not secure the fixity of the lines of operation. Similarly, so far as appears, the fundamental reality manifesting itself in the forms of matter and motion might conceivably, while remaining equal to itself, go into other lines so that the matter and motion form would disappear. Thus these doctrines, which are declared to be foundations of science, seem to float in the air as uncertain postulates — except as that peculiar a priori argument about something and nothing supports them, and the less said about that the better. In these two chapters on the indestructibility of matter and continuity of motion, there are many errors of detail, but the leading shortcoming has been mentioned.

Another difficulty should be noted, springing out of his doctrine of the Unknowable. We might ask, What is the matter that is indestructible? Is it matter as phenomenal or matter as real? Plainly it is not the former, for the material bodies about us undergo constant change and frequently disappear altogether. Our experience of phenomenal matter is throughout a changing one, and hence the matter that is really indestructible must be the noumenal matter about which, by Mr. Spencer's earlier reasoning, we can know nothing, and of which we are permitted to say nothing. But assuming that we may say something, we are at a loss to know whether the indestructible matter is the relative reality or whether it be the absolute reality itself, and we are even in some uncertainty whether the absolute reality is anything but the relative. It is conceivable that the absolute reality should be the cause of the relative reality or that it should be expressed in the relative reality, yet in such a way as to be exhausted in it. These relative realities of matter, force, and motion might conceivably not be effects produced by the absolute reality, but the modes in which the absolute reality itself exists, and in that case, except verbally, matter, force, and motion would be all, a view which would bring us around very nearly to atheism; but on this point Mr. Spencer gives us no information. It perhaps never occurred to him.

In the chapter on "The Persistence of Force," in the last edition of "First Principles," Mr. Spencer seems to help the matter somewhat by recognizing "manifestations of force of two fundamentally-different classes" — "the force by which matter demonstrates itself to us as existing, and the force by which it demonstrates itself to us as acting." This shows that Mr. Spencer had some vague sense that his proof of the indestructibility of matter had left things at such loose ends that there was no security that the Unknowable might not close out the matter business entirely and take up some new line. But the distinction itself is purely *ad hoc*. In what way would matter, or anything else, reveal or possess any existence except by acting? Moreover, since matter itself is a "symbol" of the Unknowable Reality, all its forces must depend on that Reality, and who knows that they are constant quantities? Might not the existential force and the change-producing force of matter vary? But having suggested this distinction, and taken it for granted as possible, Mr. Spencer proceeds to show that all force is persistent. In the earlier editions he says: "The persistence of Force is an ultimate truth of which no inductive proof is possible. . . . Deeper than demonstration,—deeper even than definite cognition,—deep as the very nature of mind, is the postulate at which we have arrived. Its authority transcends all other whatever; for not only is it given in the constitution of our own consciousness, but it is impossible to imagine a consciousness so constituted as not to give it." But what is the force which is persistent? In the last edition we read: "Hence the force of which we assert persistence is that Absolute Force we are obliged to postulate as the necessary correlate of the force we are conscious of. By the Persistence of Force, we really mean the persistence of some Cause which transcends our knowledge and conception. In asserting it we assert an Unconditioned Reality, without beginning or end." (Page 176.)

This is what comes of mixing physics and metaphysics. We must inquire, first, how Mr. Spencer agrees with himself, and, secondly, how he accords with sober science. On the first point the most flagrant contradiction is manifest. The doctrine really applies to that Absolute Force, that Unconditioned Reality, of which we are constantly reminded that it is inscrutable and unknowable, and that it can never be comprehended under any of the forms of our thought. But now we begin to know somewhat about it. "Every antecedent mode of the Unknowable must have an invariable connection, quantitative and qualitative, with that mode of the Unknowable which we call its consequent." (Page 177.) This is surely an important piece of information, — to use Mr. Mill's phrase again, "a prodigious amount of knowledge respecting the Unknowable," — seeing that it carries with it the affirmation of absolute and invariable law. Moreover, "In all three cases the question is one of quantity: — Does the Matter, or Motion, or Force, ever diminish in quantity? Quantitative science implies measurement, and measurement implies a unit of measure. The units of measure from which all others of any exactness are derived, are units of linear extension." (Page 173.) It would seem, then, that the Unknowable admits not only of being known in some very important respects, but also of being measured by "units of linear extension." This is certainly constraining the ineffable and unconditioned into pretty close quarters.

The scientific value of the doctrine must next be considered. Mr. Spencer is largely regarded by his disciples as an authority in this field, and he doubtless regarded himself as setting forth in these chapters the truth as it is in science. It is doubtful, however, if an equal number of scientific blunders, or looser reasoning, can be found in any other equal space in literature claiming to be scientific. For science, the indestructibility of matter means only a certain quantitative constancy in material changes. The continuity of motion is not true at all. The conservation of energy means the dynamic equivalence of antecedents and consequents in physical change. These doctrines, so far as true, are the definite results of inductive study and dynamical reasoning; and no one would be more surprised than Lord Kelvin, or any other leader in physical science, would be, to learn that the conservation of energy is "deeper than demonstration, deeper even than definite cognition, deep as the very nature of Mind." He would be surprised enough to learn than it is "given in the constitution of our own consciousness," and that "it is impossible to conceive a consciousness so constituted as not to give it." Evidently Mr. Spencer is dealing with some other doctrine, for it would be quite absurd to say these things of an inductive doctrine which was unknown before the last generation, which is so far from being an a priori truth that it is not true at all except under certain contingent conditions, and which Mr. Spencer never understood. In his case, certainly, it was "deeper even than definite cognition." Mr. Spencer's Persistence of Force is a hybrid obtained by crossing bad metaphysics and hearsay science.

From the scientific standpoint the conservation of energy is a perfectly simple doctrine. It merely affirms a certain dynamic equivalence between antecedents and consequents in physical change. If we could measure these antecedents by some quantitative dynamic standard, and then measure the consequents by the same standard, it would appear that the two were dynamically equal. This would be the case, however, only on the assumption that the system is not in any way modified from without, and that the elements of the system are subject to certain fixed conditions. That is to say, the doctrine is a hypothetical one which is found to hold within certain limits. No careful scientist, however, thinks of erecting it into absolute dogma, or of deciding what can or cannot happen; whether, for instance, the physical system admits of being modified by volitional action from without is something the scientist would decide by observation, and not by a priori reasoning from the doctrine turned into dogma. For example, do our thoughts, purposes, and volitions count for anything in the control of our bodies, and through them count for anything in the physical world? When we erect the doctrine into a dogma, then we must say No; but when we retain the doctrine, and observe its limitations, it is entirely open to us to believe that our thoughts count for something in the ongoing of things if the facts of experience seem to point that way. Some speculators, failing to see the grotesque absurdity into which they fall, have said that our purposes and volitions count for nothing and that the physical system goes along by itself; in which case, of course, it follows that any utterance or act of their own is something which comes to pass without any direction from, or origin in, thought whatever. This is not entirely incredible in some cases, but the doctrine in general is no such grotesque affair. Even Mr. Huxley himself, who commonly had a fine sense of humor, fell into this pit when he wrote his essay "On the Hypothesis for Animal Automata." He held that our volition counts for something as a condition of the course of events, but later, in his "Collected Essays," he adds the explanatory footnote, "or to conceive more accurately, the physical state of which our volition is the expression." With this rider, it follows that volition as such counts for nothing. The line of power is through the physical state, and would be all that it is if the volition were entirely away. It follows that when Mr. Huxley read and pronounced his famous essays, or had his great encounter with the Bishop of Worcester for speaking slightingly of the doctrine of descent, the real fact was that a physical organism called, for distinction's sake, Huxley, was in such a condition that a great variety of physical changes were produced, noises were made, and divers motions initiated, yet without any intervention of thought whatever, and so far as we know even without its presence. Abstract speculators like Mr. Spencer turn the doctrine of the conservation of energy into a dogma of necessity, and they make it explain everything that comes to pass, not by any insight that the dogma gives, but for the reason that otherwise the dogma could not be maintained.

After this deduction of the doctrine which Mr. Spencer declares is strictly a priori, seeing that no inductive proof of it can be given that does not beg the question, Mr. Spencer next proceeds to discuss the Transformation and Equivalence of Forces, and this also he victoriously deduces from the Persistence of Force. And here also, as in the previous discussion, he is exceedingly unclear in his scientific ideas. This Transformation and Equivalence in sound physics means only this, that in the course of physical change the antecedents are sometimes unlike the consequents, and so the force is said to be transformed; but though transformed, the new force is dynamically equivalent to the old, and hence the doctrine of the equivalence of forces. The antecedent heat may give rise to molar motions or to electricity or to chemical action, etc., and so on through the series. Mr. Spencer concludes that this transformation is absolutely necessary, because otherwise the persistence of force would be denied, and hence he fancies that he has really deduced the forces in question. But this, too, is very doubtful. If the force that is persistent be the true Unknowable, and if the force in experience be only a manifestation of that Unknowable, there seems to be no way of declaring that the necessary persistence in the Unknowable itself must lead to necessary transformation and equivalence in the forces of experience. When Mr. Spencer's doctrine is accurately taken, it leaves us without any security for the subordinate forces, just as in the case of matter and motion we saw that it left us without any security for the constancy of matter and motion. Mr. Spencer has really here simply identified these forces with the fundamental force, or else has assumed that as manifestations they are as fixed as the Unknowable itself; and thus the doctrine becomes a pure assurance on his part without anything approaching demonstration. He has practically assumed that the manifestation in space and time is and must be continuous, and that it is rooted in the Unknowable as something from which there can be no departure. In other words, it is a piece of pure dogmatism.

In illustration of the doctrine, Mr. Spencer avails himself largely of the familiar illustrations of tracing motion into heat, electricity, magnetism, light, and back into motion again. In particular it might be pointed out that there is much confusion in popular thought, and Mr. Spencer himself is not entirely free from it in this matter, in that the attractive and repulsive forces of matter are identified with its energies. Now, the real correlation is not at all among the forces of matter, such as gravitation, affinity, magnetism, etc., but among the energies which the fundamental attributes of matter give rise to. Thus gravitation never becomes affinity, and affinity never becomes cohesion or repulsion, etc., and no one of these ever becomes motion. If we should affirm a true correlation between these forces and motion, it would be conceivable that the whole universe might upon occasion turn into motion with nothing moving. Accordingly, it was long ago pointed out that the elementary forces are entirely outside the range of correlation, but all these forces meet on the field of motion where energy of movement is produced, and there they may exchange effects in certain ways; but the qualities of the elements themselves never change into anything else, and the nature of the elements, whereby they are enabled to attract or repel or manifest the various energies of heat and light, electricity, etc., remains incommensurable.

In tracing the transformation through cosmic changes, Mr. Spencer sometimes falls into mistakes as follows: He claims that the forces which have worked out geological changes all have a given genesis, namely, the heat of the sun. The changes which have been due to aqueous agencies all come back to rain and rain to vapor, and " if we ask, How came this vapor to be at that height? the reply is, It was raised by evaporation. And if we ask, What force thus raised it? the reply is, The sun's heat." (Page 189.) It is manifest that this is an extravagance, for all that the sun's heat does in the case is simply to vaporize the water. The raising of the vapor to the height from which it fell was due to gravity itself. The sun's heat had as little to do with it as it has to do with the floating of a ship. Mr. Spencer has a goodly section on this subject, in which the sun's heat is credited with a great deal more than it ever did.

Similarly, in the case of life, the forces of the organism are one with inorganic forces. Animal life is due to vegetable life and vegetable life is due to the inorganic, and ultimately to the sun again. Here also the reasoning is a little loose. It is undoubtedly true that the forces that play in the organism may be classed with the forces outside of the organism, and that these forces would not be able to accomplish anything except under certain conditions of temperature due to solar radiation. But it is altogether possible to admit this fact and yet to hold that there is a form of energy called vital, which works under certain conditions, but which can in no way be identified with those conditions.

For a long time there was a fixed determination on the part of the mechanical theorists to reduce life to a mechanical resultant and to make it correlate with the inorganic forces. The impossibility of doing this has finally become fairly manifest. There is no doubt that the general forces of the physical system also work in the organism, and to that extent the organism comes under the will of the conservation of energy; but it is equally manifest that these forces in the organism are under some unifying and controlling law, so that they work results in the organism which they nowhere else produce. In order to explain this fact, it is necessary to find some agent somewhere which shall be the source of form and the seat of control. On the other hand, it is manifest that the activity of this something, which we may call life, would be in the main directive. It would not produce physical or chemical energies, but the physical and chemical forces would have new resultants working in connection with it. In that sense we have to affirm something in an organism that is better described as vital than mechanical.

Mr. Spencer finds himself next compelled to identify mental and social forces as being transformations of the inorganic forces, or the forces that work in the inorganic field. He is a little uncertain here as to what the transformation or identification is. Thus he says in the earlier editions, "Those modes of the Unknowable which we call motion, heat, light, chemical affinity, etc., are alike transformable into each other, and into those modes of the Unknowable which we distinguish as sensation, emotion, thought: these, in their turns, being directly or indirectly re-transformable into the original shapes. That no idea or feeling arises, save as a result of some physical force expended in producing it, is fast becoming a commonplace of science; and whoever duly weighs the evidence will see that nothing but an overwhelming bias in favor of a preconceived theory can explain its non-acceptance. How this metamorphosis takes place — how a force existing as motion, heat, or light can become a mode of consciousness — how it is possible for aerial vibrations to generate the sensation we call sound, or for the forces liberated by chemical changes in the brain to give rise to emotion — these are mysteries which it is impossible to fathom. But they are not profounder mysteries than the transformations of the physical forces into each other." This appeared in the earlier editions. (Page 280, First Edition.) In the last edition the matter is a little modified, but not essentially changed.

This passage gives rise to some questions. The statement, that the change of the physical forces into thought and feeling is no more mysterious than the change of physical forces into one another, would not seem to be strictly true from Mr. Spencer's own standpoint; because the physical forces are regarded by him as modes of motion, and the change of one mode of motion into another is not obviously mysterious. Thus, rectilinear motion might become circular motion and motion might increase or diminish in velocity, and there seems to be no great mystery in the matter; but when that which is motion becomes that which is not motion, but sensation or feeling, we really seem to be introduced to a mystery of a higher order. But apart from this, in the view set forth, heat, light, etc., seem to be regarded as becoming sensation, motion, thought, so that the physical system at that moment loses something which passes into the non-physical form of mental states; and when the direction is reversed, then the physical system gains something from the return of the energy in mental states into the physical field again. This was the conception maintained by Dr. Carpenter, among others, of the doctrine of transformation, and he pointed out that in such an order we must really fix our thought upon the highest member of the series as the essential one, for if the lower forms can become the higher, it must mean that they are essentially the same as the higher from the start. We can easily conceive that a higher force might work in the form of a lower one, but we cannot conceive that a force which is essentially lower could raise itself to the higher levels. Accordingly, Dr. Carpenter held that the real force in nature, while taking on lower forms and passing down into the inorganic forms of mechanical nature, is all the while essentially correlated with the will, which is the true force in nature. The lower forces, then, are but conditioned manifestations of a supreme will from which they spring. Mr. Spencer's view, as set forth, would make a similar suggestion possible. Heat, light, etc., become sensation, emotion, and thought, and it would be quite possible from a logical standpoint to hold that the latter are the truly real forms and that the former are only these higher forms appearing in lower manifestations. But Mr. Spencer himself did not seem to hold such a view, although, even, in the last edition of "First Principles," he is unwilling to admit that mental states count for nothing in the physical ongoing. He refers to Professor Huxley's doctrine, that consciousness is outside the series of nervous changes and does not form a link in the physical chain, but is simply a "concomitant" or "collateral product." This Mr. Spencer regards as excessive, and seems inclined to think that feelings have real significance in the world of change. He says:

"Sundry facts appear to imply that consciousness is needful as an initiator in cases where there are no external stimuli to set up the coördinated nervous changes: the nervous structures, though capable of doing everything required if set going, are not set going unless there arises an idea. Now, this implies that an idea, or coördinated set of feelings, has the power of working changes in the nervous centres and setting up motions: the state of consciousness is a factor: . . . Once more, there is the question, If feeling is not a factor, how is its existence to be accounted for? To any one who holds in full the Cartesian doctrine that animals are automata, and that a howl no more implies feeling than does the bark of a toy dog, I have nothing to say. But whoever does not hold this, is obliged to hold that, as we ascribe anger and affection to our fellow men, though we literally know no such feelings save in ourselves, so must we ascribe them to animals under like conditions. If so, however, — if feelings are not factors, and the appropriate actions might be automatically performed without them, — then, on the supernatural hypothesis, it must be assumed that feelings were given to animals for no purpose, and on the natural hypothesis it must be assumed that they have arisen to do nothing." (Page 199.)

Here Mr. Spencer seems to take sides against Mr. Huxley's doctrine of animal automatism, and to insist that consciousness itself is one of the dynamic factors. At the same time, in his "Psychology" he seems to regard the mental states as a kind of inner face of the physical conditions and as truly counting for nothing in the physical movement. Ideas are spoken of as the inner aspect of nascent motor excitations in the ganglia, and the impression is given, not that physical and mental states are different things, but rather that they are different aspects of the same fact, which fact, moreover, is essentially physical, namely, a certain grouping of matter and motion. Thus Mr. Spencer leaves us somewhat in doubt, after all, as to including the mental life within the dynamic series. Some of his statements look that way and others look in the opposite direction. Possibly this was due to the fact that a very general desire possessed many of the naturalistic speculators to keep the physical series complete in itself. Any other view they regarded as a break of continuity, and this was the unpardonable sin. Professor Clifford stigmatized the theory that the physical series loses anything to pass into a mental series, or gains anything from a mental series outside itself, as the notion of a savage. He held that the physical series strictly goes along by itself, neither losing nor gaining anything from beyond itself, but moving in such a way that each physical antecedent is dynamically reproduced in the physical consequent and each such consequent can be traced to its physical antecedent. This became the general doctrine, for a time, of thinkers of this class, and Mr. Spencer oscillated rather confusedly between them. What we have just quoted respecting Professor Huxley's automatism makes feelings dynamic, but the notion of mental states as the inner aspect of physical states deprives them of all proper dynamic character. We shall return to this point later when treating of the theory of psycho-physical parallelism.

We might also point out, before leaving the subject, that, after all, Mr. Spencer does not properly make out any correlation or identification of the physical and the mental series in any case. When he gets into the psychological field, the Unknowable is presented as having two phases, a subjective aspect and an objective one, neither of which can be reduced to the other. In that case, without some further reason than has been given us, it would be possible to think that the subjective aspect, as shown in life and thought, might come from the subjective phase of the Unknowable, while the physical aspect of the world comes from the objective phase, and between these there will be no more interaction than there was in Spinoza's doctrine of the one substance with the two incommunicable attributes.

Thus, we see that Mr. Spencer is as vague and cloudy in his conception of force and the relations of the forces as in his notions of the relative realities, to which we have before referred. Nothing is clearly conceived or precisely stated, but everything seems to be continually on the point of changing into something else, the confusion being covered up by an imposing terminology which has an air of perpetually saying the right thing and hitting the nail on the head, without, however, doing so.

In leaving this subject of the persistence of force, reference may be made to a doctrine which never seems to have come within Mr. Spencer's view. The conservation of energy as a scientific doctrine is well known to be one that looks towards the running-down of a system rather than its eternal working. For a time the doctrine was thought to have proved the possibility of ceaseless energizing, and this, when combined with the indestructibility of matter, appeared to demonstrate at last the eternity of the physical system. This, however, was soon set aside by the discovery of what Lord Kelvin called the dissipation of energy, or, better, the degradation of energy. The continuance of the present dynamic system is as dependent upon the differentiation of energy as upon its conservation. As far as the meaning of the law is concerned, energy is energy, no matter what its forms; but in fact energy has many forms, as heat, light, molar motion, etc. And here the surprising fact comes out that, while it is easy to pass from some forms to some others, it is not so easy to pass back. This is preëminently the case with heat. Other forms can be entirely transformed into heat, but heat cannot be entirely re-transformed into other forms. There is as much energy as before, but it cannot be used; for heat can do work only when there is an inequality of temperature, as water can do work only when there is a difference of elevation. If water stood at the same level all around the world, there would be no loss of water, but water power would cease. Heat follows the same law, and cannot do work when it has the same level in all bodies. Now, this law points to a cessation of transformation, and therefore to the running-down of the universe as a dynamic system. A little relief might be found for a time in the wreck and clash of solar systems, until all the matter within the [range] of gravitation was gathered into one great effete lump. It and the ether may be supposed to have conserved all their energy, but to no purpose, as the transformation of energy has become impossible. We may suppose some unknown relief from this conclusion, but it must be admitted that so far as knowledge goes everything points to the running-down of the dynamic system.

Mr. Spencer, as said, has not considered this fact, unless we suppose that his chapter on "Equilibration" is such consideration. He there points out that physical processes must finally come to an end, generally for reasons unconnected with the law of energy. In a single passage, however, he does connect these final equilibrations with the persistence of force, and that only makes matters worse for his system. If by the persistence of force we mean the fundamental reality itself, we can hardly hold that it is ever going to run down, because its persistence is declared to be "deeper than demonstration, deeper even than definite knowledge, deep as the very nature of the mind itself." Hence the force that is going to run down must be something derived, and this introduces us again to our old puzzles about the relative realities and their relation to the Unknowable. This simply adds one more uncertainty to Mr. Spencer's doctrine.

Having thus established the principle of the persistence of force, Mr. Spencer proceeds to prove a rich variety of propositions. The first deduction is the uniformity of law. He says: "Every antecedent mode of the Unknowable must have an invariable connection, quantitative and qualitative, with that mode of the Unknowable which we call its consequent. For to say otherwise is to deny the persistence of force." (Page 177.) This is another case of dogmatic metaphysics for which no sufficient warrant can be found except in Mr. Spencer's own mind. The physical doctrine of the conservation of energy assumes the indestructibility of matter and the constancy of the laws of force, and on this basis it concludes to a constancy of certain dynamic relations. In itself, it warrants no metaphysical affirmation concerning the nature of matter or the uniformity of law. A more interesting application of the principle is found in the chapter on "The Direction of Motion." Simple reflection on the notion of energy reveals no differentiations in it. No such reflection, for instance, reveals that energy must appear in the various forms of light, heat, electricity, etc. This is a fact to be discovered by experience and not something that can be deduced. Similarly, the work which the energy shall do cannot be decided by any a priori reflection upon them. The energies themselves are capable of acting in a great variety of cases, so as to produce the most widely differing effects. We need, therefore, in order to get any insight into the order of things, to find some principle of direction. Some persons have thought to find this principle in intelligence, perhaps, and choice, but Mr. Spencer thinks otherwise, and proceeds to expound the principle in this chapter on "The Direction of Motion," which he says must always take the direction of the line of least resistance. This chapter is, in effect, anti-teleological, and serves to exclude all teleological interpretation.

The principle itself is somewhat of an axiom for mechanical matters, especially when we determine the line of least resistance by the direction of the motion. The principle is first traced in the inorganic world. It is then traced through organic forms, mental phenomena, social groups and movements, industrial combinations and differentiations, the movements of capital, changes of legislation, etc. These are all declared to be motions of one sort or another, and of course must follow the line of least resistance. To be sure, we cannot by reflecting on the line of least resistance discover any of these things contained in it. No reflection, for instance, on the mechanical axiom that motion takes place along the line of least resistance would reveal to us that the line must be such as to lead to the building-up of an organism, with its various parts, or to industrial changes, or to the adoption of legislation, of the dispatch of an army; but by means of a somewhat violent rhetoric we can regard these things as cases of motion and refer them to the line of least resistance, and then there is no longer any room for protest or anything to wonder about. Things must follow this line of least resistance, and the line could not have been otherwise or other-where than it is, for to suppose that it could is to deny the persistence of force. To reach any other result whatever, some force must have acted which did not or some force must have failed to act which did; and as this is impossible, everything must be as it is. In all this Mr. Spencer verily thought he was talking the language of science, whereas he was simply announcing the metaphysical dogma of necessity and using it as a means of warding off all inquiry. He gives an appearance of reasoning to some of his utterances, but the gist of it consists in falling back on the assumption of necessity. The following is an illustration: —

"Organic form is the result of motion."

"Motion takes the direction of least resistance."

"Therefore, organic form is the result of motion in the direction of least resistance." (Page 214.)

If any one had thought that organic form was a complicated matter, involving such complexity as to demand some principle of intelligence for the arrangement of its parts, he would now see from this beautifully simple syllogism how mistaken he was, and how the organic world necessarily results from elementary mechanical laws. The major premise is undeniable, the minor premise is a mechanical axiom, and the conclusion necessarily follows. To be sure, we cannot by any reflection on those laws deduce the result, but by reflection on the result we see that it must come under the law.

But the argument admits of endless application. Thus the writing of a book, say "Paradise Lost," is the result of motion in the direction of least resistance. The argument is just as good in one case as in the other, and in both cases we might say that the persistence of force demands this result. The product could not have been otherwise unless some force had acted which did not or some force had failed to act which did, and this would have been impossible, for the persistence of force forbids it. We see, then, that teleological questions may never be raised. We are in the midst of a scheme of necessity, and necessity knows no teleology. Here everything is driven from behind and nothing is led from before. There is only metaphysical causality from the past, there is no final causality which looks toward the future. This is the purely verbal trap into which Romanes fell when he wrote "The Candid Examination of Theism." Romanes escaped; Spencer never escaped, but continued to think he was talking pure speculation and deep science. Anything more naïve, whether from the scientific or the philosophic standpoint, it would be hard to find. In the work referred to, Romanes pointed out that theistic argument was worthless, because the persistence of force forbade it. The argument presupposes that things might have been otherwise, whereas they could not have been otherwise; and since they could not have been otherwise, there was nothing to wonder about. He afterward saw through the verbalism, and at the time of his death was engaged in the writing of a book to recall his earlier work. He must have felt, after coming to himself, like a man who had surrendered his valuables on being menaced with a wooden pistol. It is almost incredible that Mr. Spencer should have failed to see the superficiality of this chapter on the direction of motion, and the fact that a great many unlike things are brought together under a common word without giving them the slightest essential likeness. The principle is exemplified, as before said, in the inorganic world; then comes the deduction of organic form already given; then mental phenomena are declared to be subject to the same law; voluntary acts are next included; social aggregations and social changes are likewise brought under the law, and here we have some very familiar matter adduced in illustration. For example: —

"Fertile valleys, where water and vegetal products abound, are early peopled. Seashores, too, supplying much easily gathered food, are lines along which mankind have commonly spread. The general fact that, so far as we can judge from the traces left by them, large societies first appeared in those warm regions where the fruits of the earth are obtainable with comparatively little exertion, and where the cost of maintaining bodily heat is but slight, is a fact of like meaning. ... Similarly, with that resistance to the movements of a society which neighboring societies offer. Each of the tribes or nations inhabiting any region, increases in numbers until it outgrows its means of subsistence.... And the wars that result — the conquests of weaker tribes or nations, and the overrunning of their territories by the victors — are instances of social movements taking place in the directions of least resistance. Nor do the conquered peoples, when they escape extermination or enslavement, fail to show us movements which are similarly determined . . . . Internal social movements also may be thus interpreted. Localities naturally fitted for producing particular commodities — that is, localities in which such commodities are got at the least cost of energy — that is, localities in which the desires for these commodities meet with the least resistance; become localities devoted to the obtainment of these commodities. Where soil and climate render wheat a profitable crop, or a crop from which the greatest amount of life-sustaining power is gained by a given quantity of effort, the growth of wheat becomes a dominant industry. Where wheat cannot be economically produced, oats, or rye, or maize, or potatoes, or rice, is the agricultural staple. Along seashores men support themselves with least effort by catching fish, and hence, fishing becomes the occupation. And in places which are rich in coal or metallic ores, the population, finding that labor expended in raising these materials brings a larger return of food and clothing than when otherwise expended, becomes a population of miners. This last instance introduces us to the phenomena of exchange, which equally illustrate the general law. . . . Movement in the direction of least resistance is also seen in the establishment of the channels, along which intercourse takes place. At the outset, when goods are carried on the backs of men and horses, the paths chosen are those which combine shortness with levelness and freedom from obstacles — those which are achieved with the smallest exertion. . . . All subsequent improvements, ending in macadamized roads, canals, and railways, which reduce the antagonism of friction and gravity to a minimum, exemplify the same truth. . . . To say that artisans flock to places where, in consequence of facilities for production, an extra proportion of produce can be given in the shape of wages, is to say that they flock to places where there are the smallest obstacles to the support of themselves and families; and so growth of the social organism takes place where the resistance is least.

"Nor is the law less clearly to be traced in those functional changes daily going on. The flow of capital into businesses yielding the largest returns, the buying

in the cheapest market and selling in the dearest, the
introduction of more economical modes of manufac-
ture, the development of better agencies for distribu-
tion, exhibit movements taking place in directions
where they are met by the smallest totals of opposing
forces. For if we analyze each of these changes, — if
instead of interest on capital we read surplus of products which remains after maintenance of laborers, —
if we thus interpret large interest or large surplus to
imply labor expended with the greatest results, —
and if labor expended with the greatest results means
muscular action so directed as to evade obstacles as
far as possible, — we see that all these commercial
phenomena imply complicated motions set up along
lines of least resistance." (Pages 220–24.)

One would not have thought that so much was contained in this line of least resistance. Men live most
where they can live best. Hence, strangely enough,
they settle on good soil, on fertile river bottoms, instead of in desert places. Fishermen live along the
seashore instead of on top of hills or in the interior.
Men raise wheat where they can get most of a crop
and where it pays best. They also mine, it would
seem, in regions where there are mineral deposits.
They work, too, where they can get the most wages.
In making roads they pick out, all things considered,
the line of least resistance. When men go into business, they select the forms which promise the highest
returns, etc., etc. It is not easy at first to see how all
the various phenomena of social life can be gathered
under the one principle that motion takes place along
lines of least resistance, and indeed, they cannot well be

thus gathered except by the use of some violent metaphors whereby a mechanical principle is stretched to cover things to which it has no resemblance. But if reflections of this kind should occur to us, all doubt is completely driven away by remembering that nothing could have been otherwise unless some force had acted which did not act or some other force had failed to act which did act; and as this would contradict the persistence of force, we see with the utmost clearness that all these things come under this one principle and there is nothing left to wonder about. Reflection on the direction of motion along lines of least resistance of itself leads to nothing, but when we see the direction that motion takes, we can conclude that this must have been the line of least resistance, and then we understand everything, from the simplest mechanical change up through all individual and social action in all its details.

Thus we have the foundation stone of Mr. Spencer's system. Space, time, matter, motion, and force are given as the material out of which the system is to be built, and then we have the principle of the indestructibility of matter, the persistence of force, the correlation and equivalence of forces given as principles according to which the building is to go on. When closely considered, all of these things are left very vague and uncertain, but the one thing that is clear is that no questions may be asked or objections raised, lest we contradict the persistence of force, that is, in Mr. Spencer's understanding of the term.

And now that we have these foundation stones, we might raise one more question as to what Mr. Spencer aims to do, and here again we shall find the old uncertainty continuing. At the close of the volume on "First Principles," we have the following words: "Over and over again it has been shown, in various ways, that the deepest truths we can reach, are simply statements of the widest uniformities in our experiences of the relations of Matter, Motion, and Force; and that Matter, Motion, and Force are but symbols of the Unknown Reality. A Power of which the nature remains forever inconceivable, and to which no limits in Time or Space can be imagined, works in us certain effects. These effects have certain likenesses of kind, the most general of which we class together under the names of Matter, Motion, and Force; and between these effects there are likenesses of connection, the most constant of which we class as laws of the highest certainty. Analysis reduces these several kinds of effect to one kind of effect; and these several kinds of uniformity to one kind of uniformity. And the highest achievement of Science is the interpretation of all orders of phenomena, as differently-conditioned manifestations of this one kind of effect, under differently-conditioned modes of this one kind of uniformity. But when Science has done this, it has done nothing more than systematize our experiences, and has in no degree extended the limits of our experiences. We can say no more than before, whether the uniformities are as absolutely necessary as they have become to our thought relatively necessary. The utmost possibility for us is an interpretation of the process of things as it presents itself to our limited consciousness; but how this process is related to the actual process we are unable to conceive, much less to know. Similarly, it must be remembered that while the connection between the phenomenal order and the ontological order is forever inscrutable; so is the connection between the conditioned forms of being and the unconditioned form of being forever inscrutable. The interpretation of all phenomena in terms of Matter, Motion, and Force, is nothing more than the reduction of our complex symbols of thought to the simplest symbols; and when the equation has been brought to its lowest terms, the symbols remain symbols still." (Page 509.)

This is as confused as it is well meant. Once more, matter, motion, and force are declared to be effects in us; in which case evolution is only a process in us, and how it is "related to the actual process apart from us we are unable to conceive." These "conditioned forms of being," of which he speaks, are everywhere identified with Matter, Motion, and Force, which appear to be apart from us. Then, to complete the confusion, they are said to be "symbols of thought," and thus are made subjective again. But this point will be discussed in the next section. Here it is to be observed that the conception of explanation that runs through the paragraph is classification. This is definitely said to be the aim and end of investigation. We are, then, to arrange all of our facts under the heads of matter, motion, and force, and when this is done, we have done all that is possible. The interpretation of all phenomena in these terms is nothing more than the reduction of our complex symbols of thought to the simplest symbols, and when the equation has been brought to its lowest terms, the symbols remain symbols still. But explanation by classification is the very lowest form of explanation and really tells us nothing. It merely puts things together under certain heads of likeness and separates them into different classes, but all the while brings us no nearer to any new insight. So far, then, as this paragraph goes, we might in a way make Mr. Spencer a present of his result at the start. We are to make three classes of matter, motion, and force, of whose inner [nature] we know nothing except this, that it is totally unlike any conception we can form, and [as to] which things, moreover, we are left uncertain whether they be anything but effects in us. But granting that the classification is rightly objective, it is quite surprising to see how very little it tells us. It simply says that all things may be classed under one or another of these three heads. How their differences arise, which is a very important fact of the problem of experience, is entirely overlooked, because the differences themselves are entirely ignored. All material things may, indeed, be classed as groups of matter. A stone is a grouping. A living body is a grouping. The various machines of human invention are groupings. Houses, books, assemblies, etc., are verily cases of groupings of matter, and so we put them all together as cases of matter and motion. But a classification so general as this includes everything at the expense of meaning nothing. We might go on and include everything in the one class of the thinkable, and thus at one stroke all things would be made one. In all classification it is necessary to make sure that our work pays expenses.

318

THE INDESTRUCTIBILITY OF MATTER

There are classes and classes. Some classification is helpful, and some is so general as to be at once true and worthless. Moreover, it is far from clear how Mr. Spencer would apply this classification of all things as matter, motion, and force to life and thought and the intellectual world in general. Our conceptions are cases of matter and motion. Do we get any insight into a religious aspiration, a moral resolve, a patriotic devotion, by saying that these are cases of matter and motion? In truth, we shall see that Mr. Spencer did not confine himself to explanation by classification, but went on to something quite different; but the passage quoted serves to show how uncertain Mr. Spencer was as to his own aims.

Mr. Spencer's ideas in both physics and metaphysics were in the highest degree vague and confused. Just where precision is needed, some semi-rhetorical or metaphorical term is introduced, and we are left to grope for the meaning. There is something cramping to free movement in rigorous philosophic criticism and the precision of the mathematico-physical sciences. But possibly his genius will find a more congenial field in the broader regions of biology and sociology, and in those great evolutionary generalizations with which his name is inseparably connected. Mr. Spencer is preëminently the apostle of evolution and the great formulator of its law. Here, at all events, the disciples feel safe in giving way to their enthusiasm. We now consider his formula of evolution.

III

THE LAW OF EVOLUTION

In the first edition of "First Principles," Mr. Spencer formulated the law of evolution as follows: "Evolution is a change from an indefinite, incoherent homogeneity, to a definite, coherent heterogeneity; through continuous differentiations and integrations." (Page 216.) But this formula was highly abstract, and it was not easy to tell what the homogeneity and the heterogeneity were. It seemed to make no connection whatever with physical science. Moreover differentiation and integration also belong to those vague phrases which apply to everything without meaning much of anything; in fact, there is nothing in the heavens above or the earth beneath or in the waters under the earth in which differentiation and integration could not be traced. To screen the ashes from the furnace, to wet the flower bed, to wash one's hands, to walk about, to trim one's beard, to dress or undress, anything and everything might be brought under the head of differentiation and integration, if it were worth while. To obviate some of these difficulties, Mr. Spencer changed the definition in the second and later editions and left out differentiation and integration altogether. In the new form the definition runs as follows: "Evolution is an integration of matter and concomitant dissipation of motion, during which the matter passes from an indefinite, incoherent homogeneity, to a definite, coherent heterogeneity; and during which the retained motion undergoes a parallel transformation." In the last edition of "First Principles," Mr. Spencer fills one hundred and fifteen pages in leading up to this distinction.

This formula is to be examined, first, for meaning, and secondly, for value. In seeking to fix the meaning, we must again point out the uncertain character and whereabouts of matter and motion in Mr. Spencer's scheme. They are called symbols and relative realities, and are declared to be effects produced in us by the Unknowable. But in that case, as already pointed out, evolution has no objective significance, since all its factors are only effects in us — having an objective cause, indeed, but no objective counterpart or correspondence. This would never do, as it would land us in "the insanities of idealism." But if we make matter and motion objective "symbols" of the Unknowable, we are quite at a loss to know in what sense they are symbols. A real thing may be made a symbol of something else by mutual agreement of persons, as in telegraphic signals, but its symbolism has nothing to do with its existence. The symbolism exists only as a convention of the persons concerned, and is nothing in itself. When, then, matter and motion are called symbols, one is at a loss to know in what their symbolic character consists and for whom they are symbols. The integration of matter and dissipation of motion we can understand, when there are real moving things in space, but the integration and dissipation of symbols are unclear notions. If they are symbols, like the devices of mathematical mechanics for describing and summing up the order of experience, they are nothing in themselves, and have no more objectivity than a volume of differential and integral formulas. If, on the other hand, they are objective modes of the unknowable, we are left in some concern lest the unknowable be expressed and exhausted in these modes so as to be nothing apart from them; in which case we fall into materialism and atheism again. It will be noticed that in the definition both the Persistent Force and the Unknowable fail to appear, and nothing is left but Matter and Motion as the sole facts in the evolutionary process. To escape this result, we must continue to call them "symbols," "aspects," "relative realities," and when we do so are quite at a loss to understand our own meaning or to locate the evolutionary process.

To the popular naturalistic speculator, of course, this is unintelligible metaphysics, and we forbear. But, leaving these obscurities, the formula is still unclear in its meaning. When the homogeneity is said to be indefinite and incoherent, is it such in itself, or only with reference to some standard of our own? In the latter case the change is purely relative to ourselves again, and represents no truly objective progress. But, if it be indefinite and incoherent in itself, is it such for our senses or for the reason? In the former case we mistake appearance for reality. If indefinite and incoherent for the reason, what do the terms mean? Do they mean the absence of all definite property, law, and relation? Such a homogeneity would be nothing. Yet they must mean that or become simply relative to our plans, or senses, or powers of perception, and lose all objective significance. And the homogeneous, too, — what shall we make of that? Is it essentially or only apparently homogeneous? In the former case, it has no motion in it and refuses to differentiate. In the latter case, there is no real homogeneous, for all later differences are implicit from the start. These questions — and they are only samples of the swarming difficulties — show how confused the formula is, and how hard it is to fix a consistent and permissible meaning. And when logic has been appeased, physics objects. What is meant by the integration of matter and concomitant dissipation of motion? Certainly motion is nothing that can fly off by itself and leave matter behind. This part of the definition applies only to the contraction of a physical system through cooling, and presupposes the ether as something apart, to make it possible. The value of the formula must be declared zero. It is one of those showy generalizations which are so vague as to include everything at the expense of meaning nothing. What is there, as said, in the heavens above or the earth beneath that cannot be viewed as a case of differentiation or integration? And how much wiser is any one after such a view? Only a lover of Barmecide feasts could find satisfaction in such an unsubstantial mockery and barren show of wisdom. The formula itself leads to no insight. We merely gather under it the facts which we have elsewhere learned, without gaining any additional insight or control. That the terms mean the same thing when we are speaking of physical, mental, social, industrial, political changes is taken for granted; and all of these, on the theory, are cases of the integration of matter and concomitant dissipation of motion.

But at best, the formula is only a description. We see no reason why there should be such an order of change. Why should things move in this direction, or, indeed, move at all? This insight is furnished in the principles of the Instability of the Homogeneous, the Multiplication of Effects and Segregation, or, as Mr. Spencer sometimes calls it, the integration of correspondences. These are the principles of movement and combination in the system. On them Mr. Spencer relies to get the evolution process under way. In these principles there is a kind of parallel to the principles in Hegel's system. According to Hegel, the idea is in unstable equilibrium and tends to pass into its opposite, and thus contradict itself. This result is escaped by uniting the idea and its opposite in a higher conception. Accordingly, his scheme consists of thesis and antithesis and synthesis, each thesis producing its antithesis, and these are united in a higher synthesis, and so on indefinitely. There is a species of mechanical parallel to this in Mr. Spencer's principles. The homogeneous is unstable and passes into the heterogeneous, and then, through segregation, there is a union of opposites in some higher form, and thus the system tends to move and progress. We now consider the value of these principles.

The instability of the homogeneous is distinctly false as a general principle of thought or mechanics. Nothing whatever is unstable because it is homogeneous, but for some other reason. Iron is homogeneous and rusts. Gold or platinum is homogeneous and does not rust. Nitro-glycerine or chloride of nitrogen is heterogeneous and very unstable. Neither homogeneity nor heterogeneity has anything to do with the results, but the positive relations of chemical affinity are alone responsible. Ether is said to be supremely homogeneous, but is very stable; and indeed the homogeneous, mechanically considered, must in so far be stable, except as it is acted upon by heterogeneous forces from without. Conceiving the universe as a homogeneous whole, it must be alike in all its parts and relations. If there were differences of density or energy or direction or motion in different parts, it would be [to this degree] heterogeneous and not homogeneous. But if thus alike in all its parts, or thus symmetrically arranged, it would plainly be in balance, and without something to overturn the equilibrium would remain balanced forever. Mr. Spencer gives multitudinous examples in which the homogeneous thing is in the presence of unequal forces, and the resulting change is supposed to illustrate the instability of the homogeneous. Thus, he says a pair of scales will never remain balanced for long. One arm or the other is sure to ascend, and this is supposed to illustrate the principle; whereas, manifestly, the reason for the fact is that the arms of the scales are not strictly equal or not strictly subject to the same influences; it is heterogeneity and not homogeneity that explains the motion. Again, a vessel full of water becomes heterogeneous through the formation of distinct currents in it, but here, too, it is not homogeneity, but heterogeneity of the incident forces that explain the effect. Were the heat equal or symmetrically complete throughout the body of water, we should have no currents. The examples given illustrate instability in general and not any special instability of the homogeneous. And the argument for the principle leads to the same result. For this principle is said to be a corollary of the Persistence of Force, and this leads to constant change. Change is as continuous in the heterogeneous as in the homogeneous, but the changing heterogeneous is heterogeneous still, while the changing homogeneous is homogeneous no longer. In the latter case the name changes as well as the thing. In the former case the name does not change; but in both cases the thing changes. The change of name in one case and its constancy in the other led Mr. Spencer to think he had discovered a principle. This is well shown by an illustration given in earlier editions, but omitted in the last. The planets do not move in circular orbits, which are said to be homogeneous and would be unstable, but in elliptical orbits, which are said to be both heterogeneous and stable. The fact is that any lapse from a circular orbit makes it noncircular, but a lapse from an elliptical orbit may leave it still elliptical. This is the case with the planets. They never move in the same orbit from one instant to another, but the varying orbits admit of being reduced to a mean orbit for purposes of calculation and are all ellipses. Hence the delusion of special stability. With such science and logic one may deduce principles to order. Both the reasoning and the highly heterogeneous collection of illustrations point to instability in general, in the heterogeneous as well as in the homogeneous; and when we take the system as a whole, reflection shows that homogeneity and heterogeneity can never be increased or diminished by any action of mechanical or necessary forces. If we reason back from heterogeneity, we never come to homogeneity, but are compelled to make the heterogeneity implicit from the start. If we reason forward from homogeneity, we cannot get it to move at all. The necessary logical equivalence of cause and effect in any mechanical scheme forbids any progress. But of this also Mr. Spencer never dreamed, and under the influence of the fallacy of the universal, he passed back and forth between the homogeneous and the heterogeneous with the utmost facility and without suspecting the verbal character of the process.

Professor James Ward, in his work, "Naturalism and Agnosticism," several years ago subjected this "principle" of the Instability of the Homogeneous to a very thorough overhauling, with the result that Mr. Spencer in the last edition adds a note saying that the word "relatively" should be introduced into the definition of evolution before each of the antithetical clauses. The statement should be that "the matter passes from a *relatively* indefinite, incoherent homogeneity to a *relatively* definite, coherent heterogeneity." This does not mend the matter in the least; for logic shows that in such a system there can be no increase of heterogeneity by any action of the forces within the system itself. But the logic and metaphysics of change lay far below Mr. Spencer's soundings. When next Mr. Spencer asks if a chicken is not more heterogeneous than an egg, the answer is Yes, for the senses, and No, for the understanding; for without an immanent organic law in the egg which implied all the heterogeneities of the chicken, the chicken would not exist. In short, at any point in the past of an impersonal mechanical scheme we are bound to find all its future products in latent potentiality. If a nebula was one phase of that past, then all future products were latent in the nebula; and they were evolved only because they were potentially there. In that case, for thought there is no real progress or explanation, but only a successive manifestation of the original potentialities and implications of the system.

These considerations dispense with an examination of the two other principles mentioned. They are equally superficial and verbal and without scientific character. The Multiplication of Effects means only that, when change is once set up in the homogeneous; it proceeds more rapidly thereafter because each change becomes a ground for other changes and thus effects are multiplied. In Segregation we have his principle of combination. The two former principles tend to differentiation, and of themselves might produce chaos. This is prevented by the third principle of segregation. According to this, like tends to get with like and is then stable. Illustrations abound. In the fall the wind segregates the dead and dying leaves from a tree and leaves the green ones behind, and this is segregation. At the delta of rivers the heavier matter brought down by the current is first deposited, then the lighter, and finally, still farther out, the lightest mud, and this is segregation. When wheat and chaff are thrown up against the wind, there is also segregation. In the same way we present segregation in society, in trade, and all the divisions of labor that mark essential progress. Thus, combination and order are explained by this principle. But all of this is verbal, and unless carefully handled the principle of segregation contradicts the instability of the homogeneous, as the former seems bent on producing homogeneities, while the latter is busy in overturning them. But assuming the principles, another question arises respecting the direction of these changes. Supposing that the homogeneous must lapse into the heterogeneous, it does not follow that it must lapse into an orderly heterogeneous rather than a chaotic one. Or, supposing that there must be segregation, why should it not be amorphous segregation? The principles are quite as compatible with chaos as with creation. If they are to escape chaos, it can only be as the principles are such in the conditions of their working, that order, and the actual order, is implicit and necessary from the start. Mere change, as such, contains no principle of direction and no progress. Change might well be of a kaleidoscopic kind in which one form succeeds another form, but in which there is no movement toward an end. This question of direction, which is essentially the question of selective and directive intelligence in the cosmos, is ignored by Mr. Spencer except so far as the chapter on "The Direction of Motion" may be viewed as an answer. There it is pointed out, as already noticed, that motion must take place along the line of least resistance. All mechanical, vital, mental, and essential phenomena are identified as cases of motion, and hence are subject to the law. They could not, then, be otherwise without denying the persistence of force, which is the deepest of all truths. Thus, all things are simply called necessary, and there is nothing left to wonder about. There is no *why* to necessity, and no room for wonder. When, then, all things are seen to be necessary, teleology is out of place. Here Mr. Spencer erects a misunderstood doctrine of inductive science into an absolute and all-embracing necessity without any suspicion of the baselessness and suicidal nature of the performance. Force, then, is ever weaving and unweaving and all things pass. There is no room for stability of any kind except so far as we assume it or take it for granted. When we ask for the ground of purposelike combination in living things, Mr. Spencer goes a little way in trying to illustrate them as cases of these principles. The homogeneous germ, if unstable, falls into heterogeneity, and of the heterogeneities thus produced, the like get together and thus the organism results. Of course this is purely an assurance, for no one can trace these principles into actual results; but a veto is issued against raising any further questions, because to assume that things might have been otherwise is to presuppose that some force might have acted which did not, or some force might have failed to act which did, and this would deny the persistence of force, which is impossible. Thus we suddenly return to the doctrine of a blind necessity because of which everything is as it is because it must be. We cannot, indeed, see that it must be, but we are told it must be, and no further questions must be asked. No mind, then, is needed, but only a power. Everything flows from the persistence

of force, by ways that are, indeed, dark and sub-
terranean, so far as logic goes; but we are forbidden
to raise any questions under penalty of rebuke for
denying the persistence of force. It might be pointed
out that, since this is the gist of his argument, Mr.
Spencer might well have dispensed with a large part
of his argumentation, as it really gives us no insight.
For whenever difficulties arise, we are told that the
persistence of force makes it necessary that things
should be as they are; and in that case we might as
well have been told that at the start, and the many
volumes of the Synthetic Philosophy need not have
been written, unless, indeed, the persistence of force
required it. From the logical point of view, and so
far as insight goes, it all amounts simply to saying
that the system of things is necessary and hence must
be as it is and could not be otherwise. To be sure,
this statement is given a scientific appearance by
using scientific terminology, but that does not change
its character in the least.

From a logical standpoint Mr. Spencer's doctrine
of evolution is little more than the fallacy of the universal, that is, the mistaking of class terms for real
things and the mistaking of the classifying process for
a process of reality in itself. Logic shows that classification never makes any identity nor abolishes any
difference. We gather together a plurality of things
under a single term which serves as a name for all the
individuals. But this process does nothing to the
individuals. It simply subsumes them under a given
term which serves for our uses in thinking; but it
leaves the things just what and where they were

before. Thus, the class term becomes a sort of symbol or shorthand expression, which applies to a great many things, but which implies no one of them. The class term Man applies to all human beings, but it does not imply any one. It is merely a general name for human beings; but when we come to deal with real men and women, we always have to bring back the peculiarities and differences which we dropped out when we were forming the class term. Thus, we have in thinking a certain symbolic and shorthand process which is of great service in abbreviating thought, but which becomes a fruitful source of error unless we are on our guard against it. Man is no reality; men are the realities. And even men lose none of their individual characteristics and differences when they are classified. This every one sees with regard to class terms applied to familiar concrete beings, but not every one sees this when applied to such other class terms, as Matter, Motion, and Force, and the like. The reality in these cases is material things having definite individual forces and moving in definite relations, with definite velocities in definite directions, etc.; and these differences can never be eliminated from the real world of experience by our classifications. Yet we form such abstractions as Matter and Force, and then easily come to mistake them for the original realities of the cosmic system; and because these terms are very small and contain no concrete specification, they seem to be so low that we might well view them as the original raw material out of which the world is made, and being so low and unformed they seem to make no demands upon intelligence for explanation. Thus, the last terms of logical analysis become, because of this oversight, the first terms of real existence; and the logical subordination of individuals to the class term is mistaken for their ontological implication. That such simple originals cannot be reached by logic is manifest. Classification never eliminates, it only overlooks difference; and when we pass from symbolic thinking to concrete thinking and exhaustive thinking, we find that we can never reduce our problem to lower terms. We are compelled to pick up in the concrete all that we dropped in the abstract, and the problem remains unchanged, however much we may manipulate our classification. The principle known as the logical equivalence of cause and effect in any mechanical thinking compels us to assume, in principle, in the antecedent, all that is worked out in the consequent; for if the effect was not provided for in the cause, in the sense of being necessitated by it, it could never produce it; but if the effect is thus provided for in the cause, then the cause that explains the effect is only that which in principle contains the effect, and again there is no progress. All this was overlooked by Mr. Spencer in his evolution formula. He seemed to think it possible to reason backward from the present complex order to a simple, indefinite, incoherent homogeneity; and to reason forward from this homogeneity to the present complex order. But this is simply what we have called the fallacy of the universal, of which fallacy, moreover, Mr. Spencer's system is a monumental illustration. He can neither reach nor use his indefinite homogeneity without fallacious reasoning, and throughout he is simply mistaking, as said, the last terms of logical abstraction for the first terms of real existence, and further mistaking the fact of logical subordination for the very different fact of ontological implication.

Thus, we have examined the fundamental and scientific conceptions of Mr. Spencer's system and find them far from satisfactory. There is an abundance of learning of a sort and an appearance also of perpetually hitting the nail on the head, but when we examine the matter all this turns out to be illusory. Mr. Spencer seems to be equally far from sound science and sound reasoning. We have now to consider the use which he makes of these principles in the further development of his thought, and especially in his doctrine of life and mind.

And here the question arises whether his doctrine is to be called materialistic or not. On this point Mr. Spencer is very pronounced, and repels the charge of materialism with much warmth. This makes it sure that Mr. Spencer did not intend to be or think he was a materialist. But in attempting to decide his view the chronic difficulties of his exposition beset us. We understand that the formula of evolution is intended to cover the whole field of mind and society as well as of physics, and that formula makes evolution simply a redistribution of matter and motion. No hint is anywhere given that the formula has a new meaning when we come into the realm of life and mind, and hence it would seem that life and mind are only special cases of the redistribution of matter and motion. And a large part of the exposition agrees with this view. Mental phenomena appear only in connection with material phenomena, and both disappear together. Mental action is a function of nervous organization and disappears along with it. Thoughts and feelings are only the inner side of changes in nervous vesicles and would vanish along with them. This is undoubtedly the doctrine of a large part of Mr. Spencer's exposition, and this is what the plain man means by materialism. But the name is indifferent so long as the thing is understood. If the redistribution of matter and motion includes and accounts for all phenomena, then the world will continue to regard this system as materialistic in spite of all protests.

To put it otherwise, a system might be materialistic from its doctrine of matter or from its doctrine of mind. Common, crude materialism is based on crude physical conceptions and regards matter and motion as thus conceived as an adequate explanation of mind, a doctrine which Professor Tyndall declared to be absurd, monstrous, and fit only for the intellectual gibbet. Now, Mr. Spencer's system is not materialistic in this sense, for he insists that matter and motion are but symbols of the unknowable reality, and that surely leaves them mysterious enough. But, on the other hand, a system may be judged by its doctrine of mind; and for common sense any view which makes mental phenomena functions of physical organization is materialistic, no matter how mysterious its doctrine of matter may be. Matter may be only a symbol and mind may be only a symbol; but if the matter-symbol is relatively first and independent, and the mind-symbol is made to depend upon the matter-symbol, then we have materialism in this sense, that mind is made a function of physical organization and disappears when the organization perishes. In this sense Mr. Spencer's system is materialistic throughout. Mental phenomena are frequently spoken of as but inner aspects of the nervous changes, and in the last work which Mr. Spencer wrote, "Facts and Comments," he says definitely that he sees no ground for thinking that our conscious life may go on in separation from the organism. Here, then, is the source of those bewildering denials of materialism by Mr. Spencer which many have found so confusing. Judged by his doctrine of matter, Mr. Spencer is not a materialist; but judged by his doctrine of mind, Mr. Spencer would certainly seem to be a materialist. Thus, he says in his work on "Psychology," when considering the question: "Nevertheless, it may be as well to say here, once for all, that were we compelled to choose between the alternatives of translating mental phenomena into physical phenomena, or of translating physical phenomena into mental phenomena, the latter alternative would seem the more acceptable of the two. Mind, as known to the possessor of it, is a circumscribed aggregate of activities; and the cohesion of these activities, one with another, throughout the aggregate, compels the postulation of a something of which they are the activities. But the same experiences which make him aware of this coherent aggregate of mental activities, simultaneously make him aware of activities that are not included in it — outlying activities which become known by their effects on this aggregate, but which are experimentally proved to be not coherent with it, and to be coherent with one another." ("Principles of Psychology," vol. I, p. 159.) He continues: "If units of external force are regarded as absolutely unknown and unknowable, then to translate units of feeling into them is to translate the known into the unknown, which is absurd. And if they are what they are supposed to be by those who identify them with their symbols, then the difficulty of translating units of feeling into them is insurmountable: if Force as it objectively exists is absolutely alien in nature from that which exists subjectively as Feeling, then the transformation of Force into Feeling is unthinkable. Either way, therefore, it is impossible to interpret inner existence in terms of outer existence. . . . Hence, though of the two it seems easier to translate so-called Matter into so-called Spirit, than to translate so-called Spirit into so-called Matter (which latter is, indeed, wholly impossible); yet no translation can carry us beyond our symbols." (Pages 160–61.) "When the two modes of Being which we distinguish as Subject and Object, have been severally reduced to their lowest terms, any further comprehension must be an assimilation of these lowest terms to one another; and, as we have already seen, this is negatived by the very distinction of Subject and Object, which is itself the consciousness of a difference transcending all other differences. So far from helping us to think of them as of one kind, analysis serves but to render more manifest the impossibility of finding for them a common concept — a thought under which they can be united." (Page 157.)

Here Mr. Spencer seems very definitely to exclude
even the possibility of materialism. We have the subject and object set up as absolutely antithetical, so
that by no possibility can we unite the two under a
common class or pass from one to the other by any
dynamic relation. Both, alike, are also represented as
being incommensurable modes of the absolute being.
However, it is difficult to unite this with the formula
of evolution. There everything is given in terms of
matter and motion, and if this is to be taken seriously,
then mental facts must be looked upon as cases of
matter and motion, or at least as effects of matter and
motion. To make them cases of matter and motion is
manifestly absurd. To say that a conception in ethics
or philosophy or metaphysical speculation is a case of
matter and motion is grotesque nonsense; for in that
case an atom or molecule or group of molecules,
grouping and moving in a certain direction and with a
certain velocity, would be the conception in question.
This view Mr. Spencer seems very definitely to set
aside. And it seems equally impossible to view them
as produced by matter and motion, seeing that they
are incommensurable modes of the Unknowable. And
this makes it once more difficult to tell what the law of
evolution means when applied to these phenomena.
Certainly, only matter and motion appear in the definition of evolution, and with equal certainty mental
phenomena cannot be identified as cases or as products of matter and motion, Mr. Spencer himself
being witness. It would seem, then, that they must be
put outside of the evolution movement, if these utterances we have quoted are to be taken seriously. But

this is really only another instance of the fundamental unclearness of Mr. Spencer's system. The conception of explanation by classification, as we have seen, gives really no insight at all, and the explanation by causation is something which is not provided for in this scheme.

IV

DOCTRINE OF LIFE AND MIND

BETWEEN the inorganic and the psychological realm lies the field of Biology, to which Mr. Spencer devotes two volumes. We have no concern with this except to consider his doctrine of life. In accordance with the formula of Evolution, life is to be expressed in terms of matter and motion, and Mr. Spencer seems quite determined in his purpose to carry this notion through. We must carefully consider the process, as this progress from the inorganic to the organic is one of the crucial points in traditional naturalism. If there be failure here, the evolution formula fails to include anything beyond the inorganic.

In beginning, the critic is much embarrassed in deciding how to take matter and motion. We have before seen how uncertain their signification is in the system. According to Mr. Spencer they are symbols of the Unknowable, and we have found it very hard to tell in what this symbolism consists. But however symbolic they may be, they can mean anything to us only as there is a real movement of something called matter from point to point and grouped in certain ways. In accordance with scientific custom also, we regard this matter as at least approximately of molecular and atomic constitution. Without assuming so much, our terms have not sufficient meaning to admit of discussion. If the Unknowable interfere with the evolution process, then a transcendental factor and also one of ignorance are introduced, and our formula is made logically worthless. With this understanding of the meaning of the terms, we proceed to inquire whether we can in any way understand living organisms with their powers of propagation, heredity, etc., as explained by any possible differentiation or integration of matter and motion.

In the first edition of the "Biology," Mr. Spencer wrote, nothing doubting, but later, when pressed by critics, he refers to two volumes on Inorganic Evolution that would have helped matters if they had been written. He says: "The closing chapter of the second (of these volumes), were it written, would deal with the evolution of organic matter — the step preceding the evolution of living forms. Habitually carrying with me in thought the contents of this unwritten chapter, I have, in some cases, expressed myself as though the reader had it before him; and have thus rendered some of my statements liable to misconstructions." ("Principles of Biology," vol. i, p. 480.) It may be doubted, however, if this closing chapter would much have helped us. At all events, we have to get on with what Mr. Spencer has vouchsafed us.

In the inorganic world we can in a fashion understand things in terms of matter and motion. Given a series of atoms, we can conceive the molecule as a grouping of the same; and given a series of molecules, we can understand the mass as a grouping of the molecules. So much seems quite possible with the formula of evolution, but there the progress stops. We can pass from the atom to the molecule, and from mole-

cules to more complex molecules, and from molecules
of whatever complexity to masses of whatever size.
So far the way is clear. Mr. Spencer succeeds in getting further than this by passing from the atom to the
molecule and from the molecule to more complex molecules in terms of matter and motion, and thereafter
making the evolution depend upon the substitution of
semi-synonyms and of terms borrowed from the biological realm. In this way he passes from the complex
molecules to organic molecules, and from organic molecules to organic matter, and from organic matter to
organisms, and then, being well over into the biological realm, he brings in other biological terms, such
as propagation, heredity, and the like, and then the
deduction of life from the non-living is complete.

All of this is purely verbal. The complex molecule
is identified with the organic molecule without telling
us what the new phrase means. If it means anything
more than complex molecule we ought to have it
clearly stated, and we ought to be shown how this
difference arises. This Mr. Spencer entirely fails to
do. In a letter of his to the editor of the "North Amer-
ican Review," afterward published at the end of his
first volume on "Biology," Mr. Spencer seeks to break
the force of this criticism by showing how organic
molecules or organic matter is produced in the laboratory. He appears to think that organic matter was
first produced, though how he does not tell us. The
how would probably have been explained in the closing
chapter of the second missing volume on Inorganic
Evolution, which was to deal with the evolution of
[organic] matter — the step preceding the evolution

of living forms. But this is only a matter of surmise. In the letter in question Mr. Spencer says: "That organic matter was not produced all at once, but was reached through steps, we are well warranted in believing by the experiences of chemists. Organic matters are produced in the laboratory by what we may literally call *artificial evolution.* Chemists find themselves unable to form these complex combinations directly from their elements; but they succeed in forming them indirectly, by successive modifications of simpler combinations. . . . In this manner highly complex substances are eventually built up. Another characteristic of their method is no less significant. Two complex compounds are employed to generate, by their action upon one another, a compound of still greater complexity: different heterogeneous molecules of one stage, become parents of a molecule a stage higher in heterogeneity." (Page 482.) Here Mr. Spencer assumes that the production of organic molecules in the laboratory is significant for his doctrine of evolution. But the fact is, these organic molecules mean only complex molecules commonly found in connection with organisms, and which, until comparatively recently, could not be artificially formed by the chemist; but these molecules are not organisms. They have no power of generation, and they are not alive any more than the inorganic molecules. A molecule of uric acid is no more alive than a molecule of ferric oxide; it may be more complicated, but then its properties are all due to the definite sizes, shapes, and motions of the component elements in both cases. Such organic molecules can be described in terms of matter and motion, and they are in reality only complex molecules. Further, Mr. Spencer uses two phrases which illustrate his tendency to slide over into the biological realm without notice. He says, "Two complex compounds are employed to generate, by their action upon one another, a compound of still greater complexity." And "different heterogeneous molecules of one stage, become parents of a molecule a stage higher in heterogeneity." If we allow these phrases to remain or pass unchallenged, we might suppose that we were in the vital realm. We have generation and parentage spoken of. But here again we must insist that these phrases shall be interpreted in terms of matter and motion or else abandoned. Now, when molecules are employed to "generate" a compound of still greater complexity, the whole process admits of being described in terms of matter and motion, that is, different molecules of definite shapes and sizes and motions unite with others, also of definite shapes and sizes and motions, to produce a compound, of which also the elements have definite shapes and sizes and motions, and these could be geometrically and mathematically described, were our vision and knowledge sufficiently penetrating. But in all this is there no more of "generation" and "parentage," in the biological sense, than there is when sulphur unites with oxygen to form sulphuric acid, or when iron rusts; and the resulting compounds are no more alive in one case than in the other. With this result we reach nothing that can be called truly living, that is, nothing which has feeling or anything else that is not a matter of shape, size, and motion of the

elements. If we insist on knowing what there is more
in the case than shapes, sizes, and elements, we are
not told; or if we insist on knowing how a modification of shapes, sizes, and motions can produce the
difference between the living and the non-living,
again we are not told.

We might, then, insist upon Mr. Spencer telling us
what the distinction is between a complex molecule
and an organic molecule, and on interpreting the difference in terms of matter and motion. If the organic
is reduced to a geometrical problem of shapes, sizes,
and motions, clearly we have not reached anything
that can be called living, and if to be alive is something that is not a matter of shapes, sizes, and motions, then it stands outside of the range of Mr.
Spencer's formula of evolution. The only distinction
between the living and the dead, if matter and motion
alone are concerned, would be a purely phenomenal
one. The so-called living body would have certain
phenomena that so-called inorganic bodies do not
possess, but there would be no more true vitality in
one case than in the other. Yet Mr. Spencer, as the
result of these considerations, finds a remarkable
parallelism between evolution in the organic world
and in the vital world. He says: "See, then, the remarkable parallelism. The progress towards higher
types of organic molecules is effected by modifications upon modifications; as throughout Evolution in
general. Each of these modifications is a change of the
molecule into equilibrium with its environment — an
adaptation, as it were, to new surrounding conditions
to which it is subjected; as throughout Evolution in

general. Larger, or more integrated, aggregates (for compound molecules are such) are successively generated; as throughout Evolution in general. . . . A geometrically increasing multitude of these larger and more complex aggregates so produced, at the same time results; as throughout Evolution in general. And it is by the action of the successively higher forms on one another, joined with the action of environing conditions, that the highest forms are reached; as throughout Evolution in general." (Page 483.) Here again we see the wisdom of using the terms of organization. There is a "progress towards higher types of organic molecules which is effected by modifications upon modifications." "There is adaptation to new surrounding conditions," etc.

Here again everything is unclear. If for organic we read complex, which is all we are allowed to do, the progress ceases. The "higher types" also are things of doubtful meaning in chemical science and are really borrowed from biology. In chemistry all they could mean would be molecules of greater complexity, not molecules more nearly alive. Again, Mr. Spencer speaks of later molecules being generated and rising out of previous conditions, but these terms also are treacherous. In inorganic chemistry, when certain molecules generate other molecules or rise out of other molecules, it means only that the same elements are differently combined. There is no more generation than there is when a pile of bricks is thrown down and piled up again in another form. The same is true of the "modifications upon modifications" spoken of. It is easy, when we bear the biological goal in mind, to think that in this way we are advancing toward life, but when our thought remains clear, all that happens is that certain combinations disintegrate and certain other combinations take their place; and the same is true of the statement that through these modifications the molecule passes into equilibrium with its environment. If we have a tacit reference to living things in our thought when we use this language, we seem to be progressing again toward life, but it is only as we keep our thought unclear that this is possible. In inorganic chemical combination the equilibrium of a molecule with its environment depends upon harmonies of shape, size, and movement, and when such harmonies are broken up, new combinations are produced of other shapes, sizes, and movements; but there is nothing of life in these, and this is all that the passage of a molecule into equilibrium with its environment can mean, if the passage is to be interpreted in terms of matter and motion. But this would not help us in the least toward reaching truly biological conceptions of organisms, really alive and able to propagate themselves in one way or another.

But by these chemical illustrations, which do not really illustrate, Mr. Spencer is encouraged. It seems possible to him to produce organic matter, and then it ought not to be difficult to produce organisms. He argues as follows: "When we thus see the identity of method at the two extremes, — when we see that the general laws of evolution, as they are exemplified in known organisms, have been unconsciously conformed to by chemists in the artificial evolution of organic matter, — we can scarcely doubt that these laws were conformed to in the natural evolution of organic matter, and afterwards in the evolution of the simplest organic forms. In the early world, as in the modern laboratory, inferior types of organic substances, by their mutual actions under fit conditions, evolved the superior types of organic substances, ending in organizable protoplasm. And it can hardly be doubted that the shaping of organizable protoplasm, which is a substance modifiable in multitudinous ways with extreme facility, went on after the same manner. . . . Exposed to those innumerable modifications of conditions which the Earth's surface afforded, here in amount of light, there in amount of heat, and elsewhere in the mineral quality of its aqueous medium, this extremely changeable substance must have undergone now one, now another, of its countless metamorphoses. And to the mutual influences of its metamorphic forms under favoring conditions, we may ascribe the production of the still more composite, still more sensitive, still more variously changeable portions of organic matter, which, in masses more minute and simpler than existing Protozoa, displayed actions verging little by little into those called vital — actions which protein itself exhibits in a certain degree, and which the lowest known living things exhibit only in a greater degree. Thus, setting out with inductions from the experiences of organic chemists at the one extreme, and with inductions from the observations of biologists at the other extreme, we are enabled deductively to bridge the interval — are enabled to conceive how organic compounds were evolved, and how, by a continuance of the process, the nascent life displayed in these became gradually more pronounced." (Page 483.)

This, too, is interesting, but the matter is not helped. We observe in this long quotation some new terms and phrases creeping in, without, so far as can be discovered, any biological warrant. We have organic matter produced in abundance, and then the simplest organic forms appear. The organism is also spoken of. Inferior and superior types of organic substances are mentioned, "ending in organizable protoplasm," and this, in addition to being extremely mobile, appears to be sensitive and displays "actions verging little by little into those called vital," and thus we "are enabled to conceive how organic compounds are evolved, and how by a continuance of the process the nascent life displayed in these became gradually more and more pronounced." But it is all to no purpose. These biological terms are simply dragged in without being deduced. The complex molecule and masses of complex molecules are as far as we get, and all the rest consists simply in a substitution of semi-synonyms which are very far from being synonyms, and thus by this verbal stair we climb victoriously from the inorganic to the organic. Nothing whatever is done that throws the slightest light upon truly vital phenomena, such as feeling, propagation, growth, heredity, and the like. We are simply told that the beginnings of life were in exceedingly minute portions of organic matter, and these we subject to "innumerable modifications of condition," and then we are left to infer that in some way, not specified, something happened, we don't know what, in ways we can't tell, but nevertheless so happened that life was deduced "as in Evolution in general." However, even here the path of logic is clear. Whatever did happen must be viewed as a combination of matter and motion, and it is perfectly plain that no combination of matter and motion can ever represent that which is neither matter nor motion. Instead of laboring thus strenuously to deduce that which refuses to be deduced by any known logical method, Mr. Spencer should have fallen back upon the persistence of force, and told us that matter and motion must have produced living things because there is nothing else in the evolution formula, and to deny that they have produced living things would have been to deny the persistence of force. This would have been shorter and more effective than the way actually taken. We must say, therefore, that Mr. Spencer has not succeeded in any way in interpreting the facts of life in terms of matter and motion. As before pointed out, we can see how complex compounds arise, but we cannot see how they can display any life, or how "the nascent life which they display becomes gradually more and more pronounced," or how the highly complex molecules become "more sensitive, and display actions verging little by little into those called vital." We get stalled at the complex molecule, and we are not helped in any way by what is said about the amazing complexity and mobility of "organizable protoplasm." So long as we regard these from the mechanical side, as phases of matter and motion, nothing whatever that can be expressed in these terms is really alive. It is simply and only a highly

complicated, unstable compound without any proper
sensibility or life whatever.

And still more manifest is the failure of the formula
when we come to the facts of mind. Here again, if we
are to give matter and motion any assignable meaning,
there is no possibility of interpreting mental facts in
these terms. This we have sufficiently pointed out.
To say that a given conception or proposition, say a
theorem in geometry or a conception in mechanics,
is a case of matter and motion, or is in any way made
more intelligible to us when called a case of matter and
motion, is absurd, as Mr. Spencer himself would admit.
When, then, we are told that the evolution formula
aims to exhibit everything in terms of matter and
motion, we are very much at a loss to know what
meaning is to be given to these terms. Matter and motion in some sense we know, and thought we know,
but the impossibility of assimilating them to one another is, as Mr. Spencer has said in the quotations
already given, absolute. To formulate in terms of
matter and motion things which are absolutely incommensurable with matter and motion is certainly
a problem of great difficulty. How, then, is the formula to be retained and maintained in reference to
the mental life? We may get some sort of an answer
to this question when we come to speak of the doctrine
of psycho-physical parallelism.

Assuming, however, that we have reached the fron-
tiers of psychology, Mr. Spencer says that if evolution is true we can understand mind only by observing
how it is evolved. Mind, as it exists in man, is a late
and highly complex product. We must study it, there-

fore, in its manifestations in the earlier forms of life if we would really understand it. It is not easy to give this statement a tenable meaning, because of the fact that mind is something which can never be objectively presented, and which can be known only from the inside. Indeed, the only mind of which any one has direct knowledge is his own, and he understands all other minds only as he assimilates the activities in connection with those other minds to his own inner life. He must, therefore, have the key in himself if he is ever to understand mind at all. In connection with the lower orders of animal life the study from the outside is peculiarly difficult because of this fact. We have a tendency to fall into what we may call biological anthropomorphism. We can understand the animal mind, of course, only as we assimilate it to our own, but how far this assimilation may go is very far from self-evident. For example, shall we look upon the social life of the ants and the bees as indicating anything like the intelligence that similar combinations would imply among men? If so, we must attribute to them a very high order of mentality; but if we are not willing to do this, then all possibility of understanding them is excluded, and nothing remains but to use some such word as instinct, which is an idea without any positive contents, a word whereby we try to split the difference between the complex activities of mind and the purely mechanical activities of the inorganic world. It seems clear, then, that the attempt to understand our minds by study of the lower orders of mind must be somewhat seriously discounted. At all events, we must be con-

tinually on our guard against mistaking some interpretation of our own for the objective fact in the
animal world. The fact seems to be that that world,
though in some respects very near us, is in some other
respects very far removed. We cannot enter into its
feelings, aims, and sympathies with any measure of
justified assurance.

However, supposing evolution to be the fact, Mr.
Spencer thinks that mind will be best understood
when we assimilate it to that stage of evolution which
lies nearest to it. And this he finds in life. Accordingly, we shall get most light upon our mental life if
we study the order of life which is the adjacent phase
of the great evolution movement. Accordingly, he
reproduces the definition of life, which he now extends
to include mind. The definition of life is as follows:
"Life is the definite combination of heterogeneous
changes, both simultaneous and successive, in correspondence with external coexistences and sequences."
This, for sake of convenience, is afterward cut down
to the form that life is "the continuous adjustment
of internal relations to external relations." He next
proceeds to show that this formula applies equally
to the process of mental evolution, which also is an
adjustment of internal relations to external relations.
In a series of eleven chapters of great apparent thor-
oughness he illustrates this formula. The continuous
adjustment he calls correspondence and declares that
it grows in heterogeneity in space, in time, in specialty
(the special senses), in generality, and in complexity.
These corresponding senses are thus coördinated and
integrated. Such is mind, an adjustment of inner to

outer relations. The polyp responds only to present stimuli, and to all alike. The bee looks only for honey and wax, and stores up food for winter. Here the correspondence is extended in time. The bird corresponds to the things about it, and also to the better climate far away. As winter approaches, it leaves its home in the North and flies to the South. Here we see the correspondence increasing in space. Man corresponds variously through his special senses and also in his increasing range of knowledge through space and time. The physicist thinks of events in the past and future, thus corresponding to events at remote distances in time. He also corresponds to things in space, to changes in the sun, or to events going on in remote sidereal regions, but it is throughout correspondence. And it grows in exactness also as well as in range. The old astronomer foretold, though in a rude way, what would be. The modern astronomer fixes the day, the hour, and the minute, and when the time comes, he is on hand with his instruments to correspond to changes in Venus or Mars, or in the moon or the sun. And so through the whole field of science, the correspondence grows in space, time, exactness, complexity, etc.

This is a magnificent and very imposing formula. We see that, in a way, the mental process may be described as a correspondence of inner relations to outer relations, and we see how the correspondence grows, " as in Evolution in general," from more to more, increasing in complexity and definiteness and range, and yet it is all the while essentially a correspondence of inner relations to outer relations.

The question, however, may arise, whether this vague description, after all, gives us any real insight, whether we did not know as much before as after this new formulation. The shortcomings of the formula are manifest, first, in this: it limits the mind to the sole function of perception, or the cognition of objective fact. All sentiment and impulses of affection, or religion and æsthetics, are left out. In our experience, this judging of outward facts is a very small part of mental life; but this view excludes beauty, morals, affection, religion, wit, etc., and leaves us nothing but history and statistics. But we omit to press this question, and inquire whether the formula has any real meaning or whether it means the same thing in the case of life and mind.

First, in the case of life. The distinction, as it stands, is too broad. The elements under the law of gravitation are beautifully adjusted to one another. The oxygen that unites with iron is perfectly adjusted. The parasite that feeds on something else is adjusted. Adjustment, then, is by no means peculiar to intelligence or to life, but it is the adjustment of inner relations to outer relations. Now, what does this mean in the case of a living thing? What is meant by inner and what by outer? We certainly cannot, in the case of the organism, make inner to mean inside of the spatial limits of the body, as in that case a pin swallowed by a child would be inner, and effete matter not yet excreted would likewise be inner. But clearly, inner, organically considered, can only mean that which is comprised within the control of some vital principle. That, then, is inner which is contributing to the sum of vital functions, and that is outer which no longer assists in the performance of those functions. The organism contains a large amount of material which is not inner in this sense. All matter not yet assimilated, and all matter that has performed its functions and is now being removed from the organism, is outer. Plainly, then, we can define inner and outer not spatially, but only with reference to some vital principle; that is to say, the definition of life as a correspondence of internal relations to external relations presupposes life itself as the condition of its having any proper meaning.

That inner and outer have not the same meaning when we pass to mind is also manifest. Internal relations here again mean only thought and consciousness. In no other assignable sense are thoughts inner and things outer. The inner here is the inner of knowledge and the outer is the outer of objectivity. They have no space relations of any sort whatever. In that case, then, it is manifest that the definition of mind implies knowledge and conscious knowing itself. Given such knowledge, we may proceed to adjust ourselves to the environment and we may equally proceed to adjust the environment to ourselves. But the definition itself is meaningless until we bring into it the very thing to be defined.

This result is rather depressing. We have here a definition of mind which is made identical with that of life, whereas the two are widely different and distinct, and then we have a definition that implies mind itself as its condition. The vast range of illustration of the extension of the range of correspondence and the like is true in a fashion, but it merely puts most commonplace matter into stilted, operose language. Of course, knowledge grows, and it grows in all directions. It becomes more penetrating, more extensive, more specialized, more exact. This is fairly familiar to the wayfaring man, and it is not made any more valuable by being described as the correspondence of inner relations to outer relations, or as being said to increase in heterogeneity in space, in time, in complexity, and to be variously integrated and differentiated. All this is only trying to make familiar and commonplace matter seem new by the device of a pompous and sonorous terminology.

In leaving this topic an extraordinary passage may be quoted, in which Mr. Spencer seems to give an explanation of consciousness. He says: "For how only can the constituent changes of any complex correspondence be coördinated? Those abilities which an intelligent creature possesses, of recognizing diverse external objects and of adjusting its actions to composite phenomena of various kinds, imply a power of combining many separate impressions. These separate impressions are received by the senses — by different parts of the body. If they go no further than the places at which they are received, they are useless. Or if only some of them are brought into relation with one another, they are useless. That an effectual adjustment may be made, they must all be brought into relation with one another. But this implies some centre of communication common to them all, through which they severally pass; and as they cannot pass through it simultaneously, they must pass through

357

it in succession. So that as the external phenomena responded to become greater in number and more complicated in kind, the variety and rapidity of the changes to which this common centre of communication is subject must increase — there must result an unbroken series of these changes — there must arise a consciousness." ("Principles of Psychology," vol. I, p. 403.) It is doubtful if any one but Mr. Spencer himself could trace the connection between the premises and the conclusion; and most probably he would do it by falling back on the persistence of force and the conviction that hence it must be so.

Psycho-Physical Parallelism

Mr. Spencer begins his "Psychology" with an account in five chapters of the structure and functions of the nervous system. The scientific accuracy of this does not concern us. Then follows a chapter on "Æstho-Physiology." He says: —

"Throughout the foregoing chapters nervous phenomena have been formulated in terms of Matter and Motion. . . . Now, however, we turn to a totally distinct aspect of our subject. There lies before us a class of facts absolutely without any perceptible or conceivable community of nature with the facts that have occupied us. The truths here to be set down are truths of which the very elements are unknown to physical science. Objective observation and analysis fail us; and subjective observation and analysis must supplement them.

"In other words, we have to treat of nervous phenomena as phenomena of consciousness. The changes which, regarded as modes of the Non-Ego, have been expressed in terms of motion, have now, regarded as modes of the Ego, to be expressed in terms of feeling. Having contemplated these changes on their outsides, we have to contemplate them from their insides." ("Principles of Psychology," vol. I, p. 97.) This passage is a little embarrassing, as presenting us with truths of which the very elements are unknown to physical science and which are without any perceptible or conceivable community of nature with the facts that have occupied us. This is certainly a very distinct affirmation that the facts in question cannot be described in terms of matter and motion, however much this may be possible with nervous phenomena. We are not entirely relieved here by remembering that Mr. Spencer has called the mental phenomena and physical phenomena opposite symbols of the one unknowable reality; for that view left the mental and physical much farther apart than Mr. Spencer himself aims to do. In the passage quoted, Mr. Spencer speaks of nervous phenomena as phenomena of consciousness, or as being nervous phenomena on the outside, and forms of feeling from the inside. This introduces us to the problem of the relation of the physical and the mental series of facts and changes in Spencer's view.

The notion of a double-faced substance has existed in philosophy since the time of Spinoza, who first gave it pronounced formulation, but even in his view the matter is quite unclearly conceived. According to him, there is one substance with two attributes, thought and extension, and these two are supposed to lie parallel. On the relation of these attributes Spinoza is unclear. An attribute in his system is defined as expressing the essence of the thing. In that case, when we have two incommensurable attributes, like thought and extension, each expressing the essence of the thing, we are at a loss to know what becomes of the unity of the substance. It would seem that incommensurable attributes would imply incommensurable essences, and thus the unity of the substance would disappear. Moreover, according to Spinoza, the thing-attribute and the thought-attribute are mutually independent. All that takes place in the world of things is due to antecedent conditions in the world of things; and all that takes place in the world of thought is due to antecedent conditions in the world of thought; but neither one of these attributes affects the other. Each series goes along by itself. But in that case the thing-attribute is at once made useless in the explanation of experience, and also impossible; for all knowledge and experience lie within the thought-attribute, and as things never affect thought we have no reason whatever for affirming things. Thus we should be shut up at once to pure idealism. At times, however, Spinoza has a different view of the attributes, according to which they are the same substance seen from different points of view. The substance itself is one; but, seen from one point of view, it is extension; seen from another point of view, it is thought. But we are no better off than before; for whereas before we had two incommensurable attributes, we now have two incommensurable ways of looking at the one, so as to see it double. The doubleness, then, appears to be a kind of illusion of very obscure origin. And even the doubleness cannot be known as such unless there be something which transcends it in such a way as to unite the two, and this could be done only by thought again; in which case we should have not merely thought and extension as different ways of viewing the subject, but we should also have another thought of a higher order which should at once produce and overcome the resultant duality. How this can be, Spinoza never told us: first, because he apparently never thought of it, and, secondly, because he could not have told us had the matter been called to his attention.

In modern times this same notion of a double-faced substance has reappeared, with some difference, but with equal obscurity. With Spinoza the substance was rather statically conceived, and thought and extension were the static attributes of the one substance. With Mr. Spencer the fundamental reality is dynamically conceived. It is an all-embracing energy on which all phenomena depend and from which they forever proceed. At the same time this substance seems to have the double mode of manifestation, the mode of extension and the mode of life and thought. If we ask how there come to be two modes, we should find no answer beyond the affirmation of the fact that one and the same fundamental reality underlies the world of extension and that of life and thought. If we should next ask how the duality of these modes provides for the validity of knowledge, we should get no answer whatever, as Mr. Spencer seems never to have considered this problem.

But clearly, this doctrine of modes by no means implies that parallelism between the modes which the validity of knowledge presupposes. Thus, if the fundamental reality produces a variety of physical effects and also produces a variety of mental conceptions, there seems to be in that no assurance that the mental conceptions shall move parallel with the physical facts and rightly reproduce them. Yet, without this assumption, as said, knowledge is all at sea.

But supposing that there is a mysterious thought side in the fundamental reality, many points still remain for explanation before the view is clear. First, what would such a doctrine mean? The lowest possible meaning we could give to it would be some capacity of thought and feeling, and, indeed, we could not make much out of that without affirming some actuality of thought and feeling. An inner face or subjective aspect which did not mean this would be simply nothing to our thought. Further, what is the relation of this thought side in the fundamental reality to the relative realities, matter and motion, or to the symbols, matter and motion? Do they also have a subjective aspect, and is that aspect a mode of the subjective aspect of the fundamental reality or is it something special and individual in themselves, and do they think and feel? If not, what does the subjective aspect mean? And finally, what is the relation of these subjective aspects to the thoughts and feelings of the individuals of experience? Does the fundamental reality or the relative reality think and feel in our personal experience? Or how shall we conceive it? All of these questions are untouched by Mr. Spencer. Except in a very vague way and now and then, when the odor of materialism becomes too strong. He makes nothing of the duality in the Unknowable itself. The duality which he recognizes lies rather within the field of our finite experience, and more especially within the field of the organic world and the thought and feeling connected therewith. Here it is especially that his notion of the double aspect appears. It is really not the double aspect of the Unknowable Reality nor yet of the relative realities, but the double aspect of a series of nervous changes in living things. In general, his doctrine is that these nervous changes have what he calls sometimes an inside and sometimes an inner face or subjective aspect. This is the conception which runs through the chief part of his psychological exposition. In the passages already given, feelings are spoken of as the inside of nervous phenomena. To be sure, he differentiates at times between the physical life and the mental life; and yet the mental life is throughout regarded as a sort of attendant of the physical, and the physical is treated always as being relatively independent. The mental life attends the physical life and is not there without it. The physical life, on the other hand, is something relatively independent. Least of all is it dependent on the mental life. In the growth of intelligence the deduction of the mental life from the physical is traced through reflex action, instinct, memory, reason, the feelings and the will, and these are all shown to be but the internal aspects of physical changes in the nervous system. Thus, with respect to memory,

"The various psychical states involved in each set of motions, severally become nascent; but none of them reach that intensity which they would have were the motions performed. In the chief nervous centre the different impressions serve as different motor impulses; and these, being severally supplanted by one another before they pass into actual motor changes, will each of them consist of an incipient or faint form of that nervous state which would have accompanied the actual motor change had it occurred. But such a succession of states constitutes *remembrance* of the motor changes which thus become incipient — constitutes a *memory*. To remember a motion just made with the arm, is to have a feeble repetition of those internal states which accompanied the motion — is to have an incipient excitement of those nerves which were strongly excited during the motion. Thus, then, these nascent nervous excitements that conflict with one another, are really so many *ideas* of the motor changes which, if stronger, they would cause; or rather, they are the objective sides of those changes which are ideas on their subjective sides. Consequently, Memory necessarily comes into existence whenever automatic action is imperfect." (Volume i, p. 448.)

In like manner, reason is explained. "For though when the confusion of a complex impression with some allied one causes a confusion among the nascent motor excitations, there is entailed a certain hesitation; and though this hesitation continues as long as these nascent motor excitations, or ideas of the correlative actions, go on superseding one another; yet, ultimately, some one set of motor excitations will prevail over the rest. As the groups of antagonistic tendencies aroused will scarcely ever be exactly balanced, the strongest group will at length pass into action; and as this sequence will usually be the one that has recurred oftenest in experience, the action will, in the average of cases, be the one best adapted to the circumstances. But an action thus produced is nothing else than a rational action. Each of the actions which we call rational, presents three phases answering to those here described: — first, a certain combination of impressions signifying some combination of phenomena to which the organism is to be adjusted; second, an idea of the actions before performed under like conditions, which idea is a nascent excitation of the nervous agents before concerned in such actions, either as producers of them or as affected by the production of them; and, third, the actions themselves, which are simply the results of the nascent excitation rising into an actual excitation." (Volume I, p. 455.)

Similar reasoning identifies volition with the passage of the nascent motor excitation into action, and finally, in "Principles of Psychology," volume II, page 484, we have the subject and object defined in such a way as to bring out the same fact, that the mental subject is simply and only a peculiar nervous combination: "For, as shown in earlier parts of this work, an idea is the psychical side of what on its physical side is an involved set of molecular changes propagated through an involved set of nervous plexuses. That which makes possible this idea is the preëxistence of these plexuses, so organized that a wave of molecular motion diffused through them will produce, as its psychical correlative, the components of the conception, in due order and degree. This idea lasts while the waves of molecular motion last, ceasing when they cease; but that which remains is the set of plexuses. These constitute the potentiality of the idea, and make possible future ideas like it. Each such set of plexuses, perpetually modified in detail by perpetual new actions; capable of entering into countless combinations with others, just as the objects thought of entered into countless combinations; and capable of having its several parts variously excited just as the external object presents its combined attributes in various ways; is thus the permanent internal nexus for ideas, answering to the permanent external nexus for phenomena. And just as the external nexus is that which continues to exist amid transitory appearances, so the internal nexus is that which continues to exist amid transitory ideas."

In this last quotation the physical side is made, so far as our thought goes, the independent and abiding factor, and the mental side is simply a curious attendant of the various physical changes, which, however, have no more independence of their physical basis than the tunes and melodies of an instrument have of the instrument itself. The instrument makes possible the melodies, and when it is appropriately played the melodies exist; but they exist only as the instrument is played. And as it would be quite absurd to think of them as having a separate existence apart from the instrument, so likewise it is absurd to think of our thoughts and feelings as having any existence apart from the instrument. When the instrument is played, they exist; when the playing ceases, they cease; when the instrument is destroyed, nothing is left of thought or melody in either case.

Here, again, we see the essential materialism of Spencer's view cropping out, and we see that there is no relief in what he has said about the dual aspect of the Unknowable. What we have here on his own view is a dual aspect of organic existence; and however much mystery there may be in the nature of the organism, the dependence of the inner aspect upon the outward fact is made very manifest, in spite of all caveats or protests to the contrary.

The problem which thus emerges is not peculiar to Mr. Spencer, but is one that has haunted our materialistic monism for some time. Speculators of this school who are devoted to physical science have sought to maintain the continuity of the physical series so that each physical antecedent should be fully accounted for in the physical consequent, and each physical consequent should find its adequate explanation in its physical antecedents. Of course, on this view it was impossible to allow that thought or feeling should account for anything in the world of physical change. And hence the problem is presented, how to maintain the physical continuity, and at the same time recognize the mental order. The theory advanced became thus, that the two series are concomitant, but that each goes along by itself, so that thought and purpose account for nothing in the production of physical change; while the physical order, on the other hand, loses nothing for the production of thought and gains nothing from the thought side. But this view in this form was subject to grave difficulty. If the thought-series were really independent, then, as above pointed out, we should fall into a species of idealism, because there would be nothing in the thought-world that demanded the physical world for its explanation. The thought-world would go along by itself, and the thing-world would be only a hypostasized shadow of the thought-world. In this strait some of the speculators decided to say that the real fact was the physical series, while the mental series attended it as a kind of concomitant shadow which costs and causes nothing. As to why there should be any such duality they had no answer to give, but their view was that the physical fact was first and basal, and the mental fact was a kind of shadow, which seemed to be there for no reason whatever, but which was so implicated with its physical ground that it could have no existence apart from it.

This is the view of psycho-physical parallelism. On the one side, we have a series of subjective shadows which simply attend the physical changes, and on the other side, we have a series of physical things and movements, and the latter would be all that they are if the mental series were entirely away. Mr. Huxley sets forth this view in the essay before referred to, "On the Hypothesis that Animals are Automata." In the original view he maintained, however, that our volition counts for something in the course of events, but he was not fully grounded in the doctrine himself. He was simply expounding it. Later on, when the essay was published in his "Collected Essays," he added a footnote, as already mentioned, to the effect that the volition was simply a symbol of the nervous conditions which really produce events. Many others have set forth the same doctrine, but this view shuts us up to the most grotesque and impossible notions. It implies, for instance, that all of human history has gone on without any intervention or guidance of thought and purpose. The multitudinous activities of men in the establishment of homes, the building of cities, the making of inventions, the founding of governments, and all the complex activities that underlie civilization in general have taken place without any control of thought, and, so far as we know, without its presence. There is really no more extraordinary inversion of good sense to be found in the whole history of speculation. The function of all theorizing is to explain experience, not to explain it away. From experience all our thinking must start as its foundation and to experience it must return for its verification; but, instead of regarding this obvious fact, the theorists proceed to build abstractions without regard to experience, and then in the name of the abstractions to invert experience altogether. As soon, however, as we recall the true relation of theory to experience, we see the inverted character of this view.

On this matter, as on so many others, Mr. Spencer is uncertain. He is not willing, as we have seen, to allow that feeling counts for nothing. In a quotation before given he points out that in that case feelings have arisen to do nothing, and he rightly urges this objection against Professor Huxley's view which would make consciousness a mere collateral attendant of the nervous changes without in any way affecting them. Thus, it would seem that Mr. Spencer does not accept the doctrine in its completeness; but on the other hand, it seems impossible to say that he does not accept it, for when mental states, volitions among the rest, are declared to be only an inner aspect or face of changes among nervous vesicles, either we have the view in question, according to which feeling simply goes along with the physical series, or else we have feelings introduced as dynamic factors, and then the evolution formula, which recognizes only matter and motion, is definitely set aside. There seems to be no way out of this except to appeal with all proper gravity to the Unknowable and to the symbolic character of our knowledge; and that introduces a factor of ignorance which displaces the formula, though in another way.

Another curious thing deserves to be mentioned in connection with this double-faced character of nervous action. It is surprising that there should be a double face and still more surprising that we should know anything about it, for there is really an impassable gulf between the two faces. It is still more surprising, if possible, that, in case there should be such inner face, the inner face should rightly reproduce the outer face. If nerves be able to generate thoughts, it by no means follows that the thoughts must represent external reality. The thoughts might be as subjective as the fancies produced in dreams. And one would expect that the thoughts would represent, if

anything, the organic processes of which they are
said to be the inner face, whereas they never refer
to these and commonly refer to things entirely apart
from the organism itself. This complete silence of
the nerves as to their own existence, and the report,
instead, of what is taking place in the extra-organic
world, are very remarkable facts. Certainly, when
matter is declared to be a double-faced entity, we
should expect to find the mental face reflecting that
part of the physical face which attends it, or which
is next to it. But this it never does. The inner face
does not reproduce, except very remotely, the nervous fact of which it is said to be the inner face. The
nervous fact is a series of changes in the nervous
system, and more specifically in the gray matter of
the brain. But this is not reproduced by thoughts,
but commonly some facts external to the organism,
things and changes in the outer world. Here we have
a remarkably opaque fact. If we should suppose the
inner and the outer face to correspond, something
like the opposite sides of a relief, the imagination
would seem to have some insight into the parallelism
and its reason; but when the two faces are such that
the inner face ignores the outer face entirely, and
reports, instead, something else, the house yonder,
or the man and the landscape, and all manner of
inorganic facts, quite apart from both our mind and
our nerves, we become impressed with the extraordinary opacity of this doctrine of double-facedness.
But this problem also never occurred to Mr. Spencer.
It sufficed for him to speak of the two aspects of
matter, and later on to speak of thoughts and feelings

as the inner aspect of nervous change; and he never suspected the implications of the view. Indeed, he never had any clear idea of the view itself, but contented himself with vague pictures and such phrases as symbols, etc., and these served to carry his thought lightly over the depths.

The associational psychology has always sought to exhibit mind as a product, and especially as compounded of simpler states and ultimately of sensations. The latter are the original units out of which all mental forms and higher combinations are produced. Mr. Spencer adopts this general view, and gives a chapter on the "Composition of Mind," in which mind is exhibited as compounded of simple sensations and simple feelings which are united in such a way as to produce our actual mental structure. In the chapter on the "Substance of Mind" Mr. Spencer suggests that there may well be some ultimate mental unit, which is the original thing in mental combination. He points out that individual sensations and emotions, real or ideal, of which consciousness is built up, though they appear to be simple and unanalyzable, are not really so. He says: "There is at least one kind of feeling which, as ordinarily experienced, seems elementary, that is demonstrably not elementary. And after resolving it into its proximate components, we can scarcely help suspecting that other apparently elementary feelings are also compound, and may have proximate components like those which we can in this one instance identify." ("Principles of Psychology," vol. i, p. 148.)

Musical sound is the case to which Mr. Spencer

refers. This, he says, is clearly resolvable into simple feelings, a conclusion which he draws from the fact that when equal blows or taps are made, one after another, at a rate not exceeding some sixteen per second, the effect of each is perceived as a separate noise; but when the rapidity with which the blows follow one another exceeds this, the noises are no longer identified in separate states of consciousness, and there arises in place of them a continuous state of consciousness called a tone. Considerations of this kind lead Mr. Spencer to ask: "Can we stop short here? If the different sensations known as sounds are built out of a common unit, is it not to be rationally inferred that so likewise are the different sensations known as tastes, and the different sensations known as odors, and the different sensations known as colors? Nay, shall we not regard it as probable that there is a unit common to all these strongly contrasted classes of sensations? If the unlikenesses among the sensations of each class may be due to unlikenesses among the modes of aggregation of a unit of consciousness common to them all; so, too, may the much greater unlikenesses between the sensations of each class and those of other classes. There may be a single primordial element of consciousness, and the countless kinds of consciousness may be produced by the compounding of this element with itself and the re-compounding of its compounds with one another in higher and higher degrees; so producing increased multiplicity, variety, and complexity." (Volume I, p. 150.) Mr. Spencer thinks that this primordial element may be identified as a nervous shock. He says, "The subjective effect produced by a crack or noise that has no appreciable duration, is little else than a nervous shock"; and concludes, "It is possible, then — may we not even say probable — that something of the same order as that which we call a nervous shock is the ultimate unit of consciousness; and that all the unlikenesses among our feelings result from unlike modes of integration of this ultimate unit." (Page 151.)

This is quite in line with traditional associationalism. Mind as it exists is looked upon as a compound, and attention is directed to finding the units out of which it is compounded; and those units which seem to be given as such in consciousness are subjected to further scrutiny, with the aim of inquiring whether they are themselves not compounds of something still more ultimate; and thus, finally, there emerges the conception of some primordial unit from which by various compositions we may succeed in exhibiting the entire mind as its outcome. Mr. Spencer goes beyond the traditional doctrine in finding this unit outside of the mind in some form of nervous action, and inasmuch as there seems to be combination among nervous changes he concludes that there is parallel combination among mental changes, so that the internal change is but the inside of an external change among the nerves.

So far as his argument goes, however, there is much reason for doubting this. The illustration that is given of musical sound is very far from proving the case. There are a good many nervous changes that have no mental parallel, so far as we can see, and we are quite unable to tell when the nervous changes shall begin to have an inner face or what form the face shall have when it comes. The argument rests on the assumption that the peculiarities of the physical face must reappear on the mental side. If the physical antecedent is a series of waves, the mental consequent must also be a series of corresponding shocks, and the conscious effect can only be the integral of these shocks. This is an extremely doubtful physical analogy. Considering the unlikeness of the physical and mental series, and the arbitrary nature of their connection in general, we cannot form any rational expectation as to what mental consequent shall attend a given physical antecedent; whether it shall be as coarse-grained as the antecedent or strictly continuous must be decided by experience. The composition, too, may take place entirely in the nervous system and not in the mind. The sounds produced at a lower rate than sixteen per second affect the nerves in a certain way. When they are more rapidly produced, they affect the nerves in a certain other way. Corresponding to the lower rate, we have on the mental side a series of distinct sounds. Corresponding to the higher rate, we have on the mental side a perception of tone, but we have no reason for saying that the tone-sensation is made up of the simpler sensations. We simply have one set of sensations corresponding to one form of nervous action, and another kind of sensation corresponding to another form. And that this is really the view to be taken is shown by the fact that when sounds finally emerge in consciousness they show no tendency whatever to fuse into a common resultant. When the many notes of a piece of music are played, the notes do

not run together, otherwise there would be no music;
but they remain separate and are discriminated in
their varying quality and harmonized relations; without this, music could not exist. Similarly with colors.
When the colors of the spectrum are printed on a disc
in proper order and the disc is made to revolve rapidly,
we have a sensation of a sort of white light; but this
does not mean that the sensations of the spectrum
have fused, because, when those sensations are distinctly given, they do not fuse, but remain distinct.
We have really only a sensation resulting from one
nervous condition, just as under other circumstances
we have other sensations resulting from other nervous
conditions.

Mr. Spencer's argument, then, for the primordial
unit is unsuccessful. The real reason for it is found
in a desire to analyze difference into identity, and to
explain compounds by some unity of composition.
This is the doctrine generally held by the associational school.

After these considerations Mr. Spencer next proceeds to discuss the composition of mind as we can
detect it within experience itself. He says: "Accepting as really simple those constituents of Mind which
are not decomposable by introspection, we have to
consider what are their fundamental distinctive char-
acters, and what are the essential principles of arrangement among them." (Volume I, p. 163.) He finds that
"the proximate components of Mind are of two broadly
contrasted kinds — Feelings and the Relations between feelings." Feelings, again, are distinguished
into vivid and faint feelings, after the fashion of Hume.

According to Hume, there are some feelings which are relatively original. The chief mark of these is their vividness. Then there are other feelings which are not original, but which seem to be copies of vivid feelings. These as copies are relatively faint, and the whole of mind is made up of these vivid feelings and faint feelings and relations that arise among them. In this general view Mr. Spencer agrees with Hume, and follows in the line of the associational tradition. He gives the following account of the process: —

"The cardinal fact to be noted as of coördinate importance with the facts above noted, is that while each vivid feeling is joined to, but distinguished from, other vivid feelings, simultaneous or successive, it is joined to, and identified with, faint feelings that have resulted from foregoing similar vivid feelings. Each particular color, each special sound, each sensation of touch, taste, or smell, is at once known as unlike other sensations that limit it in space or time, and known as like the faint forms of certain sensations that have preceded it in time — unites itself with foregoing sensations from which it does not differ in quality but only in intensity.

"On this law of composition depends the orderly structure of Mind. In its absence there could be nothing but a perpetual kaleidoscopic change of feelings — an ever-transforming present without past or future. It is because of this tendency which vivid feelings have severally to cohere with the faint forms of all preceding feelings like themselves, that there arise what we call *ideas*. A vivid feeling does not by itself constitute a unit of that aggregate of ideas entitled knowledge. Nor does a single faint feeling constitute such a unit. But an idea, or unit of knowledge, results when a vivid feeling is assimilated to, or coheres with, one or more of the faint feelings left by such vivid feelings previously experienced. From moment to moment the feelings that constitute consciousness segregate — each becoming fused with the whole series of others like itself that have gone before it; and what we call knowing each feeling as such or such, is our name for this act of segregation.

"The process so carried on does not stop with the union of each feeling, as it occurs, with the faint forms of all preceding like feelings. Clusters of feelings are simultaneously joined with the faint forms of preceding like clusters. An idea of an object or act is composed of groups of similar and similarly related feelings that have arisen in consciousness from time to time, and have formed a consolidated series of which the members have partially or completely lost their individualities." (Volume I, pp. 181–83.) "Consider now, under its most general form, the process of composition of mind described in foregoing sections. It is no other than this same process carried out on higher and higher platforms, with increasing extent and complication. As we have lately seen, the feelings called sensations cannot of themselves constitute Mind, even when great numbers of various kinds are present together. Mind is constituted only when each sensation is assimilated to the faint forms of antecedent like sensations. The consolidation of successive units of feeling to form a sensation, is paralleled in a larger way by the consolidation of successive sensations to form what we call a knowledge of the sensation as such or such — to form the smallest separable portion of what we call thought, as distinguished from mere confused sentiency." (Volume I, p. 185.)

In all this, sensations appear as units of structure, or as the material out of which the developed mind is built. All mental forms and beliefs arise in this way. The ideas of space and time are traced in their genesis, and finally the self also is declared to be simply a collective term for these component states. In some of the language used, the knowing self would seem to be almost implied as something operating upon the sensations, of recognizing them in their likenesses and discriminating them in their unlikenesses and relating them to their several classes; but in general, this is not Mr. Spencer's view. In discussing the question of freedom, he points out that the notion of the self is really a collective term, and the fancy that it is anything more is an illusion. He says: "Considered as an internal perception, the illusion consists in supposing that at each moment the *ego* is something more than the aggregate of feelings and ideas, actual or nascent, which then exists. A man who, after being subject to an impulse consisting of a group of psychical states, real and ideal, performs a certain action, usually asserts that he determined to perform the action; and by speaking of his conscious self as having been something separate from the group of psychical states constituting the impulse, is led into the error of supposing that it was not the impulse which alone determined the action. But the entire group of psychical states which constituted the antecedent of the action, also constituted himself at that moment — constituted his psychical self, that is, as distinguished from his physical self. It is alike true that he determined the action and that the aggregate of his feelings and ideas determined it; since, during its existence, this aggregate constituted his then state of consciousness, that is, himself. Either the *ego* which is supposed to determine or will the action, is present in consciousness or it is not. If it is not present in consciousness, it is something of which we are unconscious — something, therefore, of whose existence we neither have nor can have any evidence. If it is present in consciousness, then, as it is ever present, it can be at each moment nothing else than the state of consciousness, simple or compound, passing at that moment." (Volume I, p. 500.) Thus, we see that sensations and feelings are all, and that all else in mind is simply the result of their combination. This is good orthodox associationalism, and this we now have to examine.

But before passing to this discussion, it may be well to notice a further extension of Mr. Spencer's doctrine that physical states and mental states are parallel, or that mental changes are simply the inner side of nervous changes. It has long been a question with the associationalists of the old school how to explain association. The process itself seems to be exceedingly obscure, and nothing remains apparently but to look upon the forms of association as ultimate facts of which no further account is to be given. But Mr. Spencer, with his notion of psycho-physical parallelism, gives us another account, in which the association takes place primarily, not in the mind, but in the nervous system. The relatively independent fact is the nerves and their changes, and here it is that we find the key to the associations on the mental side. He expounds the doctrine thus: "Changes in nerve-vesicles are the objective correlatives of what we know subjectively as feelings; and the discharges through fibres that connect nerve-vesicles are the objective correlatives of what we know subjectively as relations between feelings. It follows that just as the association of a feeling with its class, order, genus, and species, group within group, answers to the localization of the nervous change within some great mass of nerve-vesicles, within some part of that mass, within some part of that part, etc.; so the association of a relation with its class, order, genus and species, answers to the localization of the nervous discharge within some great aggregate of nerve-fibres, within some division of that aggregate, within some bundle of that division. Moreover, as we before concluded that the association of each feeling with its exact counterparts in past experience, answers to the reëxcitation of the same vesicle or vesicles; so here we conclude that the association of each relation with its exact counterparts in past experience, answers to the reëxcitation of the same connecting fibre or fibres. And since, on the recognition of any object, this reëxcitation of the plexus of fibres and vesicles before jointly excited by it, answers to the association of each constituent relation and each constituent feeling with the like relation and the like feeling contained in the previous consciousness of the object; it is clear that the whole process is comprehended under the principle alleged.

If the recognized object, now lacking one of its traits, arouses in consciousness an ideal feeling answering to some real feeling which this trait once aroused; the cause is that along with the strong discharge through the whole plexus of fibres and vesicles directly excited, there is apt to go a feeble discharge to those vesicles which answer to the missing feeling, through those fibres which answer to its missing relations, involving a representation of the feeling and its relations." ("Principles of Psychology," vol. I, p. 270.) Mr. Spencer elsewhere further extends this explanation as follows: "As the plexuses in these highest nervous centres, by exciting in distinct ways special sets of plexuses in the inferior centres, call up special sets of ideal feelings and relations; so, by simultaneously exciting in diffused ways the general sets of plexuses to which these special sets belong, they call up in vague forms the accompanying general sets of ideal feelings and relations — the emotional background appropriate to the definite conception. In the language of our illustration, we may say that the superior nervous centres in playing upon the inferior ones, bring out not only specific chords and cadences of feelings, but, in so doing, arouse reverberating echoes of all kindred chords and cadences that have been struck during an immeasurable past — producing a great volume of indefinite tones harmonizing with the definite tones." (Volume I, p. 571.)

One great difficulty with the associational doctrine has always been that it does not provide for the essential thing in memory, namely, recognition. At best, it could only lead to the successive production of similar mental states without providing for any recognition of the similarity. Particular mental states, of course, can never recur. The feeling that we had yesterday in its own particularity went away with its date and can no more recur or return than its date could. Hence we have, in this view, no recurrence of anything psychological, but rather an occurrence of certain similar mental states, with nothing, however, for their recognition as similar. To this objection there is no reply, and Mr. Spencer's physiological account of the matter in no way removes it. Supposing all these extraordinary things that are told us about the nerve vesicles and nerve fibres and nerve currents were true, we should be no nearer to the solution of the problem of memory than before, and no amount of such reproduction would ever bring us to recognition; for recognition is possible only as the mental subject relates its present experience to itself and the members of that experience to one another under the temporal form and then identifies some element of the present experience as similar to one in the past. Without this activity, memory is demonstrably impossible. We should have the occurrence of similar experiences, but this would not be for the experiences themselves, but for the observer from without, that is, it would not be memory at all. No succession of mental states can ever be identified with a consciousness of succession. The successions of consciousness are incommensurable with the consciousness of succession.

We might, then, avail ourselves of this fact to set aside Mr. Spencer's elaborate physiological explanation, but it may be well to look at it in a little more detail, in order to show how fantastic it is even on its own ground. Some philosophers, who have resorted to physiology to explain psychological problems, have been pleased to speak of nerve cells as the elements containing experience. This is the case with Professor Bain in his little work, "Mind and Body." Mr. Spencer, however, speaks of nerve vesicles which do not exactly seem to contain the elements of experience, but rather to be the physical facts involved in the production of our experience. If we should speak of an idea as stored in a nerve vesicle, it might be difficult to tell what we mean; but if we say that changes in a certain nerve vesicle are the objective basis of a given idea, we seem to escape the grotesque difficulty of supposing ideas really stored in brain cells. But we are really not very much better off, for now the idea is only the subjective side of changes in a special vesicle. It is not something produced apart from the vesicle or contained in the vesicle. It is simply the changes in that vesicle subjectively viewed. This, too, is very obscure; for where the subjective viewer comes from who can look at the nervous change in such a way as to see an inside to it, is a problem of great delicacy and difficulty. But omitting to press this, we need to know more of the relation of these vesicles to these ideas. Apparently the simple nervous changes are confined to simple vesicles, and these vesicles, by being variously grouped, produce the more complex changes which result in a more complex idea. It would seem from this as if there might be a kind of physiological preëstablished harmony between the simple vesicle and its idea. Suppose an ingoing nerve current, say from the eye, to reach the brain. Is there only one vesicle or group of vesicles for a common idea, or might other vesicles also produce the idea? We are not told; but one or the other must be true, and in either case we have exceeding difficulty. If we suppose that only one vesicle can produce the idea, then we have a most remarkable preëstablished harmony between the vesicles and the ideas. And this seems to be implied in Mr. Spencer's doctrine of the complex ideas. His notion of the origin of complex ideas is that the several vesicles which represent the combination are united by nervous fibres, along which nervous currents flow, with the result of producing the various combinations together in consciousness. In that case, it would seem that the simple ideas are confined to their own proper vesicle. Otherwise the lines of communication would be all astray, and only mental confusion would result. If we suppose that a great variety of vesicles could all produce the same idea, we should have to have the nerve fibres equally produced, and in that case, a single idea, with its possible ramifications, might almost take possession of the brain. But if, on the other hand, we should say that it is not merely a nerve vesicle, but a special form of change in the vesicle which is the real basis of the ideas, we should be at a loss to know what prevents these several forms of change from modifying one another and coalescing into a kind of resultant in which the different ideas would disappear entirely. Considerations of this kind led Professor Bain to suppose that in some way or other, when knowledge had been stored in appropriate cells, those cells were no longer open to new knowledge. When, then, a given idea had entered into cell A that cell was thereafter closed against new ideas, which must look elsewhere for a harbor. They must go to B or C or D, etc. This view further implied that the knowledge and storage tract was being gradually preëmpted so as to set a limit to further acquisition — an implication which Professor Bain recognized and sought to escape by showing that the number of nerve cells is so great that an ordinary life would not exhaust them.

This whole view is the outcome of picture-thinking. If we suppose that ideas are in some way represented in the brain, and if we next connect these nervous representatives by some kind of nervous connection, and further suppose that nervous currents play along these lines, we seem to have a kind of picturable explanation of the subject that is quite satisfactory until we examine it closely, and then it turns out, as we have already indicated, that the essential nature of the psychological facts is entirely overlooked and that anatomy knows nothing of the operations here suggested. There are, indeed, nerve cells and nervous fibres and nervous currents in the brain, but that they have any such psychological function as is here suggested is a mere assumption, which, from the nature of the case, admits of no demonstration. We have simply an appeal to the superficial imagination, with illustrations of chords and cadences struck during an indefinite past, and the imagination is satisfied with the picture. Apart from its psychological fatuity, it is doubtful if this view would have ever been held if its physiological and anatomical complexity had been duly regarded. If we suppose a single cell to register an object, it would seem that one cell might suffice for that object; but since objects are given, not as logical universals, but as particular cases in a great variety of contexts and complex relations, and each of these particular experiences has its own particular vesicle or physical function, the result is that a brief experience with the single thing might easily take up all the spare room in the brain if we are to think in this quantitative and picture fashion. We conclude, therefore, that Mr. Spencer's physiological annex to psychology is of no use in solving the special problems of psychology. There is, indeed, a certain general relation between physical conditions and mental conditions. The mind cannot act with proper energy and precision unless the brain be in a fairly normal condition, and, conversely, the brain itself may pass into an abnormal condition through mental disturbance. The widespread belief in mind cure in its various forms shows a strong reaction against this earlier notion, which made the mind purely passive so that it counts for nothing. There is, then, an order of concomitant variation between the mind and the body, a knowledge of which is important for both physical and mental health. But this extends only to certain general laws of concomitant development, laws of habit, of health, of rest and repair, of general influence of the body on the mind and of the mind on the body. Beyond these things no concomitance can be discovered, and this is far enough from the identification which is itself involved in the view of psycho-physical parallelism.

V

SPENCER'S EMPIRICAL THEORY OF THOUGHT

RETURNING now from this psychological excursion, we pass to the philosophical doctrine of mind and knowledge. A very large part of Mr. Spencer's exposition is the traditional empiricism, with sundry physiological and other additions of his own, but for the most part Mr. Spencer simply repeats the familiar traditions of the school. Two points in general are to be distinguished in discussing this matter: first, the forms of intellect and the corresponding forms of experience, and second, the ultimate warrant of knowledge. With regard to the first point, the rational psychologist holds that the form is essential to the mind and is contributed by the mind to experience. The empiricist holds that the form in both cases is the product of sensations and their laws. The rationalist then seeks to show that experience is impossible without some principle of form in the mind, and the empiricist seeks to show that form and faculty alike are the outcome of association and sensation. With regard to the other point, the rationalist claims that the ultimate test and warrant of truth are to be found in the mind itself or in its own native power to know. The empiricist, on the other hand, holds that the only warrant for believing anything whatever is the fact that it has been found valid in our experience. These two points, though quite distinct, have seldom been clearly separated by the disciples of either school, and thus differences have arisen within the schools themselves. Some rationalists have devoted themselves entirely to proving that form and faculty are innate or immanent in the mind, and have given no thought to the second question. But that their conclusion from innateness to universality is hasty is shown by the fact that Kant made the existence of innate faculties and forms the ground for denying absolute knowledge. Thus, one may be a rationalist as to the origin of faculty and a relativist or agnostic with regard to knowledge. Among the empiricists also we find like diversity of aim and purpose. Some, as Condillac and Spencer, confined their attention chiefly to the genesis of faculty and belief. They seek to identify all the mental functions, such as memory, reason, conscience, judgment, etc., as modifications of the common process of sensation. Empiricists of this type abound in appeals to heredity, and regard the law of evolution as having profound significance for the problem, expecially because it furnishes them with the time needed to work the desired transformations. Other empiricists, again, as J. S. Mill, regard such speculations as philosophically irrelevant. Chauncey Wright, in his review of Spencer, dealt very severely with him for fancying that the doctrine of heredity alters the case in the least. At bottom, he says, the crucial question is not how we come to believe, but why we believe. The debate then involves two questions, the one psychological, and the other logical or philosophical. The genesis of belief is distinguished from the grounds of believing.

389

The general aim of empiricism is to explain the higher mental forms and faculties by composition of the lower sense experiences. Sometimes they call it the genetic theory of mind. We see how mind is built up stage by stage from its crude beginnings. There is in this a certain failure to analyze the problem and its presuppositions. In general, composition may be by elements essentially related to the product, or by elements indifferent to it. In the former case, the explanation by composition presupposes the law of the product, and thus explains the same by the same. In the latter case, the product is something fortuitous so far as the explaining elements are concerned, and we have only chance as the principle of explanation, unless we assume a controlling power apart from the elements which contains the principle of their combination. A pile of stones is sufficiently accounted for by the individual stones that make up the heap, but as soon as we come to anything organic or structural, then such composition no longer serves as an explanation. In some sense the component bricks in a house explain the house, but they do not explain it except as we assume a builder apart from them. The elements in such cases are not under the law of the whole, and if we attempt to explain the composition of the whole by the elements, we do it only as we carry the law of the whole into the elements themselves. Literature, again, is in some sense explained by words, as without words and letters literature would not exist. But while words and letters are the instruments for the expression of literature, they of themselves say nothing until they are united into rational meaning by a mind that uses them. A page of print is in some sense explained by the body of type, and yet the composition of a page demands, in addition to the type themselves, the composer to put them into their proper places. Organic bodies also are not made up of the several organs and members mechanically juxtaposed, but only of those organs and members as parts of the living body. And even inorganic structures, such as buildings and machines, do not have their explanation in the component matter alone, but only in the law of the whole, which uses the inorganic matter for its realization. The same is true for all mental syntheses. If the synthesis arises from mechanically putting together things essentially unrelated, we have mere chance; but if, on the other hand, it arises from the putting together of things which are already under a higher mental idea, then we explain the higher form by assuming it in principle in the antecedents. And this whole matter of genetic procedure in general overlooks the fact that genesis in an order of law must be determined by some immanent law within the process. The growth of an organism is altogether unintelligible as an external grouping of mechanical elements. It can be understood only through an immanent law which determines the whole process from its germinal beginnings to its mature perfection. And the same must be said of mental syntheses. If we begin with sensations, without any higher rational principle, there is no assignable reason why we should ever go beyond them; and if we do go beyond them, it can be only as the mental nature is not exhausted

391

in the crude sense fact, but also involves the higher order of mental manifestation. In that case all alleged geneses or genetic procedures can be nothing more than a description of the successive order of manifestation, and are in no sense a deduction of the higher mental forms from earlier mental states which did not imply them; just as in the development of the organism we look upon the later phases, not as adventitious products mechanically taken on from without, but rather as successive manifestations of the one organic law that underlies the whole. But the empiricists in general have not been content to take this view, but rather have thought that the higher forms of mental life were produced out of the lower. The untenability of this view is already apparent. It is interesting, however, to trace the various efforts at such explanation and the failures that have resulted. We begin with the idea of space.

Herbart in Germany and the sensationalists in England have both claimed that a being capable of having sensations and representations in time must develop the idea of space. It is not plain whether the deductions are meant to deduce a knowledge of space as a reality, or only the development of the idea from non-spatial elements without any reference to its objective reality or ideality, but in both cases the psychological theory is essentially the same. As good an argument as any for their view is the following by Mr. Mill: "Suppose," he says, "two small bodies, A and B, sufficiently near together to admit of their being touched simultaneously, one with the right hand, the other with the left. Here are two tactual sensations which are simultaneous, just as a sensation of color and one of odor might be; and this makes us cognize the two objects of touch as both existing at once. The question then is, what have we in our minds, when we represent to ourselves the relation between these two objects already known to be simultaneous, in the form of Extension, or intervening Space — a relation which we do not suppose to exist between the color and the odor?" Mr. Mill next points out that the peculiarity is that in passing from A to B a series of muscular sensations must intervene, and continues: —

"When we say that there is a space between A and B, we mean that some amount of these muscular sensations must intervene; and when we say that the space is greater or less, we mean that the series of sensation (amount of muscular effort being given) is longer or shorter."

"The theory may be recapitulated as follows. The sensation of muscular motion unimpeded constitutes our notion of empty space, and the sensation of muscular motion impeded constitutes that of filled space. Space is Room — room for movement; which its German name, *Raum*, distinctly confirms. We have a sensation which accompanies the free movement of our organs, say for instance of our arm. This sensation is variously modified by the direction, and by the amount of the movement. We have different states of muscular sensation corresponding to the movements of the arm upward, downward, to right, to left, or in any radius whatever, of a sphere of which the joint, that the arm revolves around, forms the centre. We have also different states of muscular sensation according as the arm is moved *more*, whether this consists in its being moved with greater velocity or with the same velocity during a longer time; and the equivalence of these two is speedily learned by experience. These different kinds and qualities of muscular sensation, experienced in getting from one point to another (that is, obtaining in succession two sensations of touch and resistance, the objects of which are regarded as simultaneous), are all we mean by saying that the points are separated by spaces, that they are at different distances, and in different directions. . . . It appears to me that this doctrine is sound, and that the muscular sensations in question are the sources of all the notion of Extension which we should ever obtain from the tactual and muscular senses without the assistance of the eye."[1]

There is a fundamental unclearness running through this exposition which makes it uncertain whether these sensations are the sensations of space or produce it. Both possibilities run along in indefinite oscillation, so that either seems to be on the point of becoming the other. We must discuss them separately.

No sensations, muscular or otherwise, are capable of originating the space idea. The apparent success of Mill's attempt is due entirely to the space implications of the terms used. Thus we have "direction," "movement," "velocity," "downward," "upward,"

[1] *Examination of Sir William Hamilton's Philosophy*, vol. I, pp. 280-82.

"right," "left." A and B are also spoken of as coexistent bodies and sufficiently near together to be touched by each of our hands respectively at the same time, and we are supposed to pass back and forth from one to the other. Of course, if all these terms are understood in their spatial significance, it would be very easy to deduce the idea from the experience described, for we should have the idea already in a state of high development. If, now, we do not propose to beg the question, we must carefully eliminate all these terms. We know nothing of movement or velocity or direction. We must not assume that A and B coexist in space or in mutual externality, for this would beg the question. Coexistent and sequent sensations in time, like or unlike, are all that is given. If there be sensations attending movement and change of direction and velocity, they are not yet interpreted by the notions of movement, direction, and velocity. All this is to be deduced. Hence, when we speak of passing from A, all that we can mean is that the sensation, A, ceases to exist, and our return to A can only mean the occurrence of a similar sensation as when we sing the musical scale up and down. To assume that it is a movement to and from a fixed object, A, which coexists with another fixed object, V, external to it, would beg the question. We should be seeking to deduce the idea of space from muscular sensations, which, however, arise from certain movements known as movements between two bodies known to coexist in mutual externality. It would be strange, indeed, if such a deduction were not victoriously successful. But when we are careful to deny ourselves the luxury of begging the question, it turns out that we never get beyond coexistent and sequent sensations in time.

This argument has been given at much greater length by Mr. Spencer, yet without adding anything to its real strength. He is far more ambiguous than Mill in some of the leading terms and expressions employed in his discussion. Thus we have the word "serial," which may be used in speaking either of time or space, but the serial in time is not the same as the serial in space. Similarly with the phrase, "relations of position or relative positions," which may have either spatial or temporal significance. "Coexistence" and "coexistent" likewise are terms used with great ambiguity. Like Mr. Mill, he makes great use of muscular sensations and also tactual sensations. The space relation between two sensitive points on the body is discovered by the muscular feelings accompanying the motion of an organ from one to the other. He argues as follows: —

"Taking for our subject a partially developed creature, having a nervous structure that is able to receive the data for the cognition, but in which the data are not yet coördinated, let us call the two points on its body between which a relation is to be established, A and Z. Let us assume these two points to be anywhere within reach of the limbs. By the hypothesis, nothing is at present known of these points; either as coexisting in Space, as giving successive sensations in Time, or as being brought into relation by Motion. If now the creature moves a limb in such a way as to touch nothing, there is a certain vague reaction upon its consciousness — a sensation of muscular tension. This sensation has the peculiarity of being indefinite in its commencement, indefinite in its termination, and indefinite in all its intermediate changes. . . . Manifestly, such a consciousness is but a nascent consciousness. While its states are thus indistinctly separated, there can be no clear comparison of them; no classing of them; no thought, properly so called; and consequently, no ideas of Motion, Time, or Space, as we understand them. Suppose that the limb touches something. A sudden change in consciousness is produced — a change that is incisive in its commencement, and, when the limb is removed, equally incisive in its termination. In the midst of the continuous feeling of muscular tension, vaguely rising and falling in intensity, there all at once occurs a distinct feeling of another kind. This feeling, beginning and ending abruptly, constitutes a definite state of consciousness; and becomes, as it were, a *mark* in consciousness. Other such marks are produced by other such acts; and in proportion as they are multiplied there arises a possibility of comparing them, both in respect to their strengths and in respect to their relative positions. At the same time the feelings of muscular tension being, as it were, divided into lengths by these super-posed marks, become similarly comparable; and so there are acquired materials for a simple order of thought. Observe, also, that while these tactual sensations may, when several things are touched in succession, produce successive marks in consciousness, separated by intervening muscular sensations, they may also become concurrent with these muscular sensations; as when the end of the limb is drawn along a surface. And observe further, that when the surface over which the end of the limb is drawn is not a foreign body, but some part of the creature's own body, these muscular sensations, and the continuous tactual sensation joined with them, are accompanied by a series of tactual sensations proceeding from that part of the skin over which the limb is drawn.

"See, then, what happens and what is implied. When the creature moves the end of a limb along the surface of its body from A to Z, there are simultaneously impressed on its consciousness three sets of sensations — the varying series of sensations proceeding from the muscles in action: the series of tactual sensations proceeding from the points of the skin successively touched between A and Z; and the continuous sensation of touch from the end of the limb. . . . Every subsequent motion of the limb over the surface from A to Z results in the like simultaneous sets of sensations; and hence these, in course of time, become indissolubly associated. Though the series of tactual sensations, A to Z, being producible by a foreign body moving over the same surface, can be dissociated from the others; and though, if this surface (which we will suppose to be on the head) be withdrawn by a movement of the head, the same motion of the limb with its accompanying muscular sensations, may occur without any sensation of touch; yet when these two series are linked by the tactual sensation proceeding from the end of the limb, they necessarily proceed together, and become inseparably connected in thought. Consequently, the series of tactual sensations A to Z, and the series of muscular sensations which invariably accompanies it when self-produced, serve as equivalents; and being two sides of the same experience, suggest each other in consciousness. *The successive feelings on the skin being excited, association brings up ideas of the habitually-correlated feelings in the limb; and the feelings in the limb being excited, association brings up ideas of the habitually-correlated feelings on the skin.* Due attention having been paid to this fact, let us go on to consider what must happen when something touches, at the same moment, the entire surface between A and Z. This surface is supplied by a series of independent nerve-fibres, each of which separately is affected by an impression falling within a specific area of the skin, and each of which produces a separate state of consciousness. When the finger is drawn along this surface, these nerve-fibres A, B, C, D . . . Z, are excited in succession; that is — produce successive states of consciousness. But when something covers the whole surface between A and Z, they are excited simultaneously; and produce what tends to become a single state of consciousness. . . . What it now concerns us to notice is this: — *that as the series of tactual feelings A to Z, known as having sequent positions in consciousness, is found to be equivalent to the accompanying series of muscular feelings; and as it is also found to be equivalent to the simultaneous tactual feelings A to Z, which are presented in coexistent positions; it follows that these two last are found to be equivalents to each other.* A series of muscular sensations become known as corresponding to a series of coexistent positions; and being habitually joined with it, become at last unthinkable without it. Thus, the relation of coexistent positions between the points A and Z (and by implication all intermediate points), is necessarily disclosed by a comparison of experiences: the ideas of Space, Time and Motion, are evolved together. When the successive states of consciousness A to Z, are thought of as having relative positions, the notion of Time becomes nascent. When these states of consciousness occur simultaneously, their relative positions, which were before sequent, become coexistent; and there arises a nascent consciousness of Space. And when these two relations of coexistent and sequent positions are both presented to consciousness along with a series of sensations of muscular tension, a nascent idea of Motion results." ("Principles of Psychology," vol. II, pp. 220–25.)

It will be seen that this account is much more complex than that of Mr. Mill, but except in the complication it has no logical change. Mr. Mill dealt with the muscular series especially. Mr. Spencer introduces both tactual and muscular sensations and also the idea of coexistent consciousness of states. In this we have greater possibilities of confusion. The tactual and the muscular may even seem to coexist in consciousness and to have lost their sequent character altogether. In fact, however, this is only confusion. To begin with, the temporal can exist only for that which is non-temporal. A sequence of sensations is never a comprehension of sequence. If there were nothing but sequent sensations, there would never be any conception of sequence whatever; for each sensation would go off by itself and there would be no consciousness to compare the successive sensations with one another and to contrast them with the abiding self. Under these circumstances the conception of sequence would never arise, even though there should be an eternity of sequent sensations. Here Mr. Spencer simply falls into the traditional error of the associationalists in overlooking the abiding self, which is necessary even to the simplest knowledge of sequence.

For the rest, the quotation given merely confuses coexistence and sequence in consciousness with coexistence in space. After long dwelling upon this fact, that the tactual, visual, and muscular series may be spoken of as temporally coexistent, it may occur to us that space itself is an order of coexistence, and then we may fancy the problem solved. Mr. Spencer's illustration of the body, with its surface and with sensations arising from motion across the surface, merely serves to beg the question. It is very difficult to keep the idea of space involved in such metaphors from creeping into the reasoning, and then the question is triumphantly begged. But when we carefully guard against this, it is plain that we have only qualitative distinct sensations at the start. We may possibly give this a temporal order, and beyond that there is no possibility of going. These temporal sensations have in them no suggestion of space. They have no spatial qualities or relations in themselves. They are not spatially external to one another and they have no spatial position. Out of such data it is forever impossible to deduce anything totally distinct.

Mr. Spencer has elsewhere sought to deduce the

space idea from the time idea. In "First Principles," page 146, he says: "Now relations are of two orders — relations of sequence, and relations of coexistence; of which the one is original and the other derived. The relation of sequence is given in every change of consciousness. The relation of coexistence, which cannot be originally given in a consciousness of which the states are serial, becomes distinguished only when it is found that certain relations of sequence have their terms presented in consciousness in either order with equal facility; while the others are presented only in one order. Relations of which the terms are not reversible, become recognized as sequences proper; while relations of which the terms occur indifferently in both directions, become recognized as coexistences. Endless experiences, which from moment to moment present both orders of these relations, render the distinction between them perfectly definite; and at the same time generate an abstract conception of each. The abstract of all sequences is Time. The abstract of all coexistences is Space." This exposition is given in all the editions of "First Principles," and was therefore written before and retained after the quotation before given from the "Principles of Psychology." In the "Psychology," Spencer seems to regard motion as an earlier experience than that of space and time, and concludes that the three ideas develop together; but in the quotation just given it would seem that the time experience is original and the space experience is derived, and that the distinction between the space and time experience is found in the possibility of reversing the space series, which cannot be done in time.

Thus, by turning our eyes from right to left we get a given series of sensations. By turning them back again from left to right we get the same sensations reversed. The same is true for touch. We can touch a series of objects in a given order and then reverse it, but this reversibility is what distinguishes the spatial series from the temporal. The time series goes on forever and never turns back. But the space series admits of being reversed indefinitely and as often as we may desire. Thus the idea of space is reached by differentiation of the time series.

But this is equally untenable. The reversibility of a space series depends upon its being a space series. We can reverse many time series without ever getting any hint of space. Thus we can sing the musical scale up and down indefinitely, but there is nothing in that to suggest the idea of space, and there would never be in any temporal inversion a suggestion of the idea of space unless the series were already fixed as spatial.

In all this, too, it is not clear whether Mr. Spencer is trying to deduce the idea of space from non-spatial elements as something distinct from them, or whether he is calling a certain group of temporal elements space. As to his ontological theory, he holds to some form of objective reality in space. Our conception of it is indeed relative, but there is some independent fact behind what we call space as some mode of the Unknowable. This is his metaphysical view, but in his theory of knowledge he fails to justify such a conception. Whatever Mr. Spencer meant to do, he really gives us only temporal sensations in various orders, and he calls certain orders spatial. But this is

403

far enough from deducing the idea of space, and in general it is clear, as already said, that, in explaining higher mental facts by the composition of lower ones, the composition must be determined by the character of its components.

If, then, we try to construct an idea of space out of spaceless elements, it is impossible to do this unless we assume in the elements themselves some kind of spatial principle, whereby they produce, as something different from themselves, the spatial idea. But in that case we should not really deduce the idea of space from the non-spatial, but rather deduce it from elements with some immanent spatial principle in them. Unless we do this, we have to say that a certain grouping of non-spatial elements is the idea of space. This is the view before suggested as possible. We cannot admit that the space order can be deduced from the non-spatial, but we may seek to identify the space order with certain forms of our non-spatial experience. This is the view mentioned as contained in Mill's argument, — "When we say that there is a space between A and B, we mean that some amount of these muscular sensations must intervene." This implies, not that muscular sensations produce the idea of space as something apart, but that when associated, certain muscular and tactual sensations are the idea of space. But this idea refuses to be identified in any way with any kind or amount of sensations. Sensations may serve as a measure of space and they may furnish the conditions under which the space idea is educed, but no identification is possible. To see this we need only attempt to enunciate a geometrical proposition in terms of sensation, say the square of the hypothenuse is equal to the sum of the squares on the other two sides. It would be hard to translate this into terms of the relations of different groups of sensation. A geometrical representation of the square root of two is not hard to understand in space terms, but it would require the greatest penetration to identify it with temporal sensations, whether coexistent or successive.

All of these empirical attempts to reach the idea of space without appealing to some immanent spatial law in the mind fail to distinguish between our everyday space experience and the spatial intuition which underlies geometry. In the former case we might in a fashion substitute for distance, direction, etc., sundry physical experiences. And these, though not space in themselves, may yet be used as a measure of space, so much muscular effort, etc. So many organic sensations of one kind and another might in a fashion be put as the equivalent of space experience, because these things would enter into such spatial experience. At the same time they would in no way give the spatial form itself. But when we come to the spatial intuition on which geometry is based, we then have something which can in no way be related to sense experience. This is pure intuition, and the elements of this intuition cannot even be given in any sense experience. The points, lines, and surfaces of geometry cannot be discovered in sense or abstracted from sense. Here the mind is the source of both the elements and the combinations.

Mr. Spencer himself gives a very interesting passage on this matter of space, which shows a conception in his mind that his theory of knowledge would never enable him to reach, and also shows spatial conceptions far outrunning anything possible to sense experience. The passage itself is one of the last things he published, and is given in his "Facts and Comments" in the closing paragraph: —

"There is one aspect of the Great Enigma to which little attention seems given, but which has of late years more frequently impressed me. I refer not to the problems which all concrete existences, from suns down to microbes, present, but to those presented by the universal form under which these exist — the phenomena of Space.

"In youth we pass by without surprise the geometrical truths set down in our Euclids. It suffices to learn that in a right-angled triangle the square of the hypothenuse is equal to the sum of the squares of the other two sides: it is demonstrable, and that is enough. Concerning the multitudes of remarkable relations among lines and among spaces very few ever ask, Why are they so? Perhaps the question may in later years be raised, as it has been in myself, by some of the more conspicuously marvelous truths now grouped under the title of the 'Geometry of Position.' Many of these are so astounding that but for the presence of ocular proof they would be incredible; and by their marvelousness as well as by their beauty, they serve, in some minds at least, to raise the unanswerable question — How come there to exist among the parts of this seemingly-structureless vacancy we call Space, these strange relations? How does it happen that the blank form of things presents us with truths as incomprehensible as do the things it contains?

"Beyond the reach of our intelligence as are the mysteries of the objects known by our senses, those presented in this universal matrix are, if we may so say, still further beyond the reach of our intelligence; for whereas those of the one kind may be, and are, thought of by many as explicable on the hypothesis of Creation, and by the rest on the hypothesis of Evolution, those of the other kind cannot by either be regarded as thus explicable. Theist and Agnostic must agree in recognizing the properties of Space as inherent, eternal, uncreated — as anteceding all creation, if creation has taken place, and all evolution, if evolution has taken place.

"Hence, could we penetrate the mysteries of existence, there would remain still more transcendent mysteries. That which can be thought of neither as made nor evolved presents us with facts the origin of which is even more remote from conceivability than is the origin of the facts presented by visible and tangible things. It is impossible to imagine how there came to exist the marvelous space-relations referred to above. We are obliged to recognize these as having belonged to Space from all eternity.

"And then comes the thought of this universal matrix itself, anteceding alike creation or evolution, whichever be assumed, and infinitely transcending both, alike in extent and duration; since both, if conceived at all, must be conceived as having had beginnings, while Space had no beginning. The thought of this blank form of existence which, explored in all directions as far as imagination can reach, has, beyond that, an unexplored region compared with which the part which imagination has traversed is but infinitesimal — the thought of a Space compared with which our immeasurable sidereal system dwindles to a point, is a thought too overwhelming to be dwelt upon. Of late years the consciousness that without origin or cause infinite Space has ever existed and must ever exist, produces in me a feeling from which I shrink."

This is a most interesting passage in many ways. It is highly interesting in itself, as a suggestion of a deep mystery contained in the spatial intuition. It has an additional interest in Mr. Spencer's case, as showing a different state of mind from that revealed in his "First Principles," where the conception of anything infinite and eternal was especially perhorresced; and it is further interesting as showing that he could break away from his empirical theory of knowledge. The conception of space here set forth was not reached by rubbing one end of a limb over a patch of skin.

We conclude, then, that Mr. Spencer has not succeeded any better than his predecessors in deducing the higher ideas and mental forms from the lower and very simple ones. It is not necessary to consider the deduction of other ideas, such as identity, causation, etc. The example already given shows both the ingenuity of the process and its failure.

Mr. Spencer, then, succeeds no better than the traditional empiricism in deducing the higher forms of mentality from the lower elements of sensation.

He equally fails, as we now proceed to show, in deducing knowledge. In the matter just discussed, empiricism is related to psychology. In the matter now to be considered, it is related to truth. How do we distinguish truth from error and how do we learn truth in general?

In this matter, also, traditional empiricism has had much trouble. It has sought to deduce belief and conviction from habit. Things, when they come together in experience, produce expectation and ways of thinking. And thus by association habits of thought and belief are formed, and these are really what we call the intuitions of intelligence. They are slowly piled up by the long experience of the race. The principles of arithmetic and geometry, the belief in causality, and the various formal truths of reason are thought to be reached in this way. This, it will be seen, is a separate question from the other one, of the production of mental forms, and it is on this question that some of the chief debates with empiricism have raged. The aim of the empiricist is to generate the conviction of rational connection by continuous association. The strength of association varies with frequency, and hence uniform association must, it was claimed, generate necessity of thought and belief. Apart from experience the mind would know and expect nothing. The only reason we have for saying that any elements belong together is that we find them coming together in experience. How otherwise do we learn the laws of mind except by observing the laws of nature?

The plausibility of this view is largely due to its ambiguity. It may mean that conjunction is the mark of rational connection and it may mean that conjunction is the true meaning of connection. In the latter case we fall a prey to Hume's destructive criticism, and reason vanishes entirely. In the former case we say nothing to the purpose. Of course a rational mind, impelled by its nature to seek connection, will surely view a continuous coming together as a mark of belonging together. But this is not to deduce connection from conjunction; it is rather to apply the principle of rational connection to the explanation of empirical conjunctions. The truths of inductive science are, indeed, in a way, won from experience; but not by simply reading off what is given in sense, but rather by transforming the sense data through the application of a rational idea.

Any further plausibility the view may have is due to the assumption, implied or expressed, of a fixed objective order. This order has its uniformities of connection which reproduce themselves in uniformities of experience, and these in turn become uniformities of thought. This view has all the superficialities of empiricism in general, and in addition, as we shall see, has its own special inconsistencies, in that it dogmatically assumes a system of metaphysics impossible to empiricism. Nevertheless, this has become the prevailing form of empirical doctrine, and in the form of mental heredity has introduced a novelty into the discussion. This we have now to consider.

The aim of empiricism, as we have said, is to generate the conviction of connection by recurrent association. To this the rather superficial answer was given that the most assured beliefs often appear very early in the experience of the individual, and that the time was too short for association to work its wonders. To be sure, the empiricists ground away at the associational mill with the utmost briskness, but they found it exceedingly difficult to furnish a full set of beliefs in the early years of infancy and childhood.

But this particular argument had the misfortune to mislead criticism by a side issue. It suggested that the great difficulty with empiricism is the lack of time for working its transformations, which is a sad mistake. The essential difficulty with the doctrine, as we shall see, is the complete incommensurability between its data and its assumed products, and the longest time is as powerless as the shortest to remove this fact. When the doctrine is taken in earnest, it is intelligible only because it is false. But the misleading suggestion having been made that lack of time is the chief shortcoming, it was natural to look about to see if this failing could not be remedied. Here comes in Mr. Spencer's doctrine of a race experience, which is his device for removing the difficulties of empiricism and also for uniting the empirical and rational schools. He pointed out that the individual experience is really not capable of explaining all that the individual mind possesses. The facts of mental heredity forbade such a notion. We must then grant the rationalists' claim that the individual experience is no sufficient explanation of the individual's knowledge, but we may not assume that mind has always had an a priori factor in it, for that which the individual's experience cannot explain, the experience of the race may do. By combining the facts of mental heredity with the current theory of biological evolution, it seemed possible to substitute for the experience of the individual the experience of the race and even the experience of all our pre-human and sub-human ancestors. Thus a great extension of time was secured, and with the new capital acquired by the brilliant stroke, empiricism set up business again and is now operating almost exclusively on this basis. Thus apriorism and empiricism are reconciled. The former is true for the individual; the latter is true for the race. The individual's experience is preformed in its great outlines, and in this sense is innate. But there is nothing in the individual which cannot be explained by the experience of the race; for these inborn outlines in the individual are but the net result of all ancestral experience, consolidated by indefinite repetition and handed on by heredity.

The alacrity with which the empiricists flocked to the new doctrine showed the straits into which they had come through the vigorous attacks of Hamilton and others. Yet protests were not wanting from the more logical empiricists when the doctrine was first put forth. It seemed to them to be a surrender of empiricism in the only field where it can be tested, in order to recover it again by the aid of an uncertain biological speculation. But these protests, though well founded in logic, had little effect. The notion of a race experience was so peculiarly satisfying and all-explaining that it was taken up without criticism and even without understanding by the great majority of empiricists. It is a perfectly clear notion so long as thought is quiescent, but it becomes very cloudy when inspected. A brief reflection serves to show that the race is composed of an indefinite number of individuals, and that the experience of the race can only be the experiences of these individuals. At once the appearance of unity and identity vanishes into indefinite plurality. If we take a genealogical line, of which A, B, C, and D are successive members, it is plain that the line is nothing and that the members are all. There is no common experience, and, except in a figurative sense, there is no transmitted experience. The race has no experience, but only the members of the race; and the experience of each member belongs to him, and except in a figurative sense can never be transmitted. Experience cannot pass from A and it cannot pass into B. We commonly hide these difficulties from ourselves by a word. Heredity is their solution. The later members of the series inherit the experience of the earlier members. But heredity is another metaphor. The facts for which it stands are the problem itself rather than its solution. Even though it were not so, empiricism is not helped; for heredity can only transmit what is possessed; it can produce nothing. Making a will creates no property. Thus the transformation is to be worked, after all, in the experience of the individual, where analysis shows it to be impossible. In other words, suppose an individual to have existed not for seventy years, but for ages, through all the time during which the life history has been unfolded. He would be in the most favorable condition for learning all that experience could possibly give him; but this being, unless he had a rational nature, at least implicit from the start, could never by any possibility develop into a rational being. We set aside the doctrine of a race experience as only a misleading metaphor, and one which, when analyzed, is seen in its worthlessness.

But these considerations remain somewhat on the surface. We must next point out the fundamental untenability of the doctrine. Mr. Spencer himself has a very formidable metaphysical outfit. He has a fundamental reality without beginning and without end, and he has the indestructibility of matter and the persistence of force, inviolability of natural law, and a great many other things of the same kind which it would puzzle even the most determined apriorist himself to establish. Nevertheless he himself regards all this as truth which is deeper even than demonstration and deep as the very nature of the mind itself. Mr. Mill especially had a great many scruples about this extensive doctrine, and we shall later see how impossible it is for the empiricist to reach any of these first principles on which Mr. Spencer himself depends. But in general, the empiricist has never clearly decided where he begins. Green has shown, in his "Introduction to Hume," that the sensationalist doctrine rests on a fundamental ambiguity, and that all its apparent success in making out its case depends on the ambiguity in the word "sensation." By sensation we may mean simply a particular and unqualified sensation in the sensibility, or we may mean by it an experience qualified by the various categories of the reason, qualified, that is, by reference to something external as a quality of the same or as its effect, and qualified by various forms of relation of unity, plurality, identity, and the like. Now, with sensation in the first sense, as simple, unqualified impression, intelligence cannot even begin, for such impression is simply flitting, fleeting, phantasmagoric, vanishing with its date and leaving nothing behind. As Green truly says, such sensationalism must be speechless. It can say nothing, for it has nothing to say. A particular sensation as occurring in time is strictly nothing for intelligence until it is fixed into a meaning of which it is the bearer or the expression. When the sensation is thus fixed, the idea remains as the intellectual constant for grasping and expressing the sensation, but until this is done, there is nothing whatever for intelligence. Again, the sensation in this particular vanishes beyond recall. It was associated with nothing, least of all with anything recurring at a later date. When, then, we speak of associations among sensations, it is never of sensations as particular impressions, but of sensations as rationalized by being fixed into abiding meanings; that is, the sensations with which the empiricist deals have all been transformed by intelligence, and the sensations between which associations exist are just those universals of intelligence and not the particulars of empirical theory. Thus it is clear that this doctrine never begins at the beginning, and that its supposed data have all the marks of the understanding upon them. And this is still more manifest in the various rational relations which the mind establishes among them. If we should abstract these sensations from the various relations of space and time and causality and identity and number, etc., there would really be nothing articulate to them. But these relations, again, are not something which the sensations of themselves establish; they are relations established by a rational principle which comprehends the sensations in the unity of its own consciousness. So long as we remain among the plurality of sensations we have neither unity nor plurality except for some unity other than the sensations themselves. The sensations are not supposed to know themselves or one another. Each one, then, as a particular unit of consciousness is shut up to itself, and no proper rational consciousness can arise until there is something other than these particular states which is not in one nor all of them, but which comprehends them all in its own unity and establishes an order of rational relations among them. Thus a proper rational consciousness is made possible, and in no other way can this be done.

The way in which the traditional empiricist reaches rational consciousness is by taking it for granted. He continually mixes himself up with the problem, and mistakes his knowledge of the sensations and their various relations for an emergence of that knowledge among the sensations themselves as a result of their interaction. This is pure mythology so far as the sensations are concerned, and shows an utter failure to grasp the logical conditions of rational consciousness in any case. In this matter Mr. Spencer has gone with the multitude and made no improvement. As already said, he assumes an enormous metaphysical outfit which it is impossible for him to justify, and then he simply constructs a mythology of relations among the sensational units of the mental composition, then back of this another mythology respecting nerve vesicles and nerve changes which have insides to them, all of which is purely a product of picture-thinking, without any proper appreciation whether of scientific thought or of philosophic thought.

Mr. Spencer's Skepticism

When it comes to the doctrine of knowledge, empiricism, ever since the time of Hume, has been seen to end in overwhelming skepticism. In the hands of Hume it led directly to nihilism. In the hands of every other speculator who gave any attention to its bearing on knowledge the same result has been more or less dimly seen. There have been at times some rather grotesque failures to note the bearing of the doctrine on knowledge, as appears in the general union of this view with materialism. In one way the doctrine seems to lead to materialism, that is, it reduces the mind to such passivity that there is nothing but the body left. And hence persons who have thought along this line have generally tended to make physiology all; but on the other hand, it has long been clear that there is really no thoroughfare in either direction. The world of things and laws, to which materialism so confidently appeals, turns out to be something which empiricism makes impossible as an object of knowledge or even of faith. Nihilism is the doom of empiricism, as Hume showed. And to make matters worse, consistent materialism, on the other hand, overthrows empiricism. For materialism, so far as it claims to be scientific, must build on the notion of fixed elements

417

with fixed qualities and fixed laws; and hence, if matter should attain to thought, the laws of thought must be viewed as a part of the nature of things, as much so as the laws of physics and chemistry. The mental manifestation, when it comes, is as much rooted in the nature of matter as any physical manifestation. In that case antecedent experience is as little needed for intellectual insight as for chemical action. Both alike are expressions of the essential nature of matter under the circumstances, and all that is needed for either is the appropriate physical condition. This is so much the case that, if we suppose the physical double of any person produced directly from the inorganic, his mental double would also be produced. There would be the same insight, memory, and expectation in both cases. Thus the empirical deductions and explanations by reference to experience would vanish altogether. But in crude thought this is entirely unsuspected, and materialism and empiricism live along together on the best of terms, and without the slightest suspicion of their mutual contradiction. Spencer's long exposition derives what plausibility it has from the assumption, implied or expressed, of a fixed objective order. This order has its uniformities of connection, and these reproduce themselves in uniformities of experience, and these in turn become uniformities of thought, thus dogmatically assuming a system of metaphysics impossible to empiricism. According to Mr. Mill, for all we know two and two may make five in some other planet, and he holds that all natural laws must be limited in our affirmations to a reasonable degree of extension to adjacent cases, but

Mr. Spencer has absolute faith in natural laws. To question them in any way is to deny the persistence of force, and there is no deeper iniquity than this. This makes it all the more necessary for us to consider how Mr. Spencer will escape the nihilism involved in sensational doctrine, and to this we next devote ourselves.

Underlying Mr. Spencer's system we find a most formidable metaphysical apparatus. We have matter and force and law and an Unknowable without beginning or end, and various other things which it is somewhat hard for an empirical philosophy to reach. In addition, he also assumes throughout a fixed order of the world which is the original source of knowledge. In his doctrine of knowledge the problem is to reproduce the world of things in thought, and in this way he seems to get a fixed foundation. Absolute uniformities of experience, he says, must produce absolute uniformities of thought. Again, reasoning itself can be trusted only on the supposition that absolute uniformities of thought correspond to absolute uniformities of things. There is a plausibility in this which is sure to captivate the uncritical mind. Undoubtedly, in our experience a great many uniformities of thought rest upon what we call uniformities in things, The mountain range runs north and south in fact, and so we think of it as running north and south. Unsupported bodies fall to the ground and never fall up, and hence another law seems to emerge in thought. Corresponding to the fixities of things, then, we have fixities of experience. And what is this but a generation of uniformities of thought by uniformities of things?

The matter, however, is not so simple on reflection.

To begin with, these generated uniformities lie within the field of experience itself and presuppose its general possibility. In the next place, any philosophical scheme must develop its theory of knowledge out of its own resources. A given system might be such as to lead necessarily to skepticism or denial, and no such scheme should be allowed to proceed upon the general trustworthiness of knowledge in order to establish itself. This is what sensationalism has generally done. Since the time of Hume it has been clear to all critical thinkers that a consistent sensationalism can never reach any such world order as Mr. Spencer here assumes. Mr. Spencer simply picks up his doctrine of knowledge on the field of common sense and then develops a system of thinking which is incompatible with the primal assumption. Both the idealist and the epistemologist raise objections to the dogmatic realism which Mr. Spencer places at the basis of his system. Hence he is called upon to make strenuous efforts to ward off their criticism or else he must see his theory collapse. He speaks of the "insanities of idealism," and further says that "if idealism be true, evolution is a dream." He must then show that idealism is not true or see his doctrine vanish like a dream. Again, if Hume's conclusions are allowed, his doctrine falls even more hopelessly; for on Hume's theory the only reality is a set of vanishing impressions, vivid or faint, which have no proper rational connection among themselves and which spring from and point to no reality. Mr. Spencer, then, must escape both the insanities of idealism and the nihilism of Hume.

Mr. Spencer's proof of realism occupies nearly

two hundred pages. He argues, first, from priority. Realism is the oldest doctrine and is also necessary to make idealism intelligible. He also appeals to the rustic and the small child, who are requested to testify concerning the reality of objects, and they testify accordingly. From many considerations of this kind Mr. Spencer concludes that realism itself is a presupposition of idealism, and that the latter is to be looked upon as a somewhat far-fetched product of abstract reasoning, while realism is based upon the immediate deliverance of consciousness.

In support of all this, he especially appeals to what he calls the Universal Postulate, which is that the inconceivability of the opposite is the test of truth. All propositions are to be accepted whose negations are inconceivable. There is some difficulty with this view, in that it is not clear whether this inconceivability is a reason or a mark. Mr. Spencer seems to view it as a reason, but as such his long theory makes it worthless. Simple opaque inability to conceive the opposite apart from some direct rational insight is no reason in any case, and on the associational theory it is deprived of even the semblance of reason, for on that theory the inconceivability of the opposite rests entirely upon the fact that the opposite has never been given in our experience; but when we remember the brevity in time and the limitation in space of our experience, it seems in the highest degree improbable that our experience is universal enough to tell us what can or cannot be in the nature of things. Accordingly, Mr. Mill, as well as other critics, is somewhat strenuous against this test of truth as given in the inconceivability of the opposite, and the only answer Mr. Spencer could make to such criticism would be his doctrine of a race experience, and that we have before seen to be a verbal fiction.

We have before referred to the argument for realism based on the priority of realistic belief. Now that Mr. Spencer has obtained this test of truth, he gives us some extra reasons. As between two systems of thought he holds those conclusions are most probable which use the test least. The argument for realism is shorter than that for idealism and therefore it is to be accepted, there being less liability to mistake in the brief realistic reflection than there is in the long and fine-drawn idealistic reasoning. Thus he illustrates: "Let him contemplate an object, this book, for instance. He finds that he is conscious of the book existing apart from himself . . . and he cannot conceive that where he sees and feels the book there is nothing. Hence, while he continues looking at the book, his belief in it as existing really has the highest validity possible." This is a specimen of the arguments by which Mr. Spencer, with the aid of the rustic and the savage, disproves the system of idealism.

In fact, Mr. Spencer's discussion is of the most superficial and mistaken sort. The Idealism which he combats is of a kind that is practically nonexistent. There are three questions which an idealist may ask. First, is there anything other than himself? second, is the apparent object an illusion? and third, what is the nature of the world of apparent objects? Rational idealism, at least nowadays, never raises the first two questions, but deals only with the third.

Mr. Spencer's arguments are directed against an absolute or impossible idealism which is for the most part a man of straw. There is really no need of asking if there be anything other than himself, as solipsism is altogether impossible. Here we may allow Mr. Spencer's universal postulate to be valid. Neither is it necessary to inquire whether the perceived object is real or not, or whether it be only an illusion of the individual percipient. No one whose opinion is worth considering fancies that his objects belong to himself, or that he himself is all that is meant by the sun, the earth, and the stars. In some sense, then, everybody admits the reality of the objects. We are in a world of common experience which is the same for all concerned, and when Mr. Spencer brings in the rustic and the savage to testify concerning the reality of the object, he simply shows himself ignorant of the real question; for their testimony is entirely irrelevant to anything which rational idealism maintains. All their testimony amounts to is that there are objects in experience which are not illusions of the individual, but which are common to all, and we find in experience that these objects can be practically depended upon. This is all that the testimony of common sense in general means. It simply denies the fictitious and illusory character of the world of things. But this testimony, which is perfectly valid in its own field, is next extended to affirm a system of realistic metaphyics which goes far beyond any view of common sense, and here is where rational idealism parts company with it. Such idealism claims that this world of things, that is, the world of experience, shows itself upon reflection to be nothing existing apart from all intelligence and antithetical to consciousness, but rather as being something which exists for and through consciousness and is meaningless otherwise. And it will be noted that a good part of Mr. Spencer's own theory goes in the same direction. The ordinary thought of common sense is that ideas exist in the mind, and things exist out of the mind in antithesis to consciousness. And they certainly do exist in independence of our minds; and common sense views this independence of our minds as an independence of all mind; and then we have the impossible notion of a mental subject and of physical objects absolutely incommensurable and unrelated; and thus the problem of knowledge is made impossible at the start. But the progress of reflection throws increased doubt upon this idea. Mr. Spencer himself, after having used the rustic and the small child to prove the reality of things, forthwith proceeds to say that the true reality is by no means what they think; that is, they are dismissed, and a speculative realism is set up in the place of spontaneous common-sense realism.

It is interesting to notice how far we have gone in the direction of making the world of experience phenomenal, that is, subjective. The whole world of sense qualities has been handed over to phenomenality. Light, sound, heat, etc., which seem so manifestly extra-mental, are declared to exist only in our sensibility. Of course the realist hastens to remark that these qualities have objective realities corresponding to them, namely, vibrations of some sort, and with this fact he fancies he removes the paradox of his view for the unsophisticated consciousness. Heat, sound, light, are objective; of course, not as common sense supposes, but vibrations are objective, and though they are never objects themselves, still they are the reality of the object. Fortunately for our peace of mind, the rustic has been dismissed, and he is not critical in any case, but if he had remained and had been assisted by counsel, he might have asked Mr. Spencer if he regarded this as the realism to which he testified. He knows nothing of vibrations in sense experience. He knows qualities directly as properties of the objects. For him the thing is no compound of qualities partly objective and partly subjective. Transfigured realism has an altogether different set of objects from common-sense realism. The things of the latter are the phenomena of the former, and the realities of the former are undreamed of by the latter. Both believe the reality of things, but the things of one are not those of the other. The things of common sense are the objects of perception, bodies in space with various apparent properties. The things of transfigured realism are sundry deductions of theory which the senses do not give. The former realism believes in what the senses give and falls back on the unsophisticated consciousness. The latter realism sets aside what the senses seem to give and allows as real only what the senses do not and cannot give, and yet it, too, upon occasion falls back on the unsophisticated consciousness. All that the two realisms have in common is the conviction that the world of experience is not arbitrary and groundless or a private fiction of the individual, and this conviction they share with idealism.

Nor do we much mend the matter by deciding that the object is partly mental and partly extra-mental, as in the distinction of primary and secondary qualities, for the line between the subjective and the objective is hard to draw and the distinction seems like an affront to common sense. Supposing it made, however, it is not clear how the subjective qualities are to be regarded. If they are to be excluded from reality, reality itself begins to seem poverty-stricken, so much so as to be only a bare skeleton of experience without life or meaning. In that case a knowledge of the real world would reveal very little worth knowing and all the value and significance of existence would be in the unreal subjective world. The subjective qualities, which are supposed to be nothing apart from consciousness, do nevertheless appear as an important system of facts for consciousness and have the utmost practical value. This difficulty can never be escaped so long as we make the distinction of real and unreal depend upon the antithesis of mental and non-mental. In that case the real must ever grow poorer and poorer and less and less worth knowing, for the solid things of crude realism are perpetually vanishing into phenomena. We need not carry this matter into the subjectivity of space and time to see that by this time the realism of spontaneous thought has disappeared altogether, and in its place we have a so-called transfigured realism which grows more and more mysterious the more we reflect upon it. If the sense world is only an effect in us, and if the world of things is not to be thought in terms of this sense world, nor yet in terms of idealism or personality, it certainly becomes a very elusive thing, and the elusiveness grows still worse when we try to tell whereabouts this real world of Mr. Spencer's exists. The world of sense is phenomenal. The Unknowable, of course, is by hypothesis beyond us, and this real world of transfigured realism seems to lie somewhere between the two. And here we have the difficulties renewed which we pointed out in treating of the relation of matter and force to the Unknowable. They were declared at times to be effects in us, and at times they seem to be independent of us, and a kind of go-between between the Unknowable and the human world. This leaves them in the highest degree vague and uncertain as to their whereabouts. So-called reality has retreated entirely into mystery. We cannot get at it by sense or apparently by thought, and it further would seem that this reality would not be worth knowing if we could by any possibility reach it.

Further, in working out this species of realism Mr. Spencer has been forced to abandon one of his most cherished positions. In speaking of freedom, as we have before pointed out, Mr. Spencer sets aside the self as nothing but a complex of states of consciousness, which states have the ground of their connection in the brain. Either, he said, the Ego is in consciousness or it is not. If it is not in consciousness, then it is not a state of consciousness; and if it is not in consciousness, there is no evidence of its existence. Thus the self is cashiered and driven off as utterly unsubstantial, and in another passage it is declared that various nervous plexuses are the objective bond of mental states and the ground of their coördination.

427

Unfortunately, a self thus completely passive is not able to do much in the knowing line, and there is no way of saving the day against the nihilist unless something be done about it. Mere states of consciousness are neither permanent nor changeless nor external. They are simply subjective, with nothing objective in them. To meet this difficulty Mr. Spencer has recourse to the desperate measure of recalling the cashiered self in order to save the day. To find some proof of objective reality he falls back upon our own sense of power and our experience of resistance to our own power, which he views as showing the reality of the objective world. He speaks of "an indissoluble cohesion in thought between active energy as it wells up from the depths of our consciousness, and the equivalent resistance opposed to it; as well as between this resistance opposed to it and an equivalent pressure in the part of the body which resists. Hence the root-conception of existence beyond consciousness, becomes that of resistance *plus* some force which the resistance measures." ("Principles of Psychology," vol. II, p. 479.) The same thought is continued as follows: "The unknown correlative of the resistance offered by it, ever nascent in thought under the form of muscular strain, — the unknown correlative which we think of as defying our efforts to crush or rend the body, and therefore as that which holds the body together, is necessarily thought of as constituting body. On remembering how difficult we find it to conceive aëriform matter as body at all; how liquid matter, so incoherent that it cannot preserve its shape, is recognized as body in a qualified sense; and how, where the matter is solid, the notion of body is so intimately united with the notion of that which maintains continuity, that destruction of continuity is destruction of the body; we shall see clearly that this unknown correlative of the vivid state we call pressure, symbolized in the known terms of our own efforts, constitutes what we call material substance." (Page 480.) Again, "I find that as to these feelings of touch, pressure, and pain, when self-produced, there cohere those states in my consciousness which were their antecedents; it happens that when they are not self-produced, there cohere with them in my consciousness the faint forms of such antecedents — nascent thoughts of some energy akin to that which I used myself." (Page 475.) In these and various other passages which might be given, we see the notion of the self completely set forth. It is no longer a mere set of mental states, but a source of active energy producing effects and being resisted, and this sense of energy and experience of resistance are made the essential material out of which the conception of the outer world is built. But this, however good it may be as doctrine, is very far from the original empirical psychology.

We find further difficulty with Spencer's doctrine of vivid and faint states of consciousness which Spencer adapts from Hume. It will be remembered that Hume had two factors in his system, impressions and ideas. The distinction between these was that the impressions were original and vivid, while ideas were copies and faint. On this view, of course, impressions are the only source of knowledge, and nothing whatever can be looked upon as real which is not an impression. Accordingly, if any idea is presented for our consideration, and we would test its value, we inquire what is the impression from which it comes, and if no impression can be shown we can only conclude that the idea is an illusion. This was really a short and easy method of reasoning, and one readily sees what havoc it would make with moral and religious ideas. If there are no corresponding impressions of sight, sound, touch, odor, etc., then these ideas are illusory. Manifestly, ideas of God and Spirit and right and wrong, and all the metaphysical ideas of substance and cause and identity, are, on his view, pure illusions. Now, Mr. Spencer has to escape this result, and it is a matter of interest to see how he does it.

A considerable part of his discussion is in the true Humian style, and vivid and faint states of consciousness seem to be all that are recognized. The vivid states are identified with the objects and the faint states with the mind, as in the following passage: "Thus the totality of my consciousness is divisible into a faint aggregate which I call my mind; a special part of the vivid aggregate cohering with this in various ways, which I call my body; and the rest of the vivid aggregate, which has no such coherence with the faint aggregate. This special part of the vivid aggregate, which I call my body, proves to be a part through which the rest of the vivid aggregate works changes in the faint, and through which the faint works certain changes in the vivid. And in consequence of its intermediate position, I find myself now regarding this body as belonging to the vivid aggregate, and now as belonging to the same whole with the faint aggregate, to which it is so intimately related." (Page 472.) He represents himself also as sitting on a bench by the sea and having various experiences which he describes in terms of vivid and faint aggregates. [In this connection he says:] "As I rise I lay hold of my umbrella, and make the set of visual states which I know by that name, move across the sets of visual states I know as the shingle and the sea. Unlike most changes in the vivid series, which, as I sat motionless, proved to be quite independent of the faint series, and to have antecedents among themselves, these changes in the vivid series have their antecedents in the faint series. Their proximate antecedents are, indeed, the touches, pressures and muscular tensions previously set up in this peculiar portion of the vivid aggregate; but these are set up by members of the faint aggregate." (Page 472.)

In these quotations the vivid states and faint states seem to be identified respectively with the objects and the mind. The same assumption appears in a note to paragraph 450, where he speaks of the "division of all manifestations of existence into two great aggregates, implying the two existences distinguished as ego and non-ego." There is, however, some confusion arising here, as both vivid and faint aggregates are declared to be sets of consciousness and therefore both must lie within consciousness. At the same time, they are both furnished with causality and are said to act upon each other; but then comes something more in the Humian vein as follows: "Comparison shows me, then, that the vivid states are original and the faint states derived. It is true that these derivative states

admit of being combined in ways not wholly like the
ways in which the original states were combined. Having had the states yielded by trees, mountains, rocks,
cascades, etc., thoughts of these may be put together
in shapes partially new. But if none of the various
forms, colors, and distributions have been vividly presented, no faint re-combinations of them are possible.
. . . So that the vivid originals and the faint copies
are contrasted as being, the one absolutely unalter-
able while I remain physically passive, and the other
readily alterable while I remain physically passive."
(Pages 456–57.)

This doctrine of vivid and faint states of consciousness in Hume's system led directly to nihilism. According to Hume, vivid states, which he called impressions,
are the only material of knowledge; while faint states,
which he called ideas, are copies of the vivid states,
and beyond these there is nothing. In that case a
short and easy argument dispenses with every idea
that cannot be referred to any impression. Of any
idea of spiritual things, moral or religious, the soul
or God, we have only to ask, What is the impression
from which these ideas are derived? Is it a sight, a
sound, a pressure, an odor, etc.? Of course not. Then
it is an illusion, that is, it is an idea which is not based
upon impression. If the mind had some native insight
of its own, it might possibly from these states, vivid
or faint, infer something beyond themselves. But as
by hypothesis the mind has no such insight, we can
only conclude that the ideas which cannot be referred
to their original impressions are simply fictions. They
are the products of what Hume called the mental

propensity to feign. Thus at one stroke all reality is reduced to sense impressions, and all non-sensuous conceptions, which are not ideas or impressions, are shown to be fictitious and baseless. Of course the result is nihilism in speculation, sensuality for morals, and atheism for religion. Hume himself did not accept this conclusion in its rigor, but it was the conclusion of his philosophy. Spencer, however, having the same philosophy, does not allow it to reach this conclusion. But the conclusion is evaded solely by bringing in the world of causal realities outside of the vivid impressions. There is, as we have seen, a certain element of common sense running along with his own particular philosophy and saving it from self-destruction. However, this only adds one additional element of inconsistency to his general exposition. If the Spencerian takes his doctrine of vivid states and faint states of consciousness seriously, and does not allow the reason to be an original part, he must necessarily come to this result. And this goes even beyond that idealism which Spencer calls "insane" and makes evolution doubly a dream.

There are also some minor difficulties connected with the doctrine as Mr. Spencer himself works it out. The vivid states and faint states are identified respectively with the object and the subject, and this leads to the extraordinary result that in that case the object in ordinary perception is mentally subjective rather than objective, in the sense of being independent of the self. It is a commonplace of psychology that cognition is largely recognition. In perception the sense affection is to a great extent the sign rather than the thing signified; or that which is in sense is very different from that which is in thought. The thought object is the object as the mind has built it out of various experiences; while the vivid impression is simply the affection of the appropriate sense organ at the time. Thus, in the case of a picture, the sense object is merely the visual impression made on the retina or the resulting sensations, but that which is before the mind is only to a very slight extent this vivid impression. The mental object is almost exclusively made up of faint states, and hence is subjective. Hence the perceived object, that is, the object as it exists for articulate thought, is only to a very slight extent the so-called vivid impression, but is rather a function of various ideas, that is, of faint impressions which are not extra-mental at all. If we should follow out this line of reflection, it would turn out that the actual object in perception is in the Spencerian scheme subjective, being, as just said, a function of faint impressions. Just how Mr. Spencer would escape this conclusion it is not easy to say. Possibly he might hold that a vivid impression is possible in connection with faint impressions in the case of an object, and that the really objective is not the object as we perceive it, but is the complex of actual and possible vivid impressions. But if we should allow this, it would apply only to sense objects and not at all to that world of thought reality which belongs to the unpicturable ideas of the understanding and is no vivid impression and never can be one. The vivid impressions, in any case, would belong only to sense and to the sensuously presentable objects of the imagination;

434

whereas the great part of our thought of objects is drawn from the world of power, depending on ideas of cause, substance, unity, identity, etc.; and all of these in their unpicturable character lie beyond the range of impressions of any sort. Thus the failure of this view becomes manifest again, and when to this we add the generally recognized subjectivity of all the sense qualities, the whole world of vivid impressions is carried bodily over into the subject as an affection of the same, and by this time the collapse is complete.

Finally, it may be pointed out that if we should allow Mr. Spencer's whole system of metaphysics, including the Unknowable and eternal force and indestructible matter, etc., he would still be as far as ever from making out his empirical doctrine of knowledge. Mr. Spencer has assumed the whole system of metaphysical ideas in his fundamental platform, and then he has the problem, how with these, as objective facts, to secure their objective recognition. And here again there is no thoroughfare. It seems, indeed, plausible to speak of the uniformities of things as producing uniformities of thought, and the imagination finds it easy to form some fancy that the existing reality should gradually come to reproduce itself in subjective conceptions; but when we take the matter with any precision we find this doctrine vanishing also into hopeless unclearness. Given such a real world, we should first have to inquire how any subjective world of any sort should emerge. Supposing matter and motion as our original data, how do they ever become that which is neither matter nor motion, namely, conscious feeling of any kind, or vivid impressions, to use Mr. Spencer's phrase? Here also there is no thoroughfare. We can in no way represent these subjective impressions in terms of matter and motion so as to identify them with them. Mr. Spencer would, of course, fall back on his doctrine of the double-faced nature of the fundamental reality or of the nervous changes; but here again we have mainly a phrase which defies all construction in thought, and it is equally unserviceable in the solution of our problem. For at the very utmost, all that is possible on this line would be a set of coexistent or sequent impressions no matter where, and we should then have the problem, how from such impressions to build up a knowledge of them and to build up an articulate system of knowledge of any kind. We might conceivably have impressions coexistent or sequent for an observer, but the problem is to get them to be coexistent and sequent for themselves. The speculator, looking on from the outside and treating these coexistent and sequent states under the categories of coexistence and sequence and unity and identity, easily comes to mistake the coexistence, etc., which he attributes to the sensations, for a perception of these relations among themselves and by themselves. When this begging of the question is guarded against, we soon see again that there is no thoroughfare here. We have a coexistence of conscious impressions, but no knowledge of coexistence. In order to this, there must be something beyond the impressions themselves. They must be united in or for or by some principle which cannot be identified with any of the impressions themselves, but which comprehends the several impressions in the unity of its consciousness, and by discriminating and comparing them within this consciousness gives to them the relations of coexistence, sequence, etc. But in order to this, this something, which we may as well call the self, must have an essentially rational nature. The impressions as such would lie dead and reveal nothing. It is only as they are affections of a rational mind that any need arises for organizing. Left to themselves, they might coexist or follow one another in space and time for an observer, but they would organize themselves as little as a mass of type, whirled continually for an indefinite time, would organize themselves into words and develop into meanings and rational treatises. There is simply nothing in the impressions, considered in themselves, that contains meaning in abstraction from the rational nature. Thus we see that this system must be content to see all its conclusions disappear, or else to fall back on the affirmation of a rational nature which is the real source and ground of knowledge.

Thus, it is plain that Mr. Spencer does not succeed any better in developing a doctrine of knowledge than the old-fashioned empiricism of the earlier school. He gives his view something of the prestige of science by an abundant use of scientific terminology and illustration, but when the matter is taken with precision he gets on no better than the earlier prophets and apostles of the school. But given a rational nature, then the principles of association to which the empiricists refer have a real but subordinate value. We do learn many things from experience, and uniformities of experience do result in certain uniformities of thought, but this is due altogether to the fact that it is the experience of a rational being which is already determined by a rational nature.

When Hume proclaims the reduction of the self to a flux of impressions he says: "For my part, when I enter most intimately into what I call *myself*, I always stumble on some particular perception or other, of heat or cold, light or shade, love or hatred, pain or pleasure. I never can catch myself at any time without a perception, and never can observe anything but the perception. . . . If any one, upon serious and unprejudiced reflection, thinks he has a different idea of *himself*, I must confess I can reason no longer with him. All I can allow him is that he may be in the right as well as I, and that we are essentially different in this particular. He may, perhaps, perceive something simple and continued, which he calls *himself;* though I am certain there is no such principle in me."[1] In this passage the self which Hume is denying continually appears in the personal pronouns employed. If we should erase these and substitute for them the vanishing impressions which the doctrine implies, the whole passage would disappear in complete and perfect nonsense. That is, Hume had to invoke the self to be present at its own rejection and banishment. Mr. Spencer's work illustrates the same thing. The self which is to be built up is implicitly present from the start and the operation succeeds only because of this fact. In Mr. Spencer's various descriptions of the process, the self appears, as in the passage quoted from Hume, in the pronouns and substantive terms denot-

---

[1] *Treatise of Human Nature*, part IV, section VI.

ing the mind employed. This doctrine never reaches the bottom, or rather never reaches the beginning. It presupposes the very things it sets out to deduce or evolve. But after we have seen the essential failure and nothingness of the system, it is then possible to find a subordinate value in it. As an observation of the principle of association and its effects, or as a description of mental growth from the outside, the empirical theory is by no means without interest and value. Accordingly, we find in the writings of this school a great deal that is useful, only pointing out that the fundamental philosophy is untenable from the start and is completely denied on every page.

Of Mr. Spencer's system in general, it must be said that it can only be looked upon as a compound of bad science, bad logic, and bad metaphysics. In his "Autobiography," Mr. Spencer rather felicitates himself now and then on not having studied much in the history of philosophy. He sets Kant aside very peremptorily, and gives the impression that the philosophers have largely erred and strayed from the way like lost sheep, while he himself seems to have light enough within for his own purposes. But the student of philosophy, in reading Spencer, can only say that if the good man had read more widely and more carefully in philosophy, he would have saved himself from many a naïve blunder and overweening dogmatism.

In a youthful book which I published many years ago,[1] when there was not much fear of the proprieties before my eyes, I ventured to say of Mr. Spencer that he had painted a big picture with a big brush, and his

[1] *The Philosophy of Herbert Spencer*, New York, 1874.

disciples, who had found it easier to wonder than to understand, had concluded that he must be a great painter. For substance of doctrine, I still agree with this view. We have a system of great showy generalizations, but vague and baseless often, and at other times barren and leading to nothing. Mr. Spencer had the rather pathetic experience of seeing his system grow obsolete during his own life. It fell in with the naturalistic thought of his time, and for a while was the official philosophy of the naturalistic movement. But when criticism awoke and the philosophy was more carefully examined, it was seen in its true character and remanded to the fellowship of obsolete systems which for a time made a show, but passed away and left little trace or sign.

THE END